Dodge Dynasty

Dodge Dynasty

The Car and the Family That Rocked Detroit

Caroline Latham
AND David Agresta

Harcourt Brace Jovanovich, Publishers

SAN DIEGO   NEW YORK   LONDON

HBJ

Library of Congress Cataloging-in-Publication Data

Latham, Caroline.
Dodge dynasty: the car and the family that rocked Detroit /
Caroline Latham, David Agresta.—1st ed.
p.   cm.
Includes index.
ISBN 0-15-125320-X
1. Dodge family.   2. Automobile industry and trade—United States—
History.   3. Upper classes—United States—Conduct of life.
4. United States—Biography.   I. Agresta, David.   II. Title.
CT274.D62L38   1989
929'.2'0973—dc19   88-16467

Designed by Gracie Artemis
Printed in the United States of America

First edition

A B C D E

Contents

Dodge Dynasty

Introduction

It was the end of an era.

The big black hearse rolled slowly around the curved driveway of the limestone mansion built in the classic French style, past the formal rose gardens that gave the estate its name: Rose Terrace. The ornate bronze casket inside weighed more than a ton, causing the funeral director so much concern for the springs of his vehicle that he decided to station a backup hearse nearby. Yet the fine bronzework was invisible to the mourners; all they could see was the blanket of white orchids that covered the casket completely. Following the hearse through the wrought-iron gates of the Grosse Pointe estate to the old stone church in downtown Detroit were seven limousines that bore the grandchildren, nieces, former daughters-in-law, fiancés of presumed heiresses: a large and varied cast of would-be inheritors in search of a legacy. All that was missing from this assemblage of well-cut dark suits and discreetly real jewelry was any sign of genuine grief.

Anna Dodge's bronze casket is carried out of the Jefferson Avenue Presbyterian Church past a double row of her great-grandsons. (Courtesy of *The Detroit Free Press*)

It was June 6, 1970, and the occasion was the funeral of Anna Thomson Dodge, the last link with the founding of the fabulous Dodge fortune. The papers said the old lady was 103, but, like so many things that have been printed about the Dodge family, that was untrue. Anna Dodge was in fact just two months short of her ninety-ninth birthday. She had outlived her moneymaking husband, Horace, by *fifty* years; she had outlived both her children; she had outlived her brother-in-law John, the cofounder of the Dodge wealth, and all three of his wives and all but two of his six children. She had even lived long enough to see the legends about the family supplant the reality. Now there would be no one left to remember the way it all began back at the turn of the century, when the city of Detroit was youthful and optimistic and just beginning to whiff the rich greasy tang of the automobile's profit potential.

The Dodge brothers were archetypical American entrepreneurs; they and their wives and their children lived the American dream. Their story illumines the best and the worst of that most central of our cultural legends.

How did it all begin?

There was a time when John and Horace Dodge worked at their small auto parts factory for sixteen or eighteen or twenty hours at a stretch and then sought a few hours of sleep on a tool bench; when they could pay themselves less than they paid the skilled machinists who worked for them; when the grieving John was unable to find the cash to pay for his first wife's funeral. These two brawny redheaded brothers, inseparable companions throughout their lives, possessed all the virtues of the simpler age we still idealize. They were honest businessmen who never took advantage of their workers or partners. They concentrated on quality rather than price and gave their customers real value for the money. They never borrowed a penny from the bank and never owed a favor they did not repay in full measure. They built a personal reputation for dependability which complemented that of the cars they made. Their manners were rough, but their hearts were true.

In later years, sitting on a fragile antique chair that had once belonged to Queen Marie Antoinette and wearing pearls that any queen would envy, Anna liked to say that the days when she packed Horace's lunch pail every morning were the happiest of her life. And maybe she really meant it. For with the wealth came the pain of unfulfilled hopes, of early losses, of wasted lives. "Wealth is a curse," said Anna Dodge, a Scotch Calvinist who eventually learned to enjoy her income of $40,000 a day. For many members of the Dodge family, that statement was true enough. . . .

In 1900, the Dodge brothers were mechanics, workingmen on someone else's payroll. A decade later, they were already worth millions, thanks to the American virtues of working hard, taking risks and providing quality. By 1920, their car company was climbing toward the number-two position in sales and their families had every earthly possession they desired. Then, at the height of their success, John and Horace both died in the same year, under mysterious circumstances.

Thanks to the alchemy of the huge fortune they had amassed before they died in their fifties, the families of these two simple men from a small town in Michigan were able to take their place in the "best" society of two continents. The cars that Americans began to buy by the millions were translated by the Dodge heirs into paintings by great masters, jewels of dead queens, newly built homes that expressed old fantasies. Along with the possessions came the manners of people accustomed to owning such things: the attractive social graces as well as the arrogant assumptions.

The speed with which the Dodge brothers earned their fortune and the extent to which it transformed the lives of their families recall the fairy tale of the fisherman's wife who possessed a magic fish that granted her every wish, changing her hovel into a palace and covering her rags with jewels. So it should come as no surprise to learn that, like that fairy tale, the story of the Dodge family did not have a happy ending.

The ambition and single-mindedness that enabled the Dodge brothers to build up their fabulous fortune left their widows and children shut out of the reality on which the fortune was founded. The brothers' legacy was so great that their heirs quite literally could not bear its burden. The widows became gilded anachronisms, splendidly irrelevant to the modern world. The children, the first generation to grow up with the advantages of wealth, were meteorically self-destructive. Their intimates exploited and abused them, and the news media regularly chronicled their follies.

Even the next generation was largely unable to find any meaning in the money that supported its existence. The strongest, or luckiest, members settle for low-profile survival. They might ruefully agree with Anna that wealth *can* be a curse—especially when it is unaccompanied by responsibility. Now that the mind-boggling

Dodge fortune amassed by those two brothers with their genius for mechanics and their bold entrepreneurial spirit has been diluted merely to comfortable wealth, it may at last be a burden that ordinary mortals can bear.

1

Two Little Boys in Niles

"We were the poorest little urchins ever born," exclaimed the middle-aged John Dodge as he looked back on the childhood he shared with his younger brother, Horace. "Poor Mother, how she used to worry about her boys."

They were two redheads growing up in Niles, Michigan, a sleepy Midwestern town in the second half of the nineteenth century. John, the elder by four years, was the more vocal and aggressive of the two; the loyal Horace his silent shadow. Together, they walked every morning from the family's small house on the edge of town to the little brick schoolhouse a mile or so distant. After school, they might hurry down to the banks of the slow-moving river, to go ice-skating in the clean crisp air of winter, or in warmer weather to sit side by side with their homemade wooden poles and wait for the fish to bite. Most of the time the boys wore old clothes and even went without shoes, but once a week they cleaned up to look like little gentlemen for Sunday school at the Methodist church.

Even when they were slicked up in their Sunday best, no one saw in the two little Dodge boys the qualities that would later enable them to build an empire and amass a multimillion-dollar fortune.

Even for poor families like the Dodges, the town was a good place to grow up. Niles dozes on the southwest corner of Michigan's mitten. It was, and still is, an essentially rural place that owes the modest prosperity it has managed to achieve to the richness of the brown river-bottom farmland around it. The muddy St. Joseph winds through the center of town, flowing under the rounded arches of an old bridge, bringing the fertile silt that makes the corn grow tall and providing a transportation link with blue Lake Michigan and the industrial cities along its edge.

The first of the Dodges to arrive in Niles was Ezekiel, the grandfather of John and Horace. One of the youngest of twelve children born to William and Mary Dodge, Ezekiel grew up in Salem, Massachusetts, famous for its witch trials and ingrained Puritanism. The Dodges came from sturdy English yeoman stock and could trace their roots in the New World as far back as 1629. The men in the family were typically hale and hearty specimens who continued to do hard physical work well into their sixties and seventies, usually outliving two or three wives and a pathetically large number of children, who often died in infancy. The educational achievements of five generations of American Dodges might have been slight, and their material goods limited, but they were surely blessed with rugged constitutions. That was to be the heritage of John and Horace—and an important factor in their success.

A native of industrialized New England, Ezekiel Dodge was a skilled machinist. He married a local girl, Anna Cleves, and they raised a family in Salem. But sometime in the early 1830s, he decided to move westward, in search of greater economic opportunity. His pioneering spirit took him, his wife and at least six children (survivors of thirteen born to the couple, all but two of them boys) as far as the banks of the St. Joseph River.

At the time they arrived, the entire town of Niles consisted of just fourteen houses. Most of the original settlers had come in search of land to farm, but Ezekiel was drawn to the river front, and the pounding steam engines of the boats that carried goods back and forth to Chicago. He set up his machine shop on the bank of the shallow river, in an area lined with wooden sheds. As Niles grew, the flimsy sheds were replaced by two-story brick buildings, each the shape of a shoe box, which housed ship chandlers, warehouses and merchants.

Ezekiel Dodge's only enduring legacy was his skill at his machinist's trade. It passed to his sons Daniel Rugg, born in Salem in 1819, and Caleb Kimball, just one year younger. A generation later, it descended to his grandsons John and Horace. Even as children, they were able to coax inert metal and chunks of wood into objects of utility and even style. Too poor to afford the purchase of a bicycle—then every schoolboy's desire—John and Horace surprised the inhabitants of Niles by making their own high-wheeler. The big front wheel they fashioned themselves, steaming and bending a piece of wood to form a circle and then inserting the spokes to hold it rigid. The small rear wheel was scavenged from a discarded carriage. The boys got a kick out of riding their homemade cycle through the dusty streets of town.

Ezekiel and Anna's son Daniel married sometime around 1850. His wife remains nameless in the family chronology, but presumably she was from Niles or the area around it. The couple had two children: Laura, born in 1856, and Charles Francis, several years older. Then Daniel's wife died, and he was left to care for the two young children. He coped in the fashion of many a man in a similar situation: He went out and found a new wife.

She was Maria Duval Casto, three years younger than Daniel and an altogether more forceful character. Her parents, like the Dodges, were pioneer settlers in the area, and materially only a little better off. But the Castos had taught their daughter to take great pride in her mixed heritage of Pennsylvania Dutch and French ancestry. Maria was the kind of woman who insisted that her children attend school every day, whether or not they had decent clothes or shoes that fit. She inculcated in them the religious principles of her own Methodist faith, and it seems that she almost believed there was an Eleventh Commandment, which dictated, "Thou shalt work hard to get ahead." Although she lived in a little backwater, she always made an effort to acknowledge the standards of a wider world. For example, she awakened her children's interest in music, and surely must have been gratified when Horace spent some of his slowly accumulated earnings to buy himself a violin, which the nine-year-old then taught himself to play. Even the name she gave this younger son, Horace Elgin, reflects her cultural aspirations: Lord Elgin had recently returned to London with the fabulous marble he had retrieved from the Parthenon in Athens, and "Horace" was another reference to classical Greco-Roman civilization.

The redoubtable Maria married Daniel Dodge soon after she lost both her parents, in 1859, possibly as the result of an epidemic. In addition to the two children of Daniel's first marriage, the couple had three children of their own. Daughter Della was born in 1863; John Francis, on October 25, 1864, and Horace Elgin, on May 17, 1868.

By the time John and Horace were old enough to cycle through the streets, Niles had matured into a larger and more prosperous town than the one their grandparents had known. A handsome and quite sizable Episcopalian church was erected, and attractive Greek Revival and early Victorian residences went up along the high ground on the banks of the river. But the increased abundance of many of their neighbors was not shared by the Dodge family. They were squeezed together in a little house on the outskirts of town.

After they had earned a fortune in the automobile business, John and Horace Dodge made a sentimental trip back to Niles to look for the house they had grown up in. "It was gone. There was nothing on the spot but a standpipe," reported John with a hint of amusement. The year was just 1915, but already the traces of the two redheaded Dodge boys were disappearing. The town had moved out past their old house. There was an elegant mansion just down the street, a few commercial buildings where the open fields used to be—and little firsthand recollection of the family that had settled there more than eighty years earlier. By the time the auto magnates revisited Niles, the majority of the Dodges were to be found in the peaceful Silver Brook cemetery a half mile out of town.

A few residents still had Dodge memories, however. John's first-grade teacher, Miss Ella Tibbetts, remembered the husky boy who had a temper to match his fiery hair. The former principal of the Niles school still kept in touch with his most illustrious (if not his most zealous) pupils, and the record of the boys' perfect attendance could still be found on file. Another person who remembered the Dodge boys was Tom Davis, the elderly black laborer who had hired the kids to help him with his subsistence-level work—dragging heavy sacks of grain out of railroad cars to load onto river boats. "I always think of John bending over carefully to pick up a sack of bran, so as not to rip the patches on the seat of his trousers," he said, and chuckled. Stories always picture John as the outspoken leader of the pair, ready to speak up for their rights and to take on anyone who tried to give them less than their due. Horace was quieter, more introspective—and the better mechanic of the two.

Both boys spent long hours at their father's machine shop on the waterfront and typically had grease on their clothes, their hands and their faces. They watched what their father did and soon they were able to help him repair and rebuild marine engines. They were there in the hot weather, when the temperature inside the brick building was stifling, and in cold weather, when their fingers were nearly too stiff to move. The hum of the lathe, the pervasive smell of the raw crude oil that powered some of the engines, the satisfaction of seeing a machine kick back into life when they re-started it became as familiar to them as the sights and sounds of home. Equally familiar to the two brothers was the intimacy of working together, sharing their ideas, frustrations, successes and failures as they acquired the skills that would be the basis of their future achievements.

For the most part, their own company sufficed. Sometimes they let their sister, Della, one year older than John, into their private world. Della was the best student in the family, graduating from high school with honors. Her quick mind and forceful personality enabled her to hold her own with her brothers, even though she did not share their interest in machines. Older half-sister Laura acted as a baby-sitter for the boys when they were young enough to need one. But they were never especially close to her and drifted further apart after she married George W. Stineback, a local man ten years her senior. The other boy in the family, Laura's brother Charles, was too much older than John and Horace to be a play-mate, and he lacked that special spark that was characteristic of the children of Maria Casto Dodge.

There were Dodge cousins living in Niles when Horace and John were growing up, but the boys formed no emotional ties with them. No grandparents played a significant role in their childhood either. Their Casto grandparents died before Maria Casto was married; their father's mother, Anna Cleves Dodge, died in 1861, before they were born; and Ezekiel Dodge died in 1869, when Horace was less than a year old. The two boys were surprisingly self-sufficient. They had the machine shop, and they had each other.

John finished high school in 1882. He had never been a good student, but he persevered with his studies—probably at his mother's insistence. After graduation, he began to work at the shop, where his assistance was badly needed, since his uncle Caleb Kimball had died that year, predeceased by another uncle who sometimes helped out at the shop, Edwin Dodge. Of course, wherever John was, Horace was sure to be found nearby. The long hours at the machine shop caused the younger boy's school-ing to suffer, and he finally dropped out just a few months short of his high-school graduation. As the events of his later life were to prove, the time he spent at the shop was far more valuable for his career than any amount of education the Niles high school could possibly have offered.

As John and Horace grew to manhood, they took over more and more of the decision-making in the Dodge machine shop. Their father was a competent machinist, but he had a poor head for business. Furthermore, he lacked the ambition and drive that his wife, Maria, brought to the family and instilled in their children. He probably would have been quite content to live out his days in Niles and then join his parents under the tall elms out at the cemetery. But his children wanted more out of life, and instinctively they knew they were not going to find it in the town where they'd grown up.

The result was that the Dodges moved on. The pioneering spirit that took Ezekiel Dodge from the constricted world of Salem to the banks of the St. Joseph River resurfaced in his grandchildren. At their urging, the whole family (except Laura, already married and with a home of her own) packed up and left Niles with scarcely a backward glance.

After John and Horace became two of the richest men in the auto industry, their early years in Niles were obscured by clouds of myth. John loved to talk about what a "poor urchin" he'd been. Stories of how the boys worked at odd jobs, including driving a nearby farmer's cows home from the fields every night for fifty cents a week, which they dutifully gave to their mother, became part of the family legend. Like many other self-made men, the Dodge brothers preferred to emphasize the enormous disadvantages they'd had to overcome in their rise to the top. It is probably wise to take these "poor urchin" tales with a grain or two of salt. The fact that Della and John were able to finish high school (and Horace to come so close) indicates that the Dodge family had a certain economic margin. So does that purchase of a violin by young Horace. Letters and pictures preserved in the family collection suggest that the Dodge children were able to participate fully in the social activities of the community, such as Sunday-school picnics and class outings, even when these cost money.

Yet the Dodge brothers' attitude toward Niles was always ambivalent—as was Niles's attitude toward them. Once the brothers left town, they returned only infrequently. When the time came, they did bury their parents with the relatives in Niles, but they themselves chose to take their perpetual rest in Detroit, the city where they finally achieved the success they had sought.

At the height of their wealth and power, John and Horace Dodge attempted to become benefactors of Niles, but the citizenry resolutely bit the hands that tried to feed them. In 1917, John and Horace visited Niles again, no doubt arriving in one of their own black Dodge touring cars, with their initials painted on the door in gold and the special "fat-man" tilt wheel that John needed to accommodate his rich man's bulk. They emerged from a vehicle made in their own factory by some of their 22,000 employees, their diamond stickpins sparkling below their blindingly white high shirt collars. They had come, they announced, to make a gift to the city of Niles: $50,000 for a public park, to be named in honor of Daniel and Maria Dodge. Unimpressed, the city of Niles rejected the gift. They didn't really need a park, officials claimed, and besides, everyone agreed that a park could conceivably turn into a locus of crime.

So there never was a memorial or monument of any kind for the Dodges in their hometown. Visitors to the town today will see a historical plaque commemorating the sojourn in Niles of humorist Ring Lardner, and markers giving information about the old bridge, the first church, the grandest mansion. Nothing but a gas station stands near that standpipe John Dodge long ago found on the site of his boyhood home, and in the cemetery it takes a diligent search to track down the modest granite stone John and Horace erected for their parents, lying in the midst of Maria's Casto relatives. The link between Dodge and Niles has simply faded away.

The family's path away from Niles and to Detroit was not a direct one. Their first stop was Battle Creek, midway between the start and end of their journey. It is not clear what could have prompted this initial choice. Battle Creek was manifestly a prosperous area, but the people who were getting rich there in the 1880s were not machinists, but the doctors and food faddists who were catering to both the truly ill and the merely unwell who pilgrimaged from all over the Midwest to the town's health-restoring institutions. The vast Post fortune, for example, got its start when C. W. Post went to Battle Creek to recuperate in a local sanitarium and kept his mind off his nervous breakdown by devising a "wholesome" substitute for coffee, which he called "Postum." Eventually, the wives and children of the Dodge brothers would meet the inheritor of the Post fortune, Marjorie Merriweather Post, on equal terms in Palm Beach, that favorite playground for the very rich. But in 1886, the Dodges had nothing in common with Post or any of the other Battle Creek entrepreneurs, and they left the town within months of their arrival.

Their next stop was Port Huron, located on the shores of Lake Huron at its outlet into the St. Clair River, gateway to the port of Detroit. Port Huron was a bustling young city that produced its wealth by servicing the needs of the ships that moved goods up and down the Great Lakes. It was therefore likely to provide opportunity for specialists in marine engines like the Dodges.

But Port Huron did not work out either. The Dodges did not have enough capital to compete with larger and better-established firms: They lacked money to buy new tools, rent sizable premises and hire additional employees. Their little firm could never be more than marginal. Daniel took on the small pieces of work he could get, but John and Horace had to find jobs with a manufacturer of agricultural machines. They began to think about their final move, to Detroit.

Detroit in the 1880s already had a strong and diverse industrial base. Railroads linked it with Chicago to the west, New York to the east, and Canadian cities to the north, through Windsor, Ontario, on the opposite bank of the Detroit River and easily reached by ferry. The St. Marys River ship canal provided access to the mineral-rich Lake Superior district. Detroit's labor force built ships, manufactured iron and steel, processed tobacco, produced phar-maceuticals and agricultural chemicals, brewed Stroh's beer, packed meat, made boots and shoes. In 1880, foundries and machine shops were the fourth-most-important business in the city. With a pop-ulation topping 100,000, and a tenfold increase in industrial em-ployment over the previous two decades, Detroit was surely the right place for John and Horace Dodge to be.

Late in the year 1886, they arrived in the city they were even-tually to help turn into the automobile capital of America. They were young: John was twenty-two, Horace eighteen. But their skills as machinists already surpassed those of men twice their age, so they were confident that they could find well-paid positions. When the Dodge brothers went to apply for an opening, John was the one to talk up their abilities and negotiate for the wages their skills merited. The quieter Horace was the insurance that they could always deliver the caliber of work John promised.

The jobs the Dodge brothers found were in the Murphy Boiler Works. Owner Tom Murphy ran a tough but fair shop, and he quickly took to the hard-working Dodge boys. Murphy hired John at a salary of twenty dollars a week, Horace for two dollars less. Their experience with the steam engines of boats on the St. Joseph River taught them the skills that were needed at the boiler works, and the genes of their Dodge forebears gave them the strength and stamina required for the hot, sweaty work on huge cast-iron boil-ers. Decades later, a journalist trying to explain the reasons for the Dodge brothers' pre-eminence in the automobile industry, concluded:

> Work in that line and in those days was in both social and physical aspects a strength test. Only the fittest survived, and the unfit fell quickly. To their last days, the Dodge brothers retained the rugged impress of those rough and ready days, as they did the fondness for practical mechan-ics which was bred in them there.

John and Horace jointly brought home pay envelopes that totaled nearly $40 a week, and their father augmented this income by using the small stock of old tools he'd brought from Niles to do odd jobs. The family was able to live a modest lower-middle-class existence, not much different from that of the other skilled workers at Murphy's.

John and Horace probably spent their free time getting to know the exciting city that was to be their home for the rest of their lives. Perhaps they rode the streetcars (the city then had thirteen different lines) and took the ferry across the river to Canada. They would have strolled over the Belle Isle bridge to that picturesque island in the Detroit River between Detroit and the Canadian shore, just being turned into a pleasantly secluded public park where workingmen could take a young lady to free concerts on Sunday afternoons. They surely walked along the concrete sidewalks in the heart of the city's business district and appreciated the modern luxury of block after block of bright electric lights. They might even have joined their friends from Murphy's at one of the bars in the warehouse district along the waterfront, where workingmen gathered at the end of the day.

Unfortunately, we know nothing about the romances they may have had before their marriages. But it is a safe bet that their wives were not the first women to find the Dodge brothers attractive. Both men had strong healthy bodies, regular features, thatches of eye-catching red hair. John was gregarious and fun-loving; Horace was shyer, sweeter. It was easy to see they were men on their way up, good prospects as husbands.

There was a remarkable similarity about the marriages of all three of the offspring of Daniel and Maria Dodge. Oddly, all married at the same age, twenty-eight, which was relatively late. They made "sensible" choices, picking partners who shared their aspirations and were personally willing to work and sacrifice to help achieve them. They chose mates who were already autonomous and self-supporting. There is no indication that passion was a factor in any of these marriages; rather, they were deliberate rational commitments based on respect and a similarity of goals.

Della was the first in the family to marry, in February 1892, and her choice of a husband was anything but romantic. During the brief period the Dodges had lived in Port Huron, she had met the elderly widower who was the foreman at the agricultural-machinery factory where her brothers worked. Uriah Eschbach had a daughter almost Della's age—but he also had a secure income and the slightly elevated social status of being a supervisor rather than a worker. After six years of long-distance courtship, Della finally decided that Uriah was the mate who could best help her achieve her ambitions.

By that time, however, she was no longer Della. "Della" was too pedestrian a name for her tastes, too much like something you would expect of a girl from a little town like Niles. She decided instead to call herself Delphine, which sounded more sophisticated (a match for Horace Elgin). She also convinced her fiancé, Uriah, to turn himself into the more dashing Rie, while his awkwardly Germanic surname (soon to be hers as well) was smoothed out to the anglicized Ashbaugh.

Della/Delphine and Rie had no children. They lived for some years in Port Huron, although Della always remained in close touch with her family in Detroit. But her carefully laid plans for her future subsequently went awry. Her husband came down with lung trouble, a fairly common crippler in those days when all big cities were smothered in a haze of soft coal smoke, and he was unable to work. Eventually, Della and her sick husband moved to Detroit to live with her brother John. There she set about the task of making a new life for herself, succeeding admirably. Fully as able as her brothers, Della focused her considerable energies on the goal of social prominence.

John was the next of the Dodges to take a spouse, marrying on September 22, 1892. His bride was Canadian-born Ivy Hawkins, who had moved to Detroit with her family as a young woman and who earned her own living as a skilled seamstress. Ivy had dark hair, regular features and an equable disposition. She and John Dodge must have made an attractive couple on their wedding day: the groom brawny (not yet showing the stoutness he later attained), well over average height, with red-gold hair and an air of command that was already beginning to coalesce around him; the bride shorter, darker, equally self-possessed.

John and Ivy started their family soon after their marriage. Their first child, a daughter, was born in March 1894, and named Winifred for the Hawkins side of the family. Next, in February 1896, came Isabel Cleves, whose name was a link to John's grandmother, the Anna Cleves who married Ezekiel Dodge. The last of the three children of John and Ivy was a boy, born in August 1898. He was proudly named John, after his father, and given the middle name Duval, which was his Dodge grandmother's middle name and her mother's maiden name.

The newly wed John moved out of the house he had shared with his parents and brother and into a small home of his own. Naturally, it was located in the same neighborhood: The Dodge brothers could not be far apart. Marriage brought many changes to John's life, but it did not affect his intimacy with his brother.

Horace's marriage, four years later, had an equally imperceptible effect on the brothers' relationship. His bride was Anna Thomson, and the events of their wedding day speak volumes about their relationship. They were married during Horace's lunch break, and the groom had to borrow the two dollars for the marriage license. After the ceremony, the bride went home, and the groom went back to finish his day's work.

The new Mrs. Horace Dodge was born Christina Anna Thompson in Dundee, Scotland; she later dropped the p in spelling her surname and abandoned her first name altogether. She was the third child of William and Elizabeth Thompson, and her birth certificate shows her to have been born on August 7, 1871— although she later claimed to be a decade younger, and then, in the pride of old age, to be four years older. Her sister Mae was

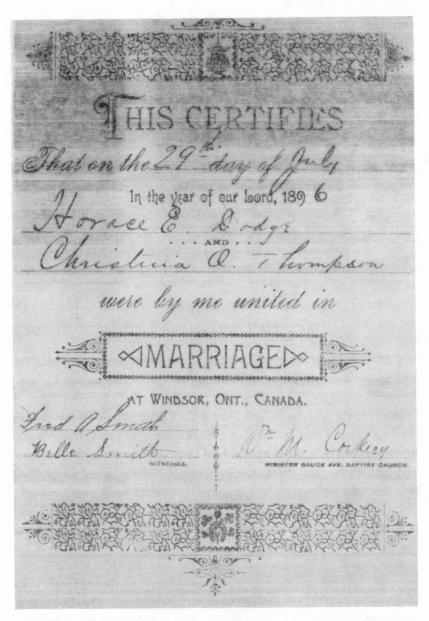

This certificate shows that Horace and Anna Dodge were married in Windsor, Ontario, by a Baptist minister. (Collection of David Agresta)

ten years her senior, and her other sister, Catherine, fit right into the middle, being five years younger than Mae and five years older than Anna.

The three girls, growing up in the dark northern city of Dundee, had a strict and joyless childhood. Piety and hard work were the virtues their parents tried to teach them. After Anna's death, a favorite book from the days she lived on Pettie Street was found among her effects. Carefully preserved by its owner for nearly ninety years, the small red volume was a moral tale for children couched in a vocabulary that would today be considered too difficult for most adults. She had neatly written her name and address on the flyleaf, along with an appropriate stanza of religious verse.

By the time Anna met Horace Dodge, she was a tall young woman who augmented her father's income as a sailmaker by giving piano lessons. Music was surely one of the things she and Horace had in common. It is unfortunate that we have no reliable evidence as to the quality of Anna's musicianship. A few years after her marriage, she fell while carrying a bottle of milk home from the store and cut a tendon in her hand on the broken glass. That put an end to her piano playing and eliminated the possibility of a documented, disinterested opinion of her talents.

Horace, the youngest child in the Dodge family and the last to marry, was the one who did not leave home. Instead, he brought his bride to live with his parents. On February 11, 1899, Horace and Anna had their first child, a baby girl they called Delphine, after the erstwhile Della, and gave the middle name Ione, an additional nod in the direction of Greece. A year and a half later, on August 2, 1900, the family was completed with the birth of a son, named Horace Elgin Dodge, Jr.

Not long after Horace and Anna married, the Dodge family circle was saddened by the loss of one of its members. Daniel R. Dodge died on July 19, 1897, at the age of seventy-nine. The family ordered black memorial cards printed in gold to mourn his passing, offering the comfort of a sentimental verse:

One precious to our hearts has gone,
The voice we loved is stilled.
The place made vacant in our home
Can never more be filled.
Our Father in His wisdom called
The boon his love had given;
And though on earth the body lies,
The soul is safe in Heaven.

By the time he died, Daniel had the satisfaction of seeing all his children settled in life, and a bright future in store for the next generation of the family. For the year of his passing was the same year that John and Horace established the first of the companies to bear the Dodge name.

2

A Bicycle
Built by Two

Every morning Horace Dodge picked up the black lunch pail Anna
had packed for him, climbed aboard his heavy bicycle and rode
off to work. As he headed down Jefferson Avenue, the rising sun
behind his back gleaming on the nearby river, he would pass many
other cyclists. Detroit in 1897 was still several decades away from
being the "Motor City." The bicycle was a convenient vehicle for
such a densely populated area, where few homes provided the space
to keep a horse. For those who could afford one, a bicycle was a
fast and easy way to commute to work.

Horace's bicycle was a more sophisticated machine than the old
high-wheeler he and his brother had put together back in Niles.
But it required constant maintenance. Grit from the unpaved roads
got in the mechanism, causing moving parts to wear out too soon
and riders to work too hard. As he pedaled along, Horace often
thought about the problem. He realized that the best solution lay
in changing the ball bearing on which the metal crankshaft rode.

How could he make a ball bearing that wouldn't clog up with dirt, but would continue to roll smoothly within its housing?

For Horace, thinking about a mechanical problem inevitably led to trying to solve it. He started to design an enclosed four-point bearing that would last longer and use the rider's energy more efficiently. He brought appropriately cast and stamped pieces of metal home with him from the shop. After dinner, he would leave Anna and his parents and go to his bench, where he shaped the hard metal as easily as if it were artists' clay. He filed, drilled and polished the shiny steel to tolerances that were precisely measured in thousandths of an inch. After hours at the bench, he would test his finished product on his own bicycle. Then it was back to the bench again to make some minute change, imperceptible to anyone else but an improvement in the way the bearing worked and lasted.

When Horace had created a dirt-resistant ball bearing that met his own exacting standards, he showed it to his brother. John was quick to see the commercial possibilities inherent in Horace's invention. It would provide a competitive edge for some bicycle manufacturer. . . . Why shouldn't that manufacturer be the Dodge brothers?

The new business opened at virtually the same time that Daniel Dodge died: The torch of entrepreneurship had passed to a new generation. It was little more than a decade after the Dodge family had moved to Detroit—a decade of experience that helped prepare John and Horace to seize the new opportunity. Their years at Tom Murphy's had taught them little they didn't already know about the machinist's trade, but the knowledge they acquired there about the men they worked for and with was invaluable.

The technical skills needed at Murphy's came easy to the brothers, but the physical labor was perpetually demanding. Sometime in the early 1890s—the most likely date is after John's marriage to Ivy and before the birth of their first child—John Dodge was no longer able to meet those physical demands. He suffered from fever and chills, from a feeling of weakness, from a racking cough that persisted for months. Eventually he learned that he had tuberculosis. Modern research tells us that the disease often afflicts barrel-chested men like the Dodges, who are particularly susceptible to lung complaints.

In those days, doctors had few effective weapons against the scourge of TB. Thanks in large part to the strength and stamina he inherited from his Dodge forebears, John made a complete recovery. He always attributed his cure to heavy consumption of a medicine made by the local pharmaceutical firm of Parke, Davis and Company. He swigged down many a bottle of Formula 131—one of the chief ingredients of which was alcohol. Whatever the remedy may have done to the TB bacteria, its effect on John was to precipitate a habit of heavy drinking that lasted the rest of his life.

John's illness forced him to quit working for a time. Horace helped his brother through the resulting financial problems by taking a part-time job in addition to his regular work at Murphy's. He found extra work at Leland & Faulconer, a leading firm of precision machinists in Detroit. Run by another pair of talented brothers, Wilfred and Henry Leland, the shop had the most modern tools of the time and specialized in hair's-breadth accuracy. For Horace, Leland & Faulconer was like a playground, in contrast to the work at Murphy's, where brute force often counted for more than finesse.

So when John was well enough to look for work again, Horace decided to join him in looking for something new, something that required less physical labor and more skill. They found what they were looking for at Dominion Typograph, located across the river in Windsor, Ontario. According to a story that has become part of the Dodge legend, John was, as usual, the one who went to talk to the owner of the company about jobs for himself and Horace. Told that the company had only one position available, John answered promptly, "Either both of us come to work, or neither of us will." The story is probably apocryphal, but the spirit is certainly authentic. The Dodge brothers always worked as a team.

Sources differ as to the exact date on which the Dodges started to work in the Dominion Typograph shop, at the foot of Ouellette Street in downtown Windsor. But the 1894 *Windsor City Directory* lists John Dodge as the foreman of the shop and Horace as a "skilled machinist." Two years later, they were still listed at the same address, but the company name had changed, to Canadian Typograph Company, and the nature of the business was described as "manufacturer of typesetting machines and bicycles." It was on this site that the Dodge bicycle company began.

It is known that it was called the Evans & Dodge Bicycle Company; that it was founded in 1897 and located in premises leased from the typographic company in the Ouellette Avenue building; that there was a partner involved, Fred S. Evans, a Windsor businessman. It is not known how Evans & Dodge was related to Canadian Typograph, nor where the financial backing for the firm came from. That might have been Evans's contribution, or it might have been an investment made by Canadian Typograph. It surely did not come from the Dodges, who were strapped by the need to support their parents and their growing families, and by the expenses and lost earnings of John's recent illness.

More is known about the product of Evans & Dodge than about the business itself. You can see the E&D bicycle that John Dodge himself owned and rode regularly until 1905, in Detroit's Fort Wayne Museum. The old E&D looks very much like the hot new mountain bikes now seen on city streets as well as back roads. The all-aluminum frame is heavy, the tires huge, the handlebars unwieldy. This bicycle was built to last, to jolt over country roads without breaking down, to take a workingman back and forth to the job every day for years. Like everything the Dodge brothers were to build, the E&D bicycle was of the highest possible quality and durability. Superior workmanship characterized not only the moving parts but even the small ornamental details, such as the metal emblem on the fork—the intertwined initials *E* and *D* on a maple leaf. Whether manufacturing bicycles or automobiles, the Dodge brothers made their marketing and design decisions in a very simple way: They manufactured the products they themselves wanted to own.

Evans & Dodge remained in business for about two years. Then, for undocumented reasons, it was taken over by the National Cycle and Automobile Company, another Canadian firm. Production of the E&D bicycle was halted, but the new owners of the company did want to put Horace's ball bearing on their own bicycles. In lieu of cash at the time the company changed hands, National Cycle offered a continuing royalty on the bearing, as well as good jobs for both brothers.

The Dodges' acceptance of this offer led to the first and only separation of their entire lives. Horace was to stay in Windsor and make his machinist's skills available to National Cycle. John was sent to manage the company's plant in Hamilton, Ontario, several hundred miles away. For more than a year, Horace and John lived apart.

At the same time that National took over Evans & Dodge, it also acquired another bicycle manufacturer, the B. C. Stearns Company of Toronto. The company's manager at the time was Frederick J. Haynes. Haynes never forgot his first meeting with John Dodge. John told him to pack up all Stearns's machinery and ship it to Hamilton. Then, in the same brusque tone, he said, "You can come down yourself if you want to." It was characteristic of John's style that he didn't try to talk Haynes into taking the job he so gruffly offered: If Haynes wanted to come, John wanted to have him, but John wouldn't try to influence his decision. It is likewise typical of John's business acumen that he had judged his man correctly. Haynes not only decided to take the job, but also became a lifelong friend and business associate—and eventually the president of the car company the Dodge brothers founded.

A little over a year after John, Ivy and the three children moved to Hamilton, National Cycle and Automobile was itself taken over. The new owner was the Canadian Cycle and Motor Company. The takeover negotiations saw the Dodge brothers walk away with a shared total of $7,500 in cash, along with the understanding that Canadian Cycle would continue to pay the royalties on Horace's ball bearing as specified in the earlier contract with National.

At long last John and Horace found themselves in possession of the one thing they still needed to succeed in business, a little capital. Their taste of entrepreneurship with the E&D bicycle had whetted their appetites for owning their own business. This time they would have the resources to do it right. They would be able to lease appropriate premises, hire skilled workers, invest in the necessary tools.

There was never any question but that the location of the new business would be Detroit. It had become home to the Dodge family, and it was also the place where they had the largest number of business contacts. These included not only manufacturers of bicycles, but also makers of the form of transportation that was going to replace them—the car. By 1900, the Dodges were already auto enthusiasts. In the fall of that year, John's wife wrote a letter from their temporary home in Hamilton to an old friend back in Detroit, describing the beginning of the long and happy Dodge love affair with the car. "John is leaving tomorrow night with a young man to go to Niagara," she remarked. "They are taking the automobile. It's such fun. They can make it in four hours! Can you believe it . . . 40 miles in 4 hours!"

That same letter of Ivy's also elucidates the agonizing problem affecting John Dodge's family at that time. "Been feeling so bad ever since we left Detroit . . ." wrote Ivy woefully. "I'm so full of rheumatism and feeling so low. Will see the Doctor tomorrow." In fact, it was not rheumatism that Ivy was suffering from, but tuberculosis.

Sadly, Ivy was not as strong as John, or as lucky. Before they left Hamilton, she got so weak that she couldn't sit up to do her sewing, by which she had added to the household income. Still, she fought hard to get well. At the time she wrote that letter to her friend back in Detroit, she certainly knew that her "rheumatism" was tuberculosis and that it was probably going to kill her.

But she speaks cheerfully of seeing her friend again in Detroit when John and Horace open their business there, and lovingly describes in her letter the antics of her son, John, playing in the yard. A "saucy rogue," she called the two-year-old, who was rolling a hoop and gathering horse chestnuts.

A pretty young woman in the prime of her life, she had everything to live for: three lively young children, a husband whom she respected and bright prospects for the future that he could create. Although she clung to life long enough to return to Detroit, Ivy died the following October, in 1901. She was only thirty-seven, and she never got the chance to enjoy the wealth that was about to wash over the entire Dodge family. In fact, at the time she died, John had all his available funds tied up in his struggling young business and was unable to come up with the cash to buy his wife a plot in Detroit's new Woodlawn Cemetery and a decent headstone to mark her grave. He was forced to borrow the money from his mother's sisters.

Like his father forty years earlier, John was left with young children to care for. The oldest, Winifred, was just seven, and John Duval, the youngest, only three. He turned for help to his mother, the doughty Maria Dodge, then almost seventy years old and confined to a wheelchair. She rose to the occasion, leaving the home where she was looked after by Horace and Anna to move into John's house on nearby Trumbull Avenue. With her usual determination and energy, she threw herself into running her son's household and raising her grandchildren.

Although worries about his children may have been a distraction for John, he was able to lose his domestic problems in the new business he and Horace had started early in 1901. With the $7,500 profit from their bicycle venture, they bought machinery, hired men and moved into rented space in the Boydell Building, situated at the corner of Lafayette and Beaubien, which put the new company right in the center of the burgeoning industrial district of Detroit. It was a good location, in an attractive and solid building (which still stands today). The ceilings were high, the façade pleasantly ornamented, the space they rented large and airy. It never occurred to them to try to hold down their initial expenses by starting out in a shabby building or an inconvenient location. From the very beginning, Dodge Brothers, as they called the company, had about it an aura of substance and success.

Records show that in 1901, Dodge Brothers employed twelve men in the Boydell shop. They paid their workers from five to forty cents an hour; their own wages were set at the level of forty cents an hour. There were only two keys to the shop door. That meant that one of the brothers had to be there in the morning to open the business, and one to close it at night. In fact, one key would have been enough, for both Dodges worked at the shop from opening to closing—and beyond. According to an article written about John Dodge in the *Evening News* in 1915:

> When the other men had called it a day and gone home, John and Horace Dodge would lock up, go out for a glass of milk and a sandwich, and then come back to the shop and work until midnight, getting out plans for machinery, estimates, designs, making tracings, studying books on mechanics for aid in solving some abstruse problem that confronted them. And John Dodge kept the accounts, made out statements, and wrote letters on the typewriter to his customers.

One of the first orders to come into the Dodge Brothers shop was for a few automobile engines, from car manufacturer Ransom Olds, the founder of the Oldsmobile Corporation: It was their earliest involvement with the business in which they were to make their fortunes.

Ransom Olds had been experimenting with cars since the mid-1880s, or about the time that the Dodges moved to Detroit. Olds's first models used steam engines, but, in 1896, he came up with a gasoline-powered engine and began to manufacture the cars in his native city, Lansing. Needing capital to expand his operation, Olds went into a partnership with Detroiter Samuel L. Smith and moved his factory to that city in 1899, out on East Jefferson, at the present site of the giant Uniroyal plant. Like most car manufacturers at the turn of the century, Olds made a small number of cars in many different models, including a topless runabout, a covered tonneau, a sturdier touring runabout and a delivery wagon for the commercial market. Competition among early auto manufacturers was fierce; there were more than 150 companies making cars in 1901, and probably a total of only 8,000 cars on the road, including foreign imports. The Oldsmobile was well accepted in the marketplace, but the very existence of the company was threatened when the factory burned to the ground in March 1901.

The only Oldsmobile model that survived the blaze was a light and inexpensive runabout with a small combustion engine, high tufted seat and curved dash. Olds decided that the way to save his company was to concentrate on producing that single model and turn out as many as he possibly could. To speed up production, he subcontracted the manufacture of some of the engines. Leland & Faulconer made a 3.7 horsepower engine for the Olds, but they couldn't work fast enough. So Ransom Olds came knocking at Dodge Brothers' door. Their version of the Olds engine developed only three horsepower, but they delivered the order on time and the engines were well made. Olds was so pleased with them that he decided to contract out to the Dodge brothers the manufacture of all the chain-and-sprocket-driven two-speed transmissions needed for his tubular-frame cars; thus his factory would be able to keep up with the rapidly increasing demand for the "merry Oldsmobile." The Oldsmobile, which sold for just $650, was in fact the first car ever to be successfully mass-produced. It is also the oldest car still manufactured under the same name.

Ransom Olds placed his order for 3,000 transmissions in early 1902, when Dodge Brothers was scarcely more than a year old. It was a huge order—probably the biggest in the auto industry at that date—for a small company. It meant that John and Horace had to expand their business immediately. They were able to acquire additional machines worth about $10,000, when Canadian Cycle and Motor Company failed. In lieu of the royalties owed by the company for the use of Horace's ball bearing, the Dodge brothers were offered their choice of the firm's stock of machinery.

New premises were also needed for the business, which had already outgrown the rented space in the Boydell Building. The brothers found a lot at the corner of Monroe and Hastings, a site now swallowed up by the construction of the Chrysler Freeway. Thanks to the security of the Oldsmobile contract, along with other work as well, including several jobs for Henry Leland, Dodge Brothers was able to build its own plant. The new quarters were modern and convenient, incorporating all that John and Horace had learned about the ideal machine shop, and there was ample room for future expansion—which, as matters turned out, would be much needed.

The Olds order made Dodge Brothers one of the largest suppliers in the automotive industry. In 1903, the total number of cars produced in the United States by all manufacturers was just over 11,000. About 30 percent of those cars were Oldsmobiles, all containing transmissions built by the Dodges. Within eighteen months of opening their own business in Detroit, the Dodge brothers were prospering mightily. They continued to put most of their profits back into the business—their rapid expansion requiring a substantial amount of working capital. Rather than borrow the money, or solicit outside investment, the Dodge brothers obtained their capital by using their large profits to fuel future growth. They were willing to defer their own enjoyment of the firm's prosperity for a few more years, perhaps because they were so certain that they would eventually be as rich as they ever dreamed of being.

The expanding business continued to require most of their waking hours. According to Clarence Burton, author of *The City of Detroit, Michigan* (1922), the definitive history of the city of Detroit and the people who founded its major industries, "Both brothers worked early and late—a habit which they never forsook even after notable success had crowned their efforts. After their workmen had left the shop for the day, the brothers would continue their efforts often until midnight. . . ." The truth of the matter was that the long hours were not really a sacrifice for John and Horace. They truly enjoyed the work, as well as one another's companionship. Probably there was no place else they would rather be than in that machine shop, tinkering to make things work better and faster the next day.

John and Horace were so engrossed in their growing business that they had little time for anything else. For Horace's wife, Anna, that meant a quiet domestic life: caring for her children, doing housework, cooking meals. She had stopped giving piano lessons after the accident with the milk bottle that damaged the tendon in her hand, but her contribution to the household income was no longer really necessary, so she was free to devote herself to the needs of her family. In later life, she was to look back sentimentally and declare that this period, when she was packing Horace's lunch pail every day, was the happiest of her existence.

A few blocks away, at John's house, Maria Dodge was finding that her physical disabilities made it impossible for her to do the actual work involved in keeping house and looking after three young children. She needed help, and her daughter-in-law Anna thought she knew just the right person. When she first moved to Detroit, she had made friends with a girl her age who lived on the same block. She and Isabelle Smith had exchanged girlish confidences, helped one another with their studies. Their intimacy did not stop when they reached adulthood, for it was "Belle" who acted as Anna's supporter on her wedding day, taking the ferry with the bride for the lunch-hour ceremony at a Baptist church in Windsor, where Horace worked at Canadian Typograph, signing the marriage certificate as a witness and then returning to Detroit with the new Mrs. Horace Dodge when the wedding was over. Belle, by this time in her thirties, had not yet married. Anna knew her to be a hard worker, a respectable woman; so she suggested that her friend Belle should be hired to help Maria Dodge. Maria was enthusiastic. She liked Belle, and Belle in turn treated her with a welcome mixture of deference and respect. John's children liked Belle too. Their grandmother was too old to enter into their play, but the addition of Belle to the household returned the children's lives to something much closer to normal.

John Dodge must also have been thankful when Belle Smith arrived at the Trumbull Avenue house. She increased the comfort of his home, solving problems rather than creating them. The situation produced a bond between the fortyish widower and the sensible woman just seven years younger who fit so readily into his family life. But at the same time, John found himself attracted to another woman who had entered his life.

In 1902, Dodge Brothers placed an advertisement in the newspaper for a secretary for the office on Beaubien—a position made necessary by the new contract with Ransom Olds. One of the applicants interviewed by John was a young woman named Matilda Rausch. Matilda, often called "Tillie" by her family, had been born on October 19, 1883, shortly after John Dodge graduated from high school. She was born in Ontario, the daughter of a working-class couple, George and Margaret Glinz Rausch, who had emigrated to Detroit about the same time the Dodges arrived there, when Matilda was still a toddler. Like the Dodges, the Rausch family had moved to Detroit in search of increased opportunity, but their marketable skills were of a humbler order. George Rausch was a saloon keeper in the warehouse district by the waterfront. His Princess Saloon was located in a two-story brick building between larger warehouses, and the family lived above the premises. Matilda and her sister, Amelia, four years younger, grew up smelling the sour tang of the barrels of beer their father served, hearing the noise of the men in the saloon—men like John and Horace Dodge—blowing off steam at the end of the day. At school, the girls were teased about their father's occupation, and it didn't help that their short, stout, bustling mother kept a boardinghouse called the "Drydock Hotel" and also took in washing to help the family get ahead.

Matilda graduated from the eighth grade at Detroit's Duffield School, but she did not finish high school, choosing instead to go to work as soon as possible. She took a secretarial course at Gorsline Business College and then found her first job as a clerk at the E. J. Kruce Cracker Company. She answered the Dodge Brothers ad because she had a long commute to Kruce; she hoped to find something closer to home.

Scions of Detroit's old society families like to claim that their mothers remembered young Tillie Rausch from when she used to deliver the washing for her mother. The patronizing undertone in their voices makes it clear why Matilda grew up yearning to have money and all the nice things it could buy: a big house, fine china and linens, clothes made of satin and velvet and, most of all, the respect that wealth commands. Amelia remembered that Matilda used to walk along the streets of the fashionable residential districts in the evenings, looking through the lighted windows at the elegant scenes being played out in those comfortable houses. In her own home, she made an almost ludicrous effort to insist that the saloon keeper's family learn to do things "correctly": set the table properly, write ladylike notes to tradesmen.

Matilda's climb up the social ladder was perforce a difficult one. A girl of no background and limited education, she lacked even the advantage of beauty, that traditional tool of ambitious young women. Short of stature, like her mother, with dark hair, a sallow complexion and heavy features, Matilda looked matronly even in the earliest photos in the family collection, and she never succeeded in appearing either elegant or fashionable. But her determination to better herself was so great, it sufficed.

When Matilda was hired by Dodge Brothers, John—then forty, with traces of gray in his sandy hair and a bit of additional bulk to his muscular frame—took an immediate interest in her. They worked together, since it was John who handled the business affairs of the company. Soon, they were also together after work. John took Matilda to concerts, for Sunday drives, and other activities traditionally associated with courtship. The self-made man was no doubt impressed by her fierce determination to better herself, and by the strength of character that was the feminine counterpart of his own aggressiveness.

But on December 9, 1903, Matilda's hopes were dashed. Her suitor married Isabelle Smith.

The reasons for his decision were complex. His mother had been urging him to take the step for months. She liked Isabelle, thought she would make a good wife, perhaps feared that she might otherwise leave the household that needed her so. Isabelle may have encouraged that fear. Traditional morality probably also played a role in his decision. It is likely that Isabelle shared not just John's home, but his bed as well, and John still had enough of that strict Methodist outlook with which he was raised to feel troubled by the fact. He may well have felt pressed by his children, who liked Isabelle, and by his sister-in-law, who could reach him through the person to whom he was closest, his brother, Horace.

Eventually he gave in to the pressure, but, being John Dodge, he did it his way. The wedding took place in the remote Ontario town of Walkerville and was performed by the local Methodist minister, with Horace and Anna acting as witnesses. His position with Isabelle was thus regularized in the eyes of God and the province of Ontario, but he didn't intend the news to go much farther. Back in Detroit (where the records of a Canadian marriage would never be stumbled upon), he insisted that Isabelle continue to call herself his housekeeper, rather than his wife—it would be interesting to know how he explained the necessity for that concealment—and he himself never referred to his marriage. So successful was he at keeping the secret that it remained publicly unknown for nearly eighty years! Not until the 1980s, when Jean Pitrone and Joan Elwart uncovered the details and published them in their book *The Dodges*, was the silence broken.

3

The Dodge Brothers
Meet Henry Ford

While John and Horace Dodge were making transmissions for
Ransom Olds's mass-produced runabout, another car company—
one of the more than 500 formed between 1900 and 1908—was
about to enter the already crowded market. Called Ford and Malcolmson, it was a partnership between an ambitious and opportu-
nistic coal merchant, Alex Y. Malcolmson, and a would-be
entrepreneur with an interest in mechanics, Henry Ford. It was
inevitable that the paths of Ford and Dodge would soon cross.

In 1902, Henry Ford was just months short of his fortieth birthday, and his business record to date was certainly less than inspir-
ing. Something of a tinkerer from boyhood on, Ford had worked
his way up from jobs as a mechanic's apprentice in his home in
Dearborn, Michigan, to hold a good position as chief engineer at
Detroit's Edison Illuminating Company. Intrigued by what he believed was the potential of the infant automobile industry, he began to build a home-made car in a shed behind his house, using

plans from an article in *The American Machinist* called "How to Build a Simple Gasoline Engine From Odds and Ends." With the help of three other mechanics from Edison—James Bishop, Edward "Spider" Huff and George Cato—Ford managed to build a rudimentary automobile, which he called the "quadricycle," by 1896. Neighbors who observed the obsessed Ford driving his car up and down the surrounding streets, sometimes chasing carriages off the road, called him "crazy Henry"; colleagues at Edison Illuminating were more likely to refer to their tall, bony colleague with the piercing blue eyes as "a queer duck."

Henry Ford left Edison in 1899 to become the mechanical superintendent of the newly formed Detroit Automobile Company, a firm whose chief distinction was that it was the first car-manufacturing company to be established in Detroit. The model the company produced was one already designed by Henry Ford. Yet he was rarely in his office, spending much of his time tinkering in the company's shop at night, along with Oliver Barthel, an experienced auto mechanic; they were building a racing car, privately owned by Ford.

The backers of this venture were leading citizens with deep pockets, so the Detroit Automobile Company began life with every advantage. Yet the car never made it into production, and when the investors tried to press their superintendent into faster action, he instructed an underling to tell them he was out of town, and continued working on his racing car. When, in early 1901, scarcely a year after it was formed, the Detroit Automobile Company was dissolved, Ford immediately criticized the backers of the venture as "exploitative," but in fact they had waited until they had endured a loss of about $86,000 before they decided that the car would never make it into production and closed the company down. Ford biographer Robert Lacey surmises that the chief problem at Detroit Automobile was that "Henry Ford got out of his depth, for producing cars to sell in quantity required very different skills from designing and producing a single prototype."

Ford saw that the publicity surrounding racing cars was the best

This rare picture shows the prototype of the car Henry Ford designed for the Detroit Automobile Company; the car never went into production. (From the collections of Henry Ford Museum & Greenfield Village)

way to attract the interest of investors and buyers for another car-manufacturing venture. Thus he decided to enter the racing car he had built with the help of Oliver Barthel, in a twenty-five-mile race for gasoline cars on October 10, 1901, at the Detroit Fairgrounds. Although his driving skills were inadequate to the task, Ford managed to surge ahead at the last moment and defeat the world speed-record holder, Alexander Winton. At the conclusion of the race, Ford jumped out of his car and muttered, "Boy, I'll never do that again. I was scared to death." It is likely that the crowd of onlookers included two men who were themselves keenly interested in the potential of the gasoline engine, John and Horace Dodge.

The success of Ford's racer persuaded a group of five wealthy men (some of them investors in the failed Detroit Automobile Company) to back a new venture, the Henry Ford Motor Company, established in November 1901. As it turned out, the racing car was also the death of that company. Rather than put his mind on the problems of producing significant numbers of a car that would sell to the masses, Ford kept on trying to perfect his racing car. The investors became annoyed with his stubbornness and all the costly delays, and brought in Henry Leland to watch over his design work.

Henry Leland was a sophisticated mechanic used to dealing in tolerances measured in hundred-thousandths of an inch, whereas Henry Ford was an intuitive problem solver who proceeded by trial and error. Ford was intimidated by Leland, found it impossible to meet his demands and, in March 1902, was forced to leave the company. It was then reorganized under the name Cadillac Automobile Company and began to produce cars based on Leland's adaptation of an early design by Ford. So in this second venture, the company succeeded, and only Ford failed. He left with a settlement of just $900 and the right to retain his designs for a racing car.

He found a new partner with whom to continue his interest in racing. Tom Cooper, a wealthy bicycling champion, financed the construction of two huge racers, the most powerful cars in the world; they were called "Arrow" and "999," after the fastest trains of the day. Cooper's cars were designed with the help of a young engineering genius, Childe Harold Wills (named after Byron's hero, and a Byronically handsome man), a draftsman, engineer and student of chemistry and metallurgy, who had worked with Ford since March 1900, when Wills helped Ford build his racer, translating

Henry's ideas to the drawing board. Wills's professional training, mechanical precision and perfectionist drive were the perfect counterpoint to Ford's sloppy intuitiveness. They wanted to enter the 999 in a race that October, to be held in the sleepy resort town of Grosse Pointe. Henry refused to drive, and owner Tom Cooper, a daredevil on a bicycle, tried a test drive in the powerful racer and promptly gave up the idea. Cooper then brought in a cyclist friend named Barney Oldfield. He had just one week to learn to drive before he took the wheel on race day and won the five-mile race with a time of five minutes and twenty-eight seconds. Henry Ford was quick to take credit for the victory, and two weeks later he tried to add to the publicity by going for a world record. By this time, he had antagonized all the other people involved in the project: Tom Cooper, the owner of the racer, refused to co-operate, and Barney Oldfield refused to drive. The partnership was dissolved, but not before Ford had turned to his old colleague Spider Huff, to drive it to a new world record—for which Ford again claimed the credit.

At the time of this victory, Ford was already planning his next business venture. In the days when he worked at Edison Illuminating, he had used Alex Malcolmson's coal company as a regular supplier, and the two men had stayed in touch thereafter. Malcolmson, who had reaped significant profits from his coal business, had invested in a number of side enterprises to increase his net worth; he was not yet a wealthy man, but he was determined to become one. Like Ford, he believed that the automobile industry was soon going to experience tremendous growth through sales to a mass market, and he intended to share in those profits.

A partnership agreement between Malcolmson and Ford was signed in August 1902, setting up a new company called Ford Malcolmson Company Ltd. It specified that Malcolmson would make an initial investment of $500, plus "such further sums of money as may be needful and necessary to complete and equip said sample Commercial Automobile." For his part, Ford would contribute not only the designs for a specific "Commercial Auto-

In 1904, Henry Ford posed in the racer that was his sole contribution to the Ford Motor Company's physical assets. John Dodge is on the far left, Alex Malcolmson at right. (From the collections of Henry Ford Museum & Greenfield Village)

mobile,'' but also all his tools, dies, models, drawings and supplies that had anything to do with manufacturing automobiles. Even the racing car, the Arrow, became the property of the partnership. To protect himself further from Ford's tendency to tinker rather than solve the problems of production, the canny Malcolmson insisted on a clause that said, "Henry Ford further agrees to devote his time to the construction of a Commercial Automobile for exhibition purposes."

The strategy of Ford and Malcolmson was to create a prototype and then use it to raise the cash to finance a car-manufacturing company. The car in question looked very much like the one Ford had designed earlier for the Henry Ford Motor Company, the car that later became the first Cadillac. The significant difference in Ford's new car was its engine. That engine was in large part the brainchild of Harold Wills who was to work with Ford until 1919. The innovative feature of the new engine was that its twin cylinders were set in the engine block vertically instead of horizontally, a change that noticeably increased the engine's power and durability.

Ford and Malcolmson were convinced the new design was a potential winner. Although they had not yet found any investors, in November they drew up an agreement to form a corporation, to be called Ford Motor Company, to manufacture the car. The designs and patents for the car itself were considered to be worth 6,900 initial shares of stock to split. Each man additionally agreed to pay $35,000 in cash "or its equivalent" in order to receive 350 more shares of stock apiece. The remaining 7,400 shares of stock in the new company were to be sold to outside investors.

In actual fact, Ford did not have $35,000, or even a fraction of that sum, to invest in the new Ford Motor Company. He could contribute nothing but his plans, his ambitions and his labor. What little cash the company possessed came from Malcolmson, and it had to be nursed carefully. To keep an eye on the business side of the company, Malcolmson appointed as its manager his tough and efficient clerk at the coal yard, James Couzens. Space was rented for seventy-five dollars a month in a one-story carpenter shop on Mack Street. Ford's first expense was buying a pot-bellied stove to heat the shed.

There was no capital to build a factory, or to buy machines needed so the company could build its cars. It would do no more than attach the rubber tires and buggy seats to the running gears manufactured by the Dodges, and then attempt to sell them. Ford and Malcolmson were engaged in a highly speculative enterprise. At that time, the total number of cars registered in the United States was barely over 30,000, and the apparently small market was crowded with car manufacturers. The seriously undercapitalized Ford Motor Company would have to turn to better-financed suppliers to do the real work of manufacturing the cars.

Thanks to Harold Wills, the innovative engine of the Ford car would be its foremost market advantage. Thus the choice of a machine shop to make the engines—and all other mechanical parts—was crucial. The supplier would have to be capable of creating the new type of engine, and doing so quickly. And if sales of the Ford cars reached their projected levels, the shop would have to be able to gear up to meet a steadily increasing demand. Of course, all this would have to be done with the supplier's own capital.

The Ford Motor Company came knocking on the Dodge Brothers' door. The Dodges already had a reputation for the quality of their work, and their contract with Olds made them one of the largest suppliers in the infant auto industry. Not only was Dodge Brothers the best choice to do the work of building the running parts of the Ford car, but their association with the project would lend it much-needed credibility.

If it is obvious why Ford needed the Dodges, it is much less clear why the Dodges agreed to work for Ford. Henry Ford had yet to prove himself to be much more than an ambitious dreamer, and the Ford Motor Company was a discernibly undercapitalized venture that might collapse at any moment. By early 1903, Dodge Brothers employed more than 150 men in the modern factory the company had just built out of its profits. Orders from Olds continued to pour in, and there was a potential order of even greater magnitude from the Great Northern Railroad. If John and Horace decided to take on the job for Ford, they would be risking all they had achieved. They would have to use their own money to retool all presses and lathes in the factory to manufacture the machines for Ford, and they would be so busy with the Ford order they would be unable to continue working for any other customer. As events were soon to demonstrate, so few people in Detroit had any real faith in Ford that Malcolmson was virtually unable to raise outside capital for the firm. If hard-headed investors declined to put their money in the speculative venture, why would John and Horace Dodge bet their entire company on it?

One thing is certain, it was not because of some positive personal chemistry between the Dodges and Henry Ford. The lanky Ford was an ascetic who never drank, remained stick-thin because he paid almost no attention to food, had few friends and supressed his emotions. He disliked confrontations and attempted instead to gain his advantage by subterfuge and manipulation. Wily and devious, possessed of an overweening ambition, Henry Ford was almost the exact opposite in every way of the Dodge brothers. John and Horace were bluff and straightforward businessmen who prided themselves on their honesty and self-reliance. They liked to meet opposition head on and thrash it to the ground. Personally, the corpulent brothers were hearty characters with loudly expressed preferences, voracious appetites for food and drink and an interest in all kinds of new experiences. One final area of incompatibility was due to Henry Ford's extremely superstitious nature. He feared the negative influence of redheaded men; every time he saw one, he had to offset bad luck by looking for a white horse. Daily meetings with the redheaded Dodge brothers must have been a serious strain! It is difficult to imagine how the three men could spend ten minutes together, let alone embark on an extended business partnership.

Some accounts suggest that the reason was the Dodges' belief in the car Ford was going to manufacture. That seems unlikely. The Ford was not a significant engineering advance over the Olds, and Horace Dodge had immediately found fault with some aspects of the car's design. He insisted on making changes to the rear axle and even the engine itself before Dodge Brothers would consider getting involved.

Robert Lacey has advanced the theory that the Dodges agreed to work with Ford because the new company was forced to offer them a better business deal than was customary. The transmissions Dodge Brothers built for Ransom Olds were delivered on standard terms, giving Olds thirty to sixty days to pay. The Ford Motor Company's poor credit rating, coupled with Henry Ford's lack of any personal fortune, meant that Ford would have to pay for its initial purchases on delivery, and all subsequent deliveries would come with bills attached that were due within five days. Certainly, the terms of sale were good ones, but there was little reason for the Dodge brothers, whose business was already generating a healthy profit, to be so anxious to get their money two to six weeks faster that they would take the manifest risk of never getting paid at all. All those favorable terms in the contract were not likely to have been the reason the Dodges decided to work with Ford, but only the protection they insisted on once they had decided to participate in such a risky venture.

The best guess at an explanation for the Dodge brothers' decision may be their appreciation of the team at Ford Motor Company. There was Couzens, with his hard-headed business sense and his strong grasp of the day-to-day operations of the company. There was the smooth-talking Malcolmson to recruit investors and lure the buyers. There was Harold Wills, with his engineering brilliance, to pin down the designs on paper. And finally there was Henry Ford, whose flair for publicity had already made his name well known to the public. At the suggestion of the Dodge brothers, the new company also tried to hire Fred Haynes as production manager, but Haynes turned down the offer; he did not believe that Ford would be able to pay him the $2,500-a-year salary he was being promised.

Beyond that, we must look to the Dodge brothers' own personalities for an answer. They liked risk, whether in fast cars or fast-growing businesses. They were men with a pronounced appetite for life, and they were also men who always loved a challenge. It was completely in character for them to choose the risky over the safe, the unfamiliar over the accustomed, the new challenge over the boring routine.

So on February 28, 1903, an agreement was signed between John F. Dodge and Horace E. Dodge, copartners as Dodge Brothers of Detroit, and Henry Ford and Alex Y. Malcolmson, copartners doing business as the Ford Motor Company. The agreement called for Dodge Brothers to manufacture, sell and deliver 650 "automobile running gears," which were to be "complete in every particular, except the wheels, tires and body." The Ford Motor Company would provide the designs, and Dodge Brothers would start delivering the machines by May 15 of that year.

The price of each machine would be $250, so the total contract was worth $162,500. The Dodges were to receive an advance payment of $5,000 on March 15, another $5,000 on April 15, and a third $5,000 payment the minute they began delivery of the machines on May 15, provided that they could demonstrate they had spent equivalent amounts of money on machinery, tools and materials needed for the job. That total advance of $15,000 was personally guaranteed by Malcolmson in a separate document, as demanded by the wary Dodges. It amounted to the purchase price of the first sixty running gears, and Ford agreed to pay cash on delivery for the next forty. A clause in the contract stipulated that if Ford ever failed to pay for the machines on time, Dodge Brothers then owned "such machines or any part thereof as may be on hand and undelivered" and could sell them as they chose, without further obligation to Ford.

As soon as they signed the contract with Ford, John and Horace Dodge began to gear up for the work. In actual fact, they spent more than $60,000 in the next few months on new machines and tools. Thus they were owed their first payment as specified in the contract on March 15, 1903. But on that date the Ford Motor Company had no cash. There were not yet any outside investors or advance orders for the car. Malcolmson's initial investment had already been spent in developing the designs, and Ford had no funds to make the $35,000 investment he had pledged. Ford Motor Company tried to stall the Dodge brothers, asking them to wait for their first payment. But John Dodge refused, and threatened to withdraw from the agreement and sell the parts so far manufactured to someone else. Thus Malcolmson was forced to honor his personal guarantee for that first payment, and the second one, due on April 15, as well. Short of funds at the time, he managed to obtain the money through a loan from his uncle, banker John S. Gray, who insisted on receiving shares in the company in return for his cash. Gray also demanded that he be made president of the new venture.

By early May, the Dodges found themselves in a disagreeable position. Although they had already spent the money needed to prepare their plant to undertake the Ford contract, they had received only $10,000 in advance payments. As is usual with newly organized companies, things at Ford were moving more slowly than predicted. The search for investors, the building of a dealer network, the organizational decisions, the planning of an advertising and marketing campaign—all took time. The delays meant that Dodge Brothers could not start delivering the machines (and therefore billing Ford for additional payments) until the first of July, six weeks later than anticipated. John and Horace were, of course, aware that part of the delay was due to Ford Motor Company's desperate lack of funds, which might cause the company to fail before it could accept delivery of the first machines. Malcolmson was doing his best to create interest in the forthcoming cars and to procure advance orders. But an ad he published in May caused the Dodge brothers to erupt, when they read that Ford Motor Company had leased the Dodge Brothers plant! An angry John Dodge forced the publisher of the paper to print a correction and received the demanded apology from Malcolmson for the falsehood, which was intended to shore up Ford Motor Company's credibility. But it seemed that John Dodge was one of the few readers to notice the ad; no money came in from eager customers.

At that point, John and Horace had two options. One was to pull out of the deal, swallow a $50,000 loss and look for other business, which might take months (and additional capital outlay) to develop. The other was to stick with Ford Motor Company and wait and hope it could find enough financing to continue as planned.

The Dodges chose the latter option, and then they committed themselves further by becoming investors in the company. They agreed jointly to invest $10,000, for which they would receive 100 shares of stock in the company, reorganized in 1903 to issue a total of just 1,000 shares. Only $3,000 of their investment had to be in cash, and that was in the form of a note, which John and Horace rather shrewdly arranged to have come due six months later, assuming the delay would give them time to see whether the company would succeed or fail. The bulk of their investment was $7,000 worth of materials that would be used for making the Ford machines.

Thus the Dodges were significant financial backers of the company as well as an important part of the manufacturing process. Their $10,000 was equal to the investment of John Gray, and greater than the amounts put in by most of the rest of the outside investors. The failure of Ford's earlier ventures discouraged Detroit's wealthy men from reaching for their checkbooks, and Malcolmson was unable to obtain so much as a dime from anyone who was not intimately connected with his own coal business. The motley crew of investors in the Ford Motor Company included Malcolmson's clerk, James Couzens; his two lawyers, John Anderson and Horace Rackham; his cousin, Vernon Fry; his bookkeeper, Charles Woodall; and Albert Strelow, the man who was renting Ford Motor Company the small carpenter shop in which the first vehicles were to be assembled. Harold Wills had no money to buy shares in the company for himself, but Henry Ford was obligated by an earlier agreement to give Wills a percentage of all that Ford personally made from the company. Malcolmson approached many of the city's businessmen, but all declined the opportunity to participate in another car company associated with Henry Ford. One of Detroit's leading citizens, Mark Stevens, remembers that his own father turned down the request, and although Stevens himself is a great admirer of Henry Ford, he concedes that his father's judg-

This 1903 photo shows the interior of the Dodge plant at Monroe and Hastings, about the time the company began to build the Ford machines. (From the collections of Henry Ford Museum & Greenfield Village)

ment was correct at the time. The Ford Motor Company was simply too speculative a venture for a responsible family man to sink his savings into.

The Ford Motor Company was incorporated on June 16, and two days later, the first stockholders meeting was called. Among the business on the agenda was the election of a board of directors, and John Dodge was one of the electees. On June 20, the Board of Directors gave formal approval to the contract between Ford Motor Company and Dodge Brothers, and on June 26, a check, written by the new firm, was sent to Dodge Brothers for the third installment of $5,000 due as an advance. On the same day, the company wrote Malcolmson a check for $10,000 to reimburse him for the money he had personally paid the Dodges earlier in the year. There was also a check to the Hartford Rubber Company, of Hartford, Connecticut, for $640, covering the purchase of sixty-four tires, enough for the first sixteen cars. Those checks almost wiped out the funds deposited to the company's account by its few investors. The only hope for the future was the quick sale of a significant number of Ford cars.

In the first week of July, Dodge Brothers began to deliver the machines. The chassis, engines and transmissions were built in the plant at Monroe and Hastings. A contemporary photograph shows a clean and well-organized space, with supplies stacked where they would be needed, overhead pulleys to move the heavy metal parts and dozens of neatly dressed workmen. Despite the prosperous appearance of the premises, cash flow into Dodge Brothers at that time was nil. Horace and John felt so strapped that they paid themselves just $43.50 per week. But their great gamble was about to pay off.

The finished machines were individually tested at Dodge Brothers and then loaded onto horse-drawn wagons for the trip to the little workshop on Mack Street that was the total physical plant of the Ford Motor Company. (A replica of the workshop at that time can be seen in Ford's Greenfield Village.) There Ford's dozen or so employees, paid $1.50 a day for their labor, would put on the bodies and upholstered seats that were purchased from Detroit carriage builder C. R. Wilson, later to become one of the largest body makers in the auto industry; add the wheels from the Prudden Company of Lansing; and then mount the Hartford Rubber Company's tires on the wheel rims. The Ford shop was so inadequately equipped for production that the heavy bodies had to be lowered onto the running gears by hand, through a series of jury-rigged ropes!

When the first order for a Ford car came in—from a Chicago dentist, who paid $850 in a check drawn on the Illinois Trust and Savings Bank—the company was ready to deliver his car. The only threat to the scheduling was Henry Ford himself, who was still trying to work out improvements to the vehicles. Manager James Couzens almost had to kidnap the finished cars from the Ford workshop, take them to the waiting freight car and nail the door shut to insure they would go out on time and provide the income needed to keep the company afloat.

The first Ford, priced to sell for $750, was a somewhat comical vehicle that looked very much like a wagon mounted on bicycle wheels. The body, for which Ford paid its supplier fifty-two dollars, was little more than a wooden platform that sat atop the Dodge-built chassis. The seat, which cost sixteen dollars, was an upholstered bench with a back, to which—for an extra $100—an optional tonneau, or cover, could be attached. The huge wheels were higher than the bottom of the seat and had the wire spokes of a bicycle wheel. The tires were thin and white. Instead of a steering wheel, there was a rod, which the driver pushed to left or right; the throttle was also controlled by hand. The car had two forward gears, as well as reverse. The Ford/Wills/Dodge engine was the only innovative feature, and it was able to produce eight horsepower from its two vertical cylinders. This car was Ford Motor Company's original Model A—and it caught the public's fancy.

Starting with that order from the Chicago dentist, sales of the Model A were gratifying. By March of 1904, nine months after the first sale, all 650 units Dodge Brothers had agreed to provide had been sold. Ford's total sales, however, were a small fraction of those for the entire auto industry, which put about 11,000 cars on the road in 1903 and twice that number in 1904. But the sales were as good as Ford Motor Company had expected them to be. With almost no capital investment and an extremely low overhead—labor costs at Ford were estimated to be no more than twenty dollars per car—the sale of a few hundred vehicles was profitable. Malcolmson estimated that the company made about $150 on each vehicle.

Early in 1904, Ford decided to step up production slightly. A new contract with Dodge Brothers was signed at the beginning of the year for 755 running gears to be delivered by May 1904. There was also an option clause, which Ford Motor Company exercised, that allowed the company to order an additional 500 by early April. To meet the increased demand, Dodge Brothers would have to expand its capacity even further.

After gambling successfully and profitably that the Ford car would sell to the public, John and Horace Dodge were easily able to expand as needed. By the middle of March 1904, Dodge Brothers had been paid the entire $162,500 called for in their initial contract. There are no records to show how much of that payment represented gross profits after all costs were paid. A reasonable rate of return at that time and in that industry was 15 percent, which would have given the Dodges a profit of about $25,000 on their venture in less than a year.

As major investors in Ford Motor Company, John and Horace Dodge stood to gain from the Ford profits as well. The first dividends were paid in November 1903, and a second installment was voted in January 1904. By June of that year, the total profit on the first 650 cars, about $100,000, had been paid out to the stockholders. That was about equal to the amount that was invested in the first place, so all parties got back what they had put in. Apparently, the Ford Board of Directors had decided that repaying investors had the highest priority. Very little of the company's profit went back into the business, for, by the end of 1904, Ford's entire stock of machinery and factory equipment was still worth less than $10,000—a fraction of the value of the Dodge Brothers plant. Part of the reason for this policy was that Henry Ford was thoroughly enjoying the first financial success of his life. He had never invested any money at all, only his designs and patents, in the company that bore his name. By the summer of 1904, he had made at least $25,000 in return. No wonder he felt able finally to buy his first dress suit and then, dressed in his purchase, to sit for a formal photograph!

John and Horace Dodge continued, as was their wont, to put most of their profits back into their business. By early 1904, they had recouped their initial outlay on the contract as well as their personal investment of $10,000, and could look forward to future profits at Dodge Brothers for the manufacture of the Ford running gears and future dividends from Ford as the reward for their risk.

4

The Money Starts
to Roll In

Together, as always, John and Horace went to see boatbuilder Peter Studer in the spring of 1904, their profits from the Ford venture already starting to burn a hole in their joint pocket. They wanted to order a steam launch, they told him, and they intended it to be the fastest on the Detroit River. Studer was at that time working on a racing boat for Ransom Olds, but he was willing to take the Dodges' order as well. To his surprise, they told him they would supply the engine themselves: Horace was building it at Dodge Brothers, fulfilling the childhood dream of the boy who worked on marine engines in his father's shop on the St. Joseph River. Horace believed his engine would push the boat through the water at the tremendous speed of forty miles an hour, in those days a difficult speed to attain even on land, let alone on water. But his chance to test that belief had to be delayed. On the morning of June 14, 1904, there was a gasoline explosion in Studer's small frame house, adjoining the boatyard. Boatyard employees were able to rescue only two small launches before the fire got out of control and forced them to leave the scene. The Dodges' boat was completely destroyed; their $1,800 investment had gone up in smoke.

By this time in their lives, John and Horace were able to laugh off a disaster of this magnitude and place an order for another boat. Their own company's profits on the Ford contract remained high, and dividends from their ownership of Ford stock kept coming in. In no way daunted, Horace decided to use some of his share of the income to buy a house in a prosperous middle-class neighborhood. The house he and Anna chose was a red-brick Victorian at 642 Forest Street, very near the present campus of Wayne State University. The wide street was lined with trees, there was a small backyard where the two children could play, and Woodward Avenue, with its commercial establishments and public transportation, was only a few blocks away.

The house had been built for Frank Robson, a Detroit lawyer, in 1891, and still stands today. There are small touches of elegance, such as a bow window in the room on the second floor over the entry porch, and gray sandstone pillars, foundation and trim to provide a pleasant contrast with the red brick. The spacious parlor was decorated with a stained-glass window, and across the hall there was a formal dining room, always an indicator of some degree of economic abundance. The second floor contained four bedrooms, which probably meant that Della/Delphine and Horace Junior each had their own room. The house was two and a half stories high, with a gable to admit light into the attic (presumably intended for use by a live-in domestic). The kitchen was located in a wing extending into the rear of the narrow lot, a common practice in the days when kitchen fires were practically routine. Even today, after decades of neglect, the house is still snug, a prime candidate for renovation.

One of the most interesting features of 642 Forest Street is its carriage house, located on the alley at the rear. That building was not original to the 1891 house, but was constructed by Horace

The house on Forest Street, where Horace and Anna and their two children lived from 1904 to 1908, still stands. (Collection of David Agresta)

Dodge after he moved in, with the aid of skilled workmen from the Dodge Brothers plant. Built of red brick and stone, to match the house, the carriage house seems to have been intended to stand for centuries. Ornamental embellishments include a central stone pediment and fancy brickwork around the doors. But the central feature is the solidity of the construction, the stamp of Dodge

Brothers quality. It appears able to withstand anything from natural disasters to aerial attack.

The records do not say whether Horace had a Ford to park in his carriage house. Its style, with wide barnlike doors, indicates that it was built to accommodate a horse-drawn carriage, but whether that was the family mode of transportation or a courtesy for visitors is not clear. In addition to its ordinary function, the carriage house was also a workshop for Horace. When he wasn't working out some design problem at the shop at Monroe and Hastings, he was doing the same thing in his own backyard.

The house itself was Anna's domain. It is a safe assumption that she had at least a "hired girl" to help with the housework and the children, if not a live-in maid. She also had the assistance of a niece. Anna's sister, Mae, ten years older than Anna and long since married to Robert McNutt, had a daughter named Ella. At the time Anna and Horace moved into the Forest Street house, Ella was a high-school student, and it was arranged that she would live with her aunt and uncle, because their home was much closer than the McNutts' to the school. Ella's recollection of this period was of a tranquil and private household, enlivened by such mild diversions as needlepoint, a game of cards and evening readings from the Bible. The heavy-boned Anna had a matching heaviness of spirit, a Scots dourness, that always pervaded her relationships.

Anna's husband's life was not so quiet. Horace and his brother had the habit of stopping off at a saloon every night after work, although by this time they were more likely to do their drinking in the expensive establishments along Woodward Avenue, such as Charlie Churchill's, rather than in cheap warehouse-district bars like the one owned by Matilda Rausch's father. The new surroundings were classier, but the evening was just as likely to end on a rowdy note. Stories of the Dodge brothers from this era are still recounted with gusto in Detroit. One tells of an evening that sounds like something out of the Wild West: The tipsy John Dodge insisted that a saloon proprietor dance for him, and when the man refused, John drew out his revolver and used it to "persuade" him. Another anecdote that is part of the Dodge legend is about the wrath of either John or Horace. One of them—there are two versions of the story, and it is hard to say which brother is the more likely protagonist—was trying to start his Ford to go home after a night of heavy drinking. Somebody standing on the sidewalk watched with amusement his efforts to turn the stiff crank, and finally burst into outright laughter at the scene, asking "What's the matter? Can't you start her?" Whichever Dodge brother it was walked straight over to the mirthful onlooker, punched him in the nose and then calmly returned to continue his cranking.

One thing all the stories, however disreputable, seem to have in common is the outcome. John or Horace Dodge would always return afterward to make amends. They paid for damages incurred, they apologized profusely and sincerely. Although some of the incidents in which they were involved have an ugly ring to them—a sense of overgrown bullies quite literally throwing their weight around—it seems that in the end even the victims forgave them. The remorse of the Dodge brothers was genuine, as was their willingness, at least by the morning after, to accept responsibility for their actions.

One of the few events in the lives of the Dodge brothers that seems out of character is the entire episode of John's second marriage. In general, he was the kind of man who did what he wanted to, and then looked other people in the eye and dared them to comment. The furtiveness of his marriage to Isabelle Smith is very un-Dodgelike. He continued to refuse to allow her to call herself Mrs. John Dodge, and treated the poor woman abominably. He came and went as he pleased, without regard for her convenience, and, worse yet, he continued to court Matilda Rausch.

It is even possible that at the same time the married John was courting Matilda, he was also interested in her sister. Matilda, presumably desirous of having her own ally on the premises, arranged for her younger sister, Amelia, to start work as a secretary at Dodge Brothers in the summer of 1904. Amelia was definitely more attractive than her sister, with more delicate features and a slimmer figure. Family photos show Amelia to be an appealing gamine under a huge mop of hair, in contrast to the dumpier Matilda, with her severe expression. Since Amelia took herself less seriously, she was more likely to laugh and to enjoy whatever came her way; surely she was more fun to be with than the soberly ambitious Matilda.

Amelia obviously thought the world of her dynamic boss. In a newspaper interview in 1980, she told a reporter, "I've worn a hair net since 1906, just to show how fussy he was. He didn't want a hair out of place on a woman. Why, I'm 93, and I still wear a hair net." In private interviews around the same period, Amelia confessed her awareness that John Dodge had been attracted to her. She also believed that the attraction was one of the reasons that her sister was determined to marry John herself.

Determined she was, and it appears that by early 1906 she and John Dodge had come to some sort of secret agreement about their future. Matilda left her job at Dodge Brothers (and, interestingly, she insisted that her sister leave as well). Although she briefly worked as a secretary at the Detroit Lumber Company, Matilda soon left that position too, and seemed instead to be making a career out of preparing herself to be a rich man's wife. She took piano lessons and studied elocution and enrolled in a class that taught young women to manage servants. Presumably these self-improvement efforts were funded by John Dodge and were based on the expectation that she would one day be mistress of his household.

Sometime in 1905, Isabelle Smith Dodge left the house on Trumbull Avenue, her situation there having become untenable. At the same time, John began building a new house for himself out on Boston Boulevard, a street in a newly developed residential area to the north of downtown Detroit. Situated on a large lot off Woodward Avenue, John's new home was an impressive red-brick house that fell just short of mansion status and reportedly cost about $250,000 to build. Three full stories high, it was richly dec-

John Dodge's old house on Boston Boulevard is now owned by the Catholic Arch-diocese of Detroit; in 1987, when the Pope visited Detroit, he stayed at the former Dodge residence. (Courtesy of the Archdiocese of Detroit)

orated with stained glass, and the major rooms on the ground floor were fully paneled. In addition to the usual living and dining rooms and a full complement of bedrooms, the house had a library and even a billiard room on the top floor. The difference in scale and luxury between the house that John Dodge felt able to build in 1906 and the much more modest house that Horace had bought in 1904 gives a clue to the speed with which prosperity was over-taking the Dodges.

The people who knew John Dodge intimately were quick to see the connection between the departure of his second wife and the building of a magnificent new home. Clearly, he was planning to marry a woman he considered a suitable mistress for such a house.

This plan was viewed with dismay and opposition by various members of his family.

Sister-in-law Anna was strongly opposed to the idea. Isabelle had been her close friend for years, and Anna was both sorry and angry to see her leave. Moreover, there was a personal slight in the situation as well: John's action seemed to imply that Anna's friends were not good enough for his social ambitions. This episode probably set the seal on Anna's personal dislike of John. She considered her husband's older, more aggressive brother a bad influence on the milder Horace, and she was sure that the Dodge brothers' after-work drinking and carousing took place at John's instigation. Anna unleashed her anger at Horace when he and John stayed out too late or behaved too outrageously. She also fought back with her Bible reading, which had a definite effect on the man who had been raised such a strict Methodist, and with her emphasis on the sanctity of home and family—a sanctity that John's dismissal of Belle seemed to throw in doubt. Horace might be temporarily abashed, but no one, not even a wife, could diminish the intimacy of the two brothers.

John's mother, Maria, was even more opposed to his plan than Anna. After Isabelle left, Maria Dodge tried to continue managing his household. But she was by this time in her seventies and increasingly debilitated by her illness, and the task was beyond her. Probably much of her resentment against John for his treatment of Isabelle was personal. She missed the presence of the daughter-in-law who had devoted her time and energy to making the elder Mrs. Dodge comfortable. Matters reached the breaking point about the time the Boston Boulevard house was finished. Maria refused to move to the new house with her son and her grandchildren. She did not even want to stay in Detroit, but went instead to live with two of her sisters in Decatur, Michigan, a small town in the vicinity of Niles.

The effect of these upheavals on John and Ivy's three children was surely negative. They had lost their mother when they were very young and then had learned to accept their grandmother and their father's second wife as substitutes. In less than a year's time, these women too were gone. When the family moved into the Boston Boulevard house in 1906, Winifred was twelve, Isabel ten, and John Duval almost nine. Suddenly, the children were virtually on their own. Their father continued to work long hours at the shop and to look for his relaxation in the man's world of the saloon. Presumably, he hired people to look after the house, do the cooking and keep an eye on the children, but essentially they had no family but themselves. Winifred and Isabel turned to one another for emotional support, creating an intimacy that would last for the rest of their lives. John Duval, his mother's "saucy rogue," was left to his own devices. For all three children, the splendors of their new home probably did little to compensate for their emotional losses.

John Dodge was surely aware of the strains within his family, but he had other things to worry about. One was Dodge Brothers' attempt to keep up with the demand from Ford Motor Company. Early in 1905, James Couzens talked to a reporter about the great success of the Ford Motor Company. "We are now turning out 25 machines a day on an average, and giving employment to 300 men." What he failed to mention was that the lion's share of the production was still being done at the Dodge Brothers plant, where almost all of the 300 men were employed.

The Ford Motor Company had finally built a small factory at Beaubien and Piquette, slightly to the north of Dodge Brothers' location. It was the work of architects Field, Hinchman & Smith, and was built at the cost of $76,500—about one-third the price tag for John Dodge's new house. The three-story brick building was a standard New England mill design, about 400 feet long and 56 wide. Engines, chassis, brakes, gears and axles were built and assembled into running gears at the Dodge Brothers plant and then sent to the new Ford plant, where workers had only to add wheels, tires and boxlike bodies. By mid-1905, Ford was asking for 400 machines a month. Obviously, Ford, which still produced none of its own parts, could work at a much faster rate than was comfortable for Dodge Brothers, which had to buy expensive machinery to build the mechanical parts of the car and train skilled machinists to operate it.

The problem was exacerbated as Ford began to turn out new models, in addition to the original Model A. The Model B was a bigger, heavier and more expensive car, aimed at the higher end of the market; it was produced during 1904 and then dropped the following year because it proved to be unpopular with the car-buying public. A later attempt at penetrating the market for expensive cars, the Model K, was also short-lived. Models C and F were updates of the A, with minor improvements and a higher price tag. At the end of 1906, Ford introduced the Model N, which was another step closer to fulfilling Henry Ford's ideal of a light but durable car with a low purchase price.

The speed with which Dodge Brothers had to expand led to occasional problems with their product. John and Horace Dodge had organized their factory on a piecework basis. Rather than pay a fixed salary to their workers, they paid them for the work they actually accomplished; they believed that was the way to get the best from their men. Henry Ford took issue with this approach, claiming that it caused workers to concentrate on quantity rather than quality. He informed the Dodges that some of the machines they were delivering were faulty and would have to be rejected by the Ford Motor Company. John was so incensed by this accusation that he rushed over to the Ford premises and dared supervisor Fred Rockelman to show him a single defective machine, threatening to knock Rockelman down if he couldn't back up Ford's complaint about Dodge workmanship. As it happened, Rockelman could, and it is characteristic of John Dodge that as soon as he was shown a few faulty engines, he laughed at his own impetuousness, apologized to Rockelman and then hurried back to his own factory to set to work solving the problem. Henry Ford later said of the incident, "Oh, those Dodge brothers, their bark is worse than their bite."

The quality-control problem was solved without changing from the piecework method of payment. The real problem was not the way employees were paid, but the rate at which everyone had to work. The pressure continued, since Ford was growing by leaps and bounds. In a letter dated April 21, 1906, the Ford Motor Company begged Dodge Brothers to rush an order of much-needed parts so production could be speeded up yet again. And on the first business day of 1907, Henry Ford wrote the Dodges a letter in which he discussed shipments of parts for the new Model N car. He said he expected to run his shops "night and day, if necessary, so as to clean up all of the model N cars by September and believe you ought to run your shop nights until you have at least a thousand of the transmissions and differentials ahead of us." It was a heavy work load, however profitable it turned out to be.

And there was worry connected with the association with Ford as well. For Henry Ford was providing dramatic evidence of the scope of his ambitions and his ruthless determination to achieve them. By mid-1905, he was making an issue of the need for Ford Motor Company to begin taking an active part in the manufacturing process. He was right, of course: It was manifestly risky for Ford to continue doing business in a position of total dependence on its suppliers. It was time for Ford Motor Company to invest some of its profits in a manufacturing capability of its own. As stockholders of Ford, the Dodge brothers could not but approve of the plan. But as suppliers, they were nervous about being squeezed out. Henry Ford, seconded by James Couzens, decided that the Ford Motor Company should begin to manufacture its own engines and chassis by 1906.

The Dodge brothers were additionally worried by the fact that Henry Ford was using the need to expand the company into manufacturing operations as an opportunity to get rid of his original partner, Alex Malcolmson. Malcolmson was the only person whose ownership of company shares was equal to Ford's. Malcolmson had believed in Ford from the beginning, despite Ford's earlier failures, and the coal merchant had done all the work of organizing the Ford Motor Company. He had brought in all the outside investment (such as it was), he had handled the advertising and sales, he had brought in Couzens, he had dealt with suppliers, he had established the small but growing network of dealers. He considered himself to be as important to the Ford Motor Company as Henry Ford, who had so far done little more than design a car, and that with the collaborative effort of Harold Wills.

But Henry Ford intended to control the Ford Motor Company, and the removal of Malcolmson was the obvious prerequisite. Ford called a meeting of all the directors of the company, with the glaring exception of Alex Malcolmson, and told them he intended to set up a second, completely independent, company to manufacture the engines and chassis needed by Ford Motor Company. The new business would be called Ford Manufacturing Company, and it would start life with the valuable asset of an exclusive contract with Ford Motor Company. Stockholders of Ford Motor Company would also become stockholders of Ford Manufacturing Company—with the notable exception of Alex Malcolmson and anyone who supported him in the ensuing fight with Henry Ford.

Ford's proposition was obviously immoral, and probably illegal. It amounted to a conspiracy by some Ford Motor Company stockholders to force out others. If Malcolmson had kept his head and fought Ford before the stockholders, he probably could have won, especially in view of the fact that most of the stockholders were his friends, relatives or protégés. But either he underestimated the threat or he overestimated the ease with which automobile companies could be started. He made the initial mistake of failing to enlist the support of James Couzens, his former clerk, who was now the business manager of the company and the only person who knew anything about the day-to-day operations of the company; Couzen's allegiance had been transferred to Henry Ford. Then he made the second mistake of announcing that he was starting a company of his own to manufacture a rival automobile. He lost the sympathy of other stockholders almost immediately.

In November of 1905, the new Ford Manufacturing Company was formed. By the following May, Malcolmson was negotiating to sell his shares of Ford Motor Company. They were purchased by the Dodge brothers, for a price of $175,000; that gave the Dodges 37.5 percent of the company. Malcolmson may have considered it a good profit on his original $25,000 investment, made a little over three years earlier. And so it was. It just wasn't as good as the profit he might have made if he had been allowed to hold on to his Ford stock a few years longer.

Shortly after Malcolmson sold out, several others followed suit. Then Ford Manufacturing Company, having served its purpose of ousting Malcolmson, was absorbed into the Ford Motor Company, and there was another reorganization. New shares were issued, for a total of 1,000. The Dodge brothers jointly held 100 shares, or one-tenth of the company. The two lawyers held another 100 shares. Banker John Gray held 105 shares, which passed to his heirs when he died in July 1906. James Couzens now held 110 shares. Harold Wills still owned no part of the company, but Henry Ford once again agreed to give Wills additional compensation out of his own share of dividends and profits. Ford himself was the big winner from the reorganization of the company. He held 585 shares, which gave him a controlling interest and allowed him always to defeat minority stockholders in any fight over policy.

John and Horace Dodge had backed Henry Ford in his manipulations to reorganize the company without Malcolmson. They had also agreed with his plans to reduce the magnitude of Dodge Brothers' contribution to the manufacturing process of the Ford car. By mid-1906, Dodge Brothers supplied only axles and transmissions for the cars; engines and chassis were built by the Ford company. The change had its good and bad aspects for the Dodges. They still had all the work they could handle, and were expanding as fast as they were able. And since they made fewer parts of the car, they could organize their factory more efficiently and reap additional economies of scale.

Yet John and Horace were too shrewd not to understand the meaning of the events they had just witnessed, and the implica-

These portraits of Ford Motor Company stockholders date from about 1907, after Alex Malcolmson had been maneuvered out and John Gray had died. (From the collections of Henry Ford Museum & Greenfield Village)

tions for the future of Dodge Brothers. Henry Ford had succeeded in snatching a controlling interest in the Ford company, and he would henceforth run it exactly as he wished. Moreover, he had made it clear that he believed the Ford company should not be dependent upon individual suppliers, but should have the capacity to manufacture cars on its own. That was good for the Ford company, but might have serious consequences for Dodge Brothers. Its entire business was restricted to producing parts for Ford cars. What would happen if Henry Ford decided next that he wanted to manufacture transmissions and axles as well?

The Dodges did what they could to protect their position. Their new contract with Ford was for a period of a year, and guaranteed that all transmissions and axles used by Ford would come from Dodge Brothers. Since John was a vice-president of Ford, and both brothers sat on the Board of Directors, they were in a position to learn of any impending changes at the earliest possible moment. For the time being, they would wait and see what Henry Ford intended to do next. The Dodge brothers never liked to make decisions under pressure. "When you have to decide a thing in a hurry, don't decide it at all," decreed John.

He himself made an important personal decision in 1907, which was obviously precipitated by the death of his mother that summer, while she was living with her sisters in Decatur. John and Horace buried Maria Dodge in the quiet country cemetery at Niles, with her husband and her Casto family. They ordered a large monument, with "Casto" on one side and "Dodge" on the other, and then bought new matching headstones for all the graves in the plot. It was their last filial gesture. John promptly went back to Detroit to arrange for an immediate divorce from Isabelle Smith Dodge.

Horace gave his brother assistance and moral support. Together, they spirited Isabelle off to a small town in northern Michigan, far away from Detroit, where she filed for divorce on the grounds of desertion. The uncontested divorce was granted on October 29, with a formal settlement for Isabelle of $2,000. Accord-

The monument to Horace's and John's parents in the cemetery at Niles is actually located in the Casto family plot, and the stone says "Casto" on the other side. (Collection of David Agresta)

ing to Pitrone and Elwart, this pittance was supplemented by a much more generous private sum; no doubt the Dodges understood that a large official settlement would attract the attention of reporters and thus lead to public knowledge of the divorce.

Six weeks after he became a free man, John Dodge married Matilda Rausch. The wedding took place on the afternoon of December 10, 1907, at the home of a minister. Horace and Anna were the only witnesses at the 44-year-old John's third marriage, as they were at his second. None of Matilda's family was invited. After the wedding, John took Matilda to his Boston Boulevard home and, for the first time, introduced her to his three children, whose response to the event was understandably cool. Then all the Dodges sat down to a wedding supper. Matilda, then just twenty-three and (except in her imagination) unaccustomed to the level of luxury present in her new home, must have required every bit of her nerve to carry off this social occasion. It is hard to imagine that Anna was anything but disapproving, and John's children must have been stunned and angry to meet their new stepmother in this fashion. What a bold young woman Matilda must have been, and how determined to marry John Dodge!

5

A Man's World

John had been determined to marry Matilda, no matter what the obstacles. But even after the marriage, his only constant companion was his brother. John and Horace still spent most of their waking hours together and were so close that they seemed like two halves of one entity. They did often quarrel; at the plant, they would sometimes get so angry at one another that profane shouts filled the air. But they made a point of reconciling their differences before they left—usually together—at the end of the day. Employees called them "the Gold Dust Twins" (a name taken from a popular comic strip) and noted how they were able to predict each other's responses, sometimes even to finish one another's sentences. The physical resemblance between these two stout and florid men, with their round faces, was heightened by their manner of dress. The Dodge brothers bought identical suits from the same tailor; they wore the same high white collars, Dodge Broth-

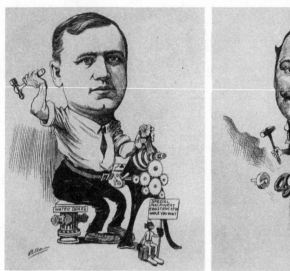

An early automotive magazine featured these caricatures of the well-known Dodge brothers of Detroit. (From the collections of Henry Ford Museum & Greenfield Village)

ers emblem in their lapels and diamond stickpins in their ties; even their derby hats were exactly alike.

Those who knew the brothers well did notice a difference in their personalities. Said veteran Dodge employee Fred Lamborn, "John was always up to something; he had a helluva sense of humor. Horace? He was quieter . . . a musician and more refined. You had to be careful what you said around Horace. His neck could get red awfully easy. But John was a mixer."

John and Horace had the habit of eating lunch together every day at John's Boston Boulevard house. (Matilda supervised the preparation of the meal but never joined them.) They also went out drinking together in the evening. They spent their weekends together, either resolving problems at the plant or enjoying one another's company while engaged in their hobbies. Even their vacations were shared, often in some remote spot dedicated to hunting and fishing.

The Dodge brothers used their wealth to create a man's world, in which they played like boys. Then, to keep the peace at home, they allowed their wives to spend freely to achieve their own social ambitions. Every year, there was more and more money to spend.

In the fall of 1908, Ford Motor Company introduced the Model T, one of the biggest marketing successes in the history of the automobile business. For a mere $825, buyers got a sturdy car that could carry them over the mud-and-gravel roads that were then the norm. Most breakdowns of the simple engine and planetary transmission could be fixed by any amateur mechanic. From the very beginning, the car broke sales records, and by its tenth birthday, nearly half of all the automobiles in the world were Model Ts. Thanks to that seemingly endless line of funny-looking black "Tin Lizzies," the Dodges could afford to buy anything they could work up a desire for.

One thing they definitely wanted was more fresh air. At about the time of his marriage to Matilda, John bought a farm in the rural area of Rochester, Michigan, a few hours from Grosse Pointe by car. He paid the owner of Meadow Brook Farm, George Higgins, $50,000 for the farmhouse, complete with furniture, the land and the Shorthorn cattle and Yorkshire pigs that were on it. Then he set to work to turn that working farm into a refuge for himself, his brother and their cronies. The farm provided an escape from business worries, from social pressures and even from family life. Over the years, John remodeled the white frame house, adding verandas and sleeping porches but keeping it simple and unadorned. The old cellar was turned into storage space for a large inventory of casks of whiskey and beer, as well as countless bottles of wine: never a fear of running out of drink during a weekend with John Dodge. A short distance away, there was a massive root cellar for food storage (sectioned for wet foods and dry), since John Dodge didn't want to go hungry either. Eventually, John also built a $50,000 greenhouse for out-of-season produce as well as flowers to make the house more welcoming. The farm, still called Meadow Brook, had its own power plant—built, like every-

The farmhouse at Meadow Brook probably looked more rustic in John Dodge's day than it does in this 1957 photo, but the air of tranquility was the same. (Detroit Free Press)

thing the Dodge brothers undertook, to withstand centuries of hard use.

Meadow Brook Farm was as self-sufficient as John Dodge could make it. The meat and butter on the table, the fruits and vegetables, even the honey came from the farm. To insure that everything was in good working order and that the farm would always be ready for his spur-of-the-moment visits, John sent his wife's parents to live at Meadow Brook, despite the fact that neither George nor Margaret Rausch cared for country life. Never one to play the hypocrite, John had made it abundantly clear that his acceptance of his in-laws was limited: The Rausches would have to follow his orders if they expected him to support them. A gauge of the distance between Dodge and Rausch was that throughout his entire life, John never once sat down to a meal with his in-laws. Matilda was so comfortable with the treatment of her parents as poor relatives that she continued it even after John's death.

Although old family photographs taken at Meadow Brook show that wives and children sometimes visited the farm, its real purpose was for John, his brother and his friends to get away together. This function of the farm was emphasized by the later construction of a nine-hole golf course near the house: In fact, the front walk of the house led to the first tee. There are those who say that John built the course after he was blackballed for membership in the prestigious Bloomfield Hills Country Club, and that may be true, but surely John was just as happy to have his own course and his own club. He even had his own scorecards printed. The clubhouse was like a playhouse for grown men. The decor was rustic; the furniture consisted of plain and sturdy Stickley pieces—now collectors' items—that could take any amount of drunken abuse. In the main room, there was a timbered ceiling, tapestries on the walls and a huge fireplace, which was ornamented by Dodge hunting and fishing trophies. The next room off the hallway was the locker room, with steps leading down to an Olympic-size swimming pool tiled in white with a green wave motif. There are no records of the kind of golfers the Dodge brothers were, but it is a safe bet that they were stars in the clubhouse if not on the course.

Meadow Brook was John's property and pet project, but Horace joined him there frequently. And when they tired of the fresh country air, they simply moved the never-ending party onto the water. Horace was the one who particularly loved boats, but his brother was amenable to going out on the water with him. It was always more fun to do things together.

Horace quickly found himself dissatisfied with the *Lotus*, the boat that was built after fire burned Peter Studer's boatyard to the ground in 1904, and also with its companion, the forty-foot *Hornet*. He raced both boats, but never achieved the speeds he sought. So early in 1910, he commissioned a new steam yacht, the *Hornet*

Horace (left) *and John enjoy a day out on the boat.* (Collection of David Agresta)

II, to be constructed at the Great Lakes Boat Works by builder Alfred Seymour. The yacht, although Horace's pet project, was actually jointly owned by Horace and John.

The new *Hornet* was more than twice as long as its predecessor, measuring 100 feet. It was powered by twin 1,000 horsepower engines designed and built by Horace at the new Dodge Brothers Marine Division he had established, the better to pursue his hobby. One of those engines has been restored and is now in the permanent collection of the Smithsonian Institution. The huge four-cylinder quadruple-expansion steam engine had a ten-inch stroke and cylinders of 7.5, 10.5, 17 and 24 inches. The two Dodge engines could propel the *Hornet II* through the water at a top speed of forty-one miles per hour. That made it the fastest boat in the world at the time it was built; the runner up, with a top speed of 39.98 mph, was a United States Navy torpedo boat. Even today, such speeds are rarely achieved by a yacht that size.

The yacht, christened by Winifred Dodge late in 1910, was intended primarily for day cruising. Its long low cabin featured comfortable sitting accommodations and a large dining area; there were no cabins for sleeping. The open stern area allowed passengers to enjoy the fresh air, while a canvas cover protected them from sun and rain.

But even the *Hornet II* didn't satisfy Horace Dodge for long. By 1913 he had commissioned naval architects Gielow & Orr to design a new steam yacht, the *Nokomis*. One hundred and eighty feet long, the yacht carried two masts for sails and a big power plant. The *Nokomis* was an elegant vessel, with gilded prow and elongated bowsprit, and could provide comfortable overnight accommodations for a large number of guests. The ship was launched from the Brooklyn shipyard of Robins Dry Dock and Repair Company on December 20, 1913, after being christened by Horace's daughter, Delphine. That same month, Horace was elected commodore of the Detroit Motor Boat Club. (When he ordered his new commodore's uniform, his tailor was so used to making two of everything for the Dodge brothers that he made a second uniform, for John.) Commodore Horace Dodge brought the *Nokomis* back to Detroit, where it was used for business entertaining on behalf of Dodge Brothers and for pleasure by the Dodge brothers themselves.

Since the Dodge brothers enjoyed hunting and fishing, they frequently drove off to remote spots in northern Michigan, or to the Upper Peninsula, for a few days in the woods. Eventually, John decided that he wanted a hunting lodge of his own, so he bought acreage in the Upper Peninsula, about fifteen miles east of Pickford, and built a place to his own specifications. He called it Munuscong Lodge, and invited his brother and their friends to join the Munuscong Hunting and Fishing Club.

Munuscong Lodge consisted of a main building, a smaller lodge for a caretaker and five guest cabins that were probably built somewhat later. All the buildings were of native white pine covered with cedar siding that was coated with linseed oil and then treated with creosote. The interiors were white pine, varnished and stained; the floors were bird's-eye maple. The main lodge had four comfortable bedrooms, and a big front porch with a sturdy porch swing. There was a beamed ceiling in the living room, and bookcases with glass doors and more of the Stickley furniture that was John's preference. Supplies were kept in a tin-lined locker that prevented wild animals from helping themselves when the lodge was vacant. As usual, there was also ample storage space for a copious liquor supply. Family photos of the Dodge brothers at Munuscong show them with throngs of friends.

Who were the friends who accompanied John and Horace on such outings? Despite their increasing wealth and power, the Dodge brothers were still not accepted in the "best circles" of Detroit society. Although John and Horace eventually became members of the all-male Detroit Athletic Club, acceptance in the locker room was one thing, but in the drawing room quite another. It is hard to imagine that these two men knew how to behave in polite society, and they certainly never seemed inclined to live by its rules. If they had any desire to mix with high society, it was only because they quite naturally did not like the feeling of being rejected. Their wives were socially ambitious, but Horace and John were content to keep their old friends. Horace liked to boast that he had hardly a friend he hadn't known for at least several decades: Both brothers were well known for their loyalty to their old pals.

Some of their friends were men they had known when they first moved to Detroit and started drinking in the warehouse-district bars. Others were fellow businessmen: suppliers, competitors and even employees. A close friend was Fred Haynes, a Cornell graduate who had briefly worked for John in Hamilton at the National Cycle Company. After turning down a job with Ford, Haynes had gone to work for the Franklin Auto Company, but in 1912, Dodge Brothers made him an offer he could not refuse, and he joined the company. Fred Haynes was a frequent guest at Meadow Brook, on the *Hornet II* and at Munuscong Lodge.

Other friends were politicians to whom the Dodge brothers had given their support. John and Horace were both staunch Republicans, of the populist sort often found in the Midwest at that time. They had two valuable assets in the eyes of Detroit's Republican officials. One was their money, which they gave freely to candidates of their choice. The other was their work force, over which they could—and did—exercise a considerable influence. They saw nothing wrong in printing pay envelopes that said, "Vote Republican," a linkage of jobs and votes that must have struck many workers as persuasive.

Horace's political interests were largely confined to playing cops-and-robbers. He was appointed to the post of deputy sheriff, and loved to ride around with his siren blaring, scattering pedestrians in the breeze. Old-timers tell of seeing Horace roaring up the drive and around and around the flagpole circle of the Grosse Pointe Country Club, with assistant deputies hanging on to his car for dear life. One of his favorite duties was taking criminals away to prison. He would hire a gang of assistants (all friends, of course), board the train and escort the malefactor to wherever he was to serve his sentence. The cost of these trips often ran into the thousands of dollars—paid for out of Horace's pocket.

John's political interests were a bit more serious. One of his close friends and regular companions was the Republican mayor, Oscar B. Marx. Like many municipal governments of the time, the Marx administration was characterized by a combination of inefficiency and corruption. John's friendship with Marx grew out of John's appointment by the previous mayor in 1905 to be a member of the Water Board. Subsequently, Marx named him, along with Ford business manager James Couzens, to be a member of the Detroit Railway Commission, which had the job of overseeing Detroit's public transportation. After several years, John was named commissioner.

As a public administrator, John behaved very much the way he

A formal portrait of Horace Dodge (left), *probably taken around 1910.* (Collection of David Agresta) *John Dodge was a tough negotiator, with a reputation for fairness in all his dealings.* (Collection of David Agresta)

did as president of Dodge Brothers. Wary of so-called experts, he preferred a hands-on approach. According to one published story, he watched one day as a city workman filled a trench dug for Detroit's water pipes and became so disgusted with the man's inefficiency that he jumped in the ditch, seized the tamping ram and demonstrated the way to do the job properly. John, along with his friend James Wilkie, whom he had brought to the Water Board in 1908, were the chief planners of a completely overhauled water system for Detroit. For nearly a year, they met two or three nights a week to draw up blueprints for a new pumping station and additional miles of pipes. The result was a supply of city water that was sufficient for several decades of heavy growth in Detroit. City water rates were among the lowest in the country, and the $15-million waterworks carried less than $2 million in debt.

As member and later commissioner of the Detroit Railway Commission, John Dodge was also high-handed—and effective. The work was complicated by the fact that at that time the streetcar system was operated by a private company, Detroit Urban Railway. (The DUR was later taken over by the city.) The streetcar workers were unionized, and union leaders usually took a tough stand against what they saw as abuses by the company. The city commission, caught in the middle, could do little more than wring its hands as invective filled the air and strikes were threatened. But John Dodge was used to dealing with workers, he understood their point of view and he knew just what to say to them. He ended one strike quickly in a spirited address to members of the union:

I'm looking forward to the day when there won't be any DUR. You help us to get possession of the car lines for you and the trouble between you and your employers will end. I say this because I know all you want is a square deal. You're entitled to a square deal. As long as I am on the board and the city owns the lines, you men can come into our meetings and state your grievances. There won't be any delay or technicalities. It won't take six months or six days to settle a question. It will take six minutes. You will be treated like gentlemen, and my experience has been that when men are treated that way, there is never any doubt that they will be fair.

Boys, I had 8000 men who walked to work yesterday morning. Those fellows are workingmen, just like you and I. Some of them walked seven miles to the shop, and did it without a murmur. We hauled them home the best way we could last night, but a lot of them walked again today.

After all, these men and you are all part of one big corporation. We're all part of the city of Detroit. That's why
municipal ownership of the street railways will succeed.
You'll be working for yourself and for the men you haul
on the cars.

That's how John Dodge ended the strike in 1914—the union
workers voted to return to work and submit their grievances to
arbitration—and also set the stage for the city's takeover of the
DUR.

Unquestionably, John put in long hours of hard work at his city
posts. He received no pay, but he enjoyed the sense of importance
they brought, the public recognition and the access to power. And
he did not hesitate to use that access when he needed it. Take the
case of his accident in October 1913. He was driving his Packard,
a huge, heavy car made heavier by some special adaptations he
had carried out at Dodge Brothers, with Oscar Marx in the passenger seat. Apparently, John became incensed by the driver of a
little Hupmobile, who seemed to be driving too close to the center
line. John made his point by ramming right into the hapless Hup-
mobiler and saying loudly, "That will teach 'em to keep to the
right!" The victim of this "accident" called the police, and a mo-
torcycle policeman sped after Dodge and Marx. When he caught
up with them, he found them "laboring under some kind of excitement" and promptly gave John Dodge a ticket. The incident
was then reported in the newspaper, in a tone of disapproval at
the lordly ways of the rich and powerful. Marx responded by telling the editor that "John Dodge could buy your newspaper and
turn it into a machine shop." The paper told its readers about that
incident as well, whereupon Marx denied that his remark had been
meant as a threat. The whole episode came to a close a few days
later when, by prearrangement, John Dodge appeared in private
at the home of a city judge to plead guilty to the charge of speeding. Nothing further was said about his "excitement" at the time
of the accident, and he was given a routine fine of fifty dollars.

By this time, John and Horace Dodge were among the richest men in Detroit. By 1913, their joint net worth was estimated at $50 million. Only Henry Ford was making money faster than they were. The continued success of the Model T caused Dodge Brothers to expand year by year. Fred Haynes later recollected—in a deposition for a tax case in the 1920s by Ford stockholders against the IRS—how breathtakingly fast that expansion had been:

> Mr. Haynes states that he came to Dodge Brothers on June 15, 1912. At that time, the plant was making 400 sets of parts a day for Mr. Ford. Mr. John Dodge told Mr. Haynes his first job would be to tool the plant and equip it so it would take care of 800 sets of parts as soon as possible. This was done in short order [but failed to keep the nose of Dodge Brothers above water as the demands from Ford increased so fast they could not keep pace with them.]
>
> Toward the latter part of 1912, the Dodge Brothers were called upon to prepare to furnish 1800 sets of parts a day for Ford, beginning with 1913. When Mr. Haynes came to Dodge Brothers, they had been equipped for 10 hours of work, but they increased their shifts and equipment in 1912 as rapidly as possible, and in the early part of 1913 ran up as high as 1600 sets of parts per day.

Almost as soon as the Model T hit the market, it was obvious that the Dodge Brothers' building at Monroe and Hastings had become inadequate. While Henry Ford was opening up the new Highland Park plant on Woodward Avenue, John Dodge looked for a new site for Dodge Brothers. In 1909, John and Horace bought a thirty-acre parcel of land to the north of their existing plant, in the Polish enclave of Hamtramck. Located north of Dunn Road, the site was bounded by Joseph Campau Avenue on one side and Conant Avenue on the other. In that year, a total of 123,000 cars were built, nearly a third of them Fords with parts manufactured by Dodge Brothers.

To design the new plant, they chose up-and-coming industrial architect Albert Kahn. Around the turn of the century, Kahn had designed a group of buildings that served as production facilities for Packard Motor Company. Struck by the limitations of the standard mill construction material he was forced to use, Kahn enlisted the aid of his brother, a trained engineer, and perfected the technique of reinforcing concrete, turning it into a construction material nearly as strong as steel and just as fireproof, at a fraction of the cost. He demonstrated the possibilities of reinforced-concrete construction in the Ford Motor Company's new plant at Highland Park, and both he and the Dodges wanted to see if that model could be improved upon.

For Dodge Brothers, Albert Kahn designed a group of buildings to house the complex operations of machining, forging and casting required for production of axles and transmissions for Ford. The Ford contract was then bringing Dodge Brothers about $10 million annually.

The most important building at the new Hamtramck plant was the machine shop, a four-story reinforced-concrete building with flat-slab framing. Two wings, each 405 feet long and 65 feet wide, were joined by a third segment, 65 feet by 235 feet. Ten-sided reinforced-concrete columns with flared capitals provided vertical thrust; the building had a steel sash and a flat roof. Initially, there was an open grass-covered courtyard between the two long arms of the machine shop, but in 1914 a single-story building was added there. Horace and John Dodge insisted that the machine shop, like all the buildings at the site, have good light and ventilation, for the benefit of the men who spent ten-hour shifts near hot machines.

Other buildings in the complex were two 400-foot steel-framed shops, one for the forge and one for the smithy. They were two stories high, with gabled roofs and glass clerestory windows, and brick façades at the ends. A steel-and-brick powerhouse was designed for the two huge Corliss engines that supplied the power necessary for production and were vented by a brick smokestack

The Dodge plant in Hamtramck ("Dodge Main") was designed by Albert Kahn and built in 1910. (Albert Kahn Associates, Architects & Engineers)

in the center of the building. An attractive but modest brick building, 120 feet long, served as the main office, and there was a smaller brick building for the watchman's post.

John Dodge's diary provides a day-by-day perspective on the process of design and construction. On April 26, 1910, he recorded that he had met with Albert Kahn to give him the first sketches of the new factory. Between that date and June 3, when John approved the final plans, they met ten times. The project was opened to bids on June 21. Shortly thereafter, general contractors Bryant & Detweiler, a Detroit firm, broke ground on the site; subcontractors built the steel frames, did the masonry, poured concrete and roofed the buildings. On November 28, John noted that they had fired the boilers in the powerhouse and produced a few sample forgings. Dodge Brothers was operating out of this facility by the end of the year. The company was by then the largest parts-manufacturing firm in the United States.

In 1912, a foundry was added, designed by another leading Detroit architectural firm, Smith, Hinchman & Grylls; and the next

This photo of the interior of the new Dodge plant in Hamtramck was taken at the time of its completion, before work had started there. (Albert Kahn Associates, Architects & Engineers)

year, the same firm drew up plans for a heat-treatment building. The office was expanded by two stories, plus two-story extensions at each end. All together, the Dodge Brothers plant (later to be known as Dodge Main) was one of the biggest manufacturing operations in the Midwest. Some statistics from mid-1914 give an idea of its capacity. The plant

—employed 5,000 men
—used 3 million gallons of crude oil and 25,000 tons of coal each year
—cast 25 tons of brass and 75 tons of gray iron every day
—made 7 million clutch discs per year
—cut 34,000 gears a day
—used 10,000 pounds of potassium cyanide every week to harden steel

—produced 855,000 connecting rods every year

—met an annual payroll that exceeded $6 million.

The writer of an article that appeared in *Automobile Topics* in 1914 was noticeably impressed by the efficiency of the Dodge Brothers plant. "Human haste, sweat and anxiety have been reduced to a minimum by a combination of ripe experience, farsighted planning, and bold expenditure of money, and whatever strain is involved in enormous production falls on the machinery, not on the men." That element of Dodge Brothers' operation came from Horace and John Dodge's instinctive identification with the workingman, which was reflected in many aspects of the company. There was a well-equipped clinic on the premises, with doctors and nurses in constant attendance to treat both work-related injuries and general health problems. A welfare department stood ready to help workers and their families with a variety of problems, and it had a $5-million trust fund, set up by the brothers, to make sure it could do the job. Each and every single file from that department crossed John Dodge's desk. A large well-equipped machine shop called "the Playpen" was available to any worker who wanted to tinker on his own time, whether to repair a child's broken toy or try to invent a new machine. Each day at noon, all Dodge Brothers workers were served platters of overstuffed sandwiches and big pitchers of beer, at the company expense. On hot summer days, more beer was served throughout the afternoon, to help the men working at foundry and forge quench their thirst.

While John Dodge was in his office at one end of the plant, dealing with issues of fairness and social welfare for the workers, Horace was ensconced at the other end of the plant ("That's so we won't fight," John said, chuckling), devising ways to put the work on the machines instead of the men. Horace designed new equipment and innovative systems, such as a way to keep the tempering oil used in the heat-treatment plant at a constant temperature, and an elaborate internal system for handling materials within the foundry. He utilized locomotives, a huge overhead monorail crane and two traveling magnetic cranes to move the large daily tonnage of scrap metal in the forge, blacksmith and heat-treatment areas. Dodge ingenuity never failed: For example, Horace even found a way to harness the steam that was given off by the steam hammers to run a turbine that drove a 750-kilowatt generator.

Dodge Main was an enduring monument to the Dodge brothers, and a reminder that a sense of play can be a valuable adjunct to serious work. For John and Horace, the line between work and play in the man's world they devised for themselves was almost nonexistent. The plant created by these two overgrown boys, who still remembered very clearly what it was like to be an ordinary workingman, was so well built and so far ahead of its time in its innovative approach to the requirements of a large industrial facility that it was used for the production of parts and, later, entire cars for many decades, long after it was sold to Chrysler Corporation in 1926. Dodge Main was finally closed on January 4, 1980, and torn down shortly thereafter.

6

The Home Front

While John and Horace Dodge worked and played together, their wives were left to pursue their own agendas. Surely Anna and Matilda must often have felt painfully excluded by the brothers' intimacy, which was so much greater than that they shared with their wives and children. Both women knew that whenever there was a conflict of loyalties, John and Horace would invariably rank the fraternal bond above the conjugal. John's divorce from Isabelle was a case in point. As Isabelle's close friend, and an advocate of the marriage from the start, Anna could only have viewed John's desire for a divorce with deep disapproval. But her feelings counted for less with her husband than did John's need for an ally, so Horace helped his brother do the deed of which his wife disapproved.

Many such conflicts must have been played out in both households. Even the little routines of daily living served continually to emphasize the closeness of the brothers over that with their wives and children. There was, for example, John and Horace's habit of eating lunch together—a lunch from which all others were barred. The quintessence of the family relationship can be seen in the way the Dodge family traditionally observed New Year's Eve. On that night, the whole family gathered at John's home on Boston Boulevard, although Anna and Matilda probably may well have preferred separate celebrations. Just before midnight, John and Horace would go into the library for a little time alone, to survey their shared past and contemplate what they were sure would be their shared future. Alone together, the two brothers toasted in the New Year at the stroke of midnight—and only then did they rejoin their families.

In later years, both Anna and Matilda were to display an emotional coldness, a psychological distance from the people with whom they should have been most intimate, that could at times turn into absolute cruelty. It is impossible to know whether the two women were always of that temperament, or whether the repeated experience of being ignored by husbands who turned to one another for all their emotional needs taught Anna and Matilda to withdraw into a chilly distance.

It does not take much reflection to realize that although John and Horace were excellent providers for their families, they could not possibly have been very good husbands, or fathers either. Theirs is not the typical story of the self-made man who must sacrifice family in order to achieve business success. For the Dodge brothers, spending time at the plant was never a sacrifice but, instead, their first and best choice. They would have spent all their time together, with the machines they both loved, even if Dodge Brothers had never grown beyond that first small shop with twelve employees on Beaubien. Their preference for one another's company exacted a high emotional toll on their wives and children.

For Anna and Matilda, the compensation for their emotional losses was the money they had at their disposal, money that enabled them to create their own world parallel to the man's world of the Dodge brothers. As the millions started to roll in, Anna and

Matilda embarked on their separate efforts, often blatantly competitive, to scale the social heights they had always dreamed of occupying.

Matilda at last was the mistress of the Boston Boulevard house, but at times it must have seemed to her very much like her mother's boardinghouse. After her marriage, her parents sold the saloon and the boardinghouse and moved in with John and Matilda, occupying the apartment over the carriage house. Margaret Rausch helped her daughter with the mundane tasks of housekeeping, and George acted as a combination superintendent and handyman around the place. Socially, they were completely ignored, by Dodge family and Dodge friends, so perhaps it was with some relief that they agreed to take on the responsibility of living at Meadow Brook Farm as caretakers.

Matilda's sister, Amelia, also lived at Boston Boulevard for a time. She went back to work at Dodge Brothers shortly before John and Matilda's marriage, and Amelia and John drove to work together nearly every morning. In the evening, the lively Amelia provided company for Matilda while John was away—which was often. She also provided company for John when he was at home. "After dinner," she later recalled, "we'd sit in the living room and he'd make me play grand opera records. He didn't like popular music too well." She concluded, "Mr. Dodge was rather stern. He was not a jolly fellow." Presumably, this type of stern behavior was limited to the hearthside, for those who met John Dodge at a club or saloon had a very different story to tell. The long evenings at home must have been hard for everyone to get through.

Winifred, Isabel and John Duval were also in residence, and no doubt took every opportunity to demonstrate their lack of regard for their new stepmother. Of the three children from John Dodge's marriage to Ivy Hawkins, John Duval was the one who had the most trouble adjusting to the presence of a new stepmother. In part because of his behavior problems, John was sent to Manlius, a military academy in upstate New York. He did poorly there, as he did at Culver Military Academy, to which he was subsequently dispatched. Winifred and Isabel fared better because they had one another, and they also had all the social interests of teenage girls of the day to occupy them. Both girls were students at Liggett School, in Grosse Pointe, where they made friends with other girls from wealthy families and learned to conduct themselves like proper young ladies. As is often the case with families moving up in the world, the children were more comfortable in their new social milieu than were the parents. Matilda wisely made only perfunctory efforts to supervise her husband's daughters, and they possessed an unusual degree of freedom, which gave them a very attractive air of self-possession. While still at Liggett, Winifred drove her own electric runabout (which was in the newspapers once, when it caught on fire near the Boston Boulevard house), and she and her sister used it to come and go on their own.

John's sister, Della/Delphine, also lived in the Boston Boulevard house, with her ill husband; she was already there, having established her husband's sickbed upstairs, when Matilda came as a bride. Rie Ashbaugh (the former Uriah Eschbach) had become another victim of tuberculosis and finally died in May 1915, at the home of his brother-in-law. Della then threw her considerable energies into a career as a clubwoman. She initiated a project of providing housing for homeless young girls through the Salvation Army, and quickly became president of the Women's Auxiliary of the Salvation Army. She raised funds for a modern hospital for the poor (her brother John was a major contributor) and succeeded in getting Salvation Army head Evangeline Booth to come dedicate it. A newspaper article said she was "as successful in her own way as her brothers in theirs" and mentioned that John had given the Detroit Federation of Women's Clubs, of which Della was then president, a gift of $35,000 to build a clubhouse, as "a token of his regard for her." Della also did a great deal of work for the American Red Cross, raising funds to fight tuberculosis, a cause also supported by her brothers. Another of her accomplishments was being named president of a group called Detroit Women

Writers. Clever and literate, Della fancied herself a poet, and published a lavishly illustrated volume of her work at her brother John's expense. Although Della's husband was an impoverished invalid, and she lived on her brother's charity, Della nevertheless succeeded in winning the admiration of Detroit society, due not only to her aggressiveness, but also to her hard work for the causes she supported and her ability to turn herself into a sophisticated and worldly woman.

While Matilda was learning to run the large and tension-ridden establishment on Boston Boulevard, Anna was busy moving into a new house. Mr. and Mrs. Horace Dodge had obviously outgrown the comfortable middle-class home on Forest Street. It was time for a real mansion—preferably one that would outstrip Matilda's. Horace bought a piece of riverfront land in Grosse Pointe, at the very spot where Lake St. Clair feeds into the Detroit River. Aside from its natural advantages as a future homesite, it was right next door to the exclusive Grosse Pointe Country Club. At Anna's urging, Horace had applied for membership there and had been firmly rejected. Detroit's old money was not amused by the rowdy Dodge brothers and the tales of their after-work carousing. Horace promptly bought the land next door to the club and then told a reporter that he planned to build a home there that would make the clubhouse look like his garage.

By the end of 1908, Anna and Horace had moved out of the house on Forest Street and into the original white farmhouse left standing on the Grosse Pointe site. From that vantage point, they were able to watch their new house going up. The architect they chose for the task was Albert Kahn. Although Kahn at that time was known primarily as an industrial architect, he was also interested in residential buildings and had begun to execute some commissions for private homes. His complete blueprint of the new house was presented to Horace on March 30, 1910, and construction began soon thereafter. Although some changes were made as work progressed, the house took shape speedily, and the last of

Albert Kahn designed the 1910 Rose Terrace for Horace and Anna Dodge in the Early English Renaissance style. (Albert Kahn Associates, Architects & Engineers)

the drawings is dated June 22. Horace, Anna, Delphine and Horace Junior were able to celebrate Christmas of 1910 in their new home.

Kahn took full advantage of the magnificent site Horace had purchased, which sloped from Jefferson Avenue down to the shore of Lake St. Clair. He placed the house at the end of a long curved driveway, looking out over the water. Between the house and the lake was an elaborately landscaped formal garden, with a double flight of broad steps descending from a balustraded upper terrace outside the house to a lower terrace level extensively planted with formal rose gardens. This feature gave the house its name, Rose Terrace.

In his domestic architecture, Albert Kahn employed a variety of architectural idioms, ranging from classical Georgian to the modern Prairie style. For Rose Terrace, he opted for the style called Early English Renaissance, a more symmetrical and orderly cousin of the then-popular Tudor architecture (which was the style of the house Kahn had designed next door in 1903 for businessman Henry Swift). The exterior of Rose Terrace was a deep-red sandstone trimmed with light-gray granite. Peaks of the sandstone façade extended beyond the real roof line, emphasizing a sense of mass. Although the design was visually somber, scores of mullioned windows let in all the light the Michigan weather provided—which in the summer was so much that the waterfront exposures had to be protected by canvas awnings. In his decorative details, Kahn allowed himself to eschew stylistic purism and include Italianate elements as well, such as a classical Tuscan portico on the water side of the house and balustraded porches opening off rooms of the second story.

The interior of Rose Terrace was as grand as Kahn could make it. The floor plans of the basement alone are enough to announce that Rose Terrace was designed for extravagance. There was a vegetable cellar, a workroom, one room for the ice machine and another for laundry and another for indoor drying of clothes. For the men of the family, there was a gym (although to judge by Horace's rotund figure, it could not have seen very frequent use).

On the main floor, there was an abundance of ornamentation. Every reception room was fully paneled, and the ceilings were coffered, except in the dining room, which featured an elaborate plaster molding. Classical columns of linen-fold paneling were surmounted by carved pediments, the whole in turn topped by one or two layers of carved cornice that extended right up into the ceiling. Fireplaces called forth an encircling riot of carved garlands, shields and escutcheons. In the dining room, there were built-in display cabinets for a collection of china and glass yet to be purchased. The massive kitchen was surrounded by a warren of serving pantries, larders and rooms for the use of servants. There were also a den, a study and a music room in which Horace in-

Interior photos of Rose Terrace at the time Horace and Anna moved in show the dining room (above) *and the entrance hall* (opposite). (Albert Kahn Associates, Architects & Engineers)

stalled an excellent organ. In that era, the instrument was virtually *de rigueur* in the homes of the rich, but for Horace it meant much more than merely following fashion. He had always loved music, and he wanted not just to hear it but to play it as well. From contemporary accounts, we know that he was able to play the organ, but it is not clear how he learned, or what level of mastery he achieved. It is possible that Anna, the former music teacher, gave him lessons. It is probable that, like the other skills he acquired, learning to play the organ was for Horace a matter of trial and error.

On the second floor, there were large bedrooms for Delphine

and Horace Junior, guest rooms and even guest suites. The master bedroom suite faced the water and caught the sun at the end of the day; the bedroom and sitting room opened onto a big deck covered by a canvas awning. The third floor contained a large playroom, which ran the length of the house on the water side; a sewing room; rooms for trunks to store out-of-season clothing, and small bedrooms for servants.

Anna Dodge, who only a few years earlier had passed quiet hours at home doing needlework and reading the Bible, was suddenly the mistress of one of Detroit's most elegant mansions (although new competitors were being built every month). Just shopping for the things needed to furnish Rose Terrace must have been a tremendous undertaking. Period photographs show heavy carved tables in the Jacobean style, high-backed chairs with tapestry-covered seats, chandeliers and sconces nearly appropriate for the vastness of the rooms, and a magnificent cased clock on the stair landing. Presumably, all these furnishings were bought in the relatively short period when the house was being built. It is possible that Albert Kahn helped find or select some of these new possessions, but more likely that Anna did it all herself.

But the photos show something else as well. The furnishings are surprisingly sparse for a house of that time and place. Most of them are brand-new machine-made pieces that are not authentic enough in their details to qualify even as reproductions. The scale of the furniture is not correct; chairs are dwarfed by high mantels, and tables look insignificant in the center of wide-open spaces. The den features overstuffed chairs mismatched with a lumpy sofa, all covered in a hideous print. This furniture, along with the pseudo-Tiffany lamp visible on the table, must surely have come from the old Forest Street house.

It all adds up to the picture of a woman with little or no innate taste, and equally little exposure to beautiful things, who is trying apprehensively to live up to her new status. Unlike her new sister-in-law, Anna Dodge did not take classes to learn to manage a wealthy man's household, and it is reasonable to conclude that her life thus far had provided few models of rich women for her to observe. Her mother and her sisters, the women to whom she was closest, were little help, since all they knew about good taste and high society came from watching Anna herself. She certainly couldn't turn to the women she hoped to emulate. The one woman who was in a position to understand Anna's difficulties in learning her new role was Matilda Dodge, but the sisters-in-law never overcame their initial antipathy.

In this rather remarkable state of social isolation, Anna Dodge labored to invent herself all over again, with nothing but ladies' magazines and newspaper articles about high society to guide her efforts. Perhaps that is why pictures of Albert Kahn's Rose Terrace project a sense of unreality. Rather than building a house that grew out of the family's existing tastes and activities, Horace and Anna Dodge built a house they would have to learn to inhabit. It was a stage set for a life they did not yet live. The only genuine reflections of the owners' interests at Rose Terrace were Horace's organ and his boathouse on the lake. When Horace bought the property, he acquired the old boathouse that had been part of the Grosse Pointe Country Club. The channel and bay were in good condition, but the building itself was not up to the new Dodge standards. In the summer of 1911, the boathouse was remodeled by Albert Kahn. It became the home of the launch for Horace's new boat, the *Hornet II*, which was anchored offshore. Horace loved to sit on the lower level of the terrace and watch the traffic on the lake, as well as his own pride and joy riding at anchor.

The basic artificiality of the setting was underscored by the painful fact that Anna had no one to entertain in those magnificent rooms of her new house. Her only guests were poor relatives and business or political associates of her husband and his brother—and they generally preferred to do without female companionship. Then in her forties, with matronly clothes and few social graces, Anna lacked the ability to go out and make new friends. It took her several years to discover that essential strategy of the social climber—the charitable cause. Slowly, she learned to use Horace's contributions as a means of advancing her own social ambitions. She served as chairman of the Red Cross Christmas Seal campaign, and she entertained fellow committee members at luncheon. She capitalized on Horace's interest in music to get him to support the Detroit Symphony Orchestra (at one time, the musicians were almost literally on the Dodge Brothers' payroll) and to give money for and assist in the quick construction of a new, acoustically superior, Symphony Hall, at which the family occupied a conspicuous box. The Dodges were still not invited to the "best" parties, nor were they members of the prestigious clubs. But little by little, Anna managed to be at least on speaking terms with many prominent Detroit socialites.

Meanwhile, what about the children? It is interesting to note that Anna's social ambitions seem to have been in large part for herself. She was by no means ready to concede her own defeat and concentrate on hopes for the next generation, as many wives of self-made men have done. But she recognized that her children could be a help to her own upward climb.

Delphine was eleven when the family moved into Rose Terrace, an attractive girl on the brink of adolescence. She was smaller and slimmer than her mother, and prettier as well, with rich chestnut hair and elfin features. She always had an air of the tomboy about her. She was in fact quite close to her brother, who was just one year younger, but she was soon to move away from outdoor games and sports and into the hothouse world of the "proper young lady." Delphine attended day school at the Convent of the Sacred Heart. It was considered to be the best private school in Grosse Pointe, and many non-Catholics sent their daughters there. The nuns gave Delphine piano lessons and told her parents she was musically talented. Later, Delphine went to Springside School, a boarding school near Philadelphia. Animated and self-confident, she seemed like the kind of girl who was destined to be "popular." Perhaps that is why she and her mother never developed any particular closeness.

Anna's warmest maternal feelings were reserved for her son, Horace Junior. He was an intelligent boy with more than his share of charm. Not precisely good-looking, he was gregarious and had an appealing personality and a warm grin. He also had the knack of getting what he wanted. A characteristic picture of the whole family picnicking at Meadow Brook Farm shows Horace Junior in tears while the others try to appease him. The family's increasing wealth brought Horace Junior all manner of opportunities, for the most part never balanced by any responsibilities. His father did

Horace Junior looked unusually serious when he posed for this photo in his uniform at Manlius Academy. (Burton Historical Collection, Detroit Public Library)

little to share his own interests in mechanics and business with the boy. In fact, he saw very little of his son. Anna doted on him, and she was probably a good mother when he was small. But she had no idea of how to prepare a rich young man to handle wealth and power; she still didn't quite know how to handle them herself. In his teens, Horace was sent to Manlius Military Academy, along with his cousin John Duval. It was an attempt to introduce the young Dodge heirs to the concept of discipline, but it failed miserably. Although Horace looked quite splendid in his academy uniform, he learned almost nothing about self-control while he was wearing it.

The younger generation of Dodges was sought after socially. Its members may not have learned self-discipline at school, but they had learned the social graces. And their parents used the Dodge fortune to provide a suitable background for them. All the girls had lavish debuts. Winifred came out over the Christmas season of 1914. Whatever Matilda's deficiencies as a stepmother, this was an opportunity she intended to exploit to the fullest. She and John Dodge hosted a dinner dance at the elegant Pontchartrain Hotel. Decorators had turned the ballroom into a replica of an English garden, complete right down to the recorded songs of appropriate birds. Winifred, standing in the receiving line with her father and stepmother, wore a frothy confection of white net over white chiffon embroidered with pearls, and carried a bouquet of fashionable Hillington roses. Matilda had opted for primrose, one of her favorite colors, though it was not kind to her sallow complexion, and she carried huge purple orchids. The guest list reflected the increased importance of the Dodges in Detroit: Only the very upper echelon of society was absent.

Once she was officially "out," the pretty and spirited Winifred made the most of her increased independence and threw herself into a social whirl. There were parties, outings and romances. One of her beaus was the socially prominent Jack Currie, but she chose to marry William Gray, Jr., a relative of the banker who had put up the $10,000 that kept Ford Motor Company afloat way back in 1903. John Dodge was satisfied because her prospective husband was financially acceptable, and Matilda was happy because of his social status. The wedding took place on October 30, 1915, and it was as opulent as John Dodge's money could make it. Winifred was a beautiful bride in a long fitted white dress and a silk helmet topped with a crown of antique lace over her dark hair. Her bridesmaids included Josephine Clay (later to become the wife of Ernest Kanzler, a top Ford executive, who was the older sister of

Eleanor Clay, later Edsel Ford's wife) and Josephine's sister, Isabel.

It is easy enough to understand why Winifred chose to marry young. There was a vacuum in her emotional life that no amount of luxury could fill. But she hated to leave Isabel. Even after Winifred's marriage, the sisters remained close. When Isabel, who had attended finishing school at Briarcliff in New York, made her debut in December 1915, Winifred, now a young society hostess was very much in charge. And when Winifred and William Gray moved into their new house, Isabel became an almost perpetual house guest.

The new house was a wedding gift from John Dodge. It was situated on a large corner lot in the new neighborhood of Indian Village, three or four blocks wide and about twice that long, which had suddenly become the most stylish address for young couples. Many of Winifred's friends lived in Indian Village, some of them on the same street. Ernest and Josephine Kanzler, and Edsel and Eleanor Ford were neighbors on Iroquois Avenue; Jack Currie and his wife, and Jack's sister Gwen and her husband, Wesson Seyburn, were also Indian Village residents. The Indian Village Association put in its own stylish street lamps and even paved its own streets, covering the concrete foundation with large cedar blocks to dampen the noise of passing traffic.

Winifred's house, which still stands at 1723 Iroquois Avenue, was designed by Smith, Hinchman & Grylls, the firm that was then doing all of the architectural work at the Dodge Brothers plant. It was set over to one side of the lot, thus creating a large side yard on the corner, which was made private by a brick-and-wrought-iron fence. The three-story house was also brick, with a big wrought-iron door. The style was predominantly Tudor, with tall brick chimneys and arched windows; bay windows in the front helped catch the light. An entry tunnel, on the side of the house away from the corner, led to a large carriage house that had a second-floor apartment for servants.

The interior was designed by William Kapp, of Smith, Hinchman & Grylls. Floors were reinforced concrete topped with six
inches of cork under the subflooring, and the all-copper roof was
covered with inch-thick slate. There was a refrigerated vault for
furs, a walk-in refrigerator, oak paneling in the nine-passenger el-
evator to the third-floor ballroom, and a turntable in the garage to
point Winifred's car back in the direction of the exit. The drawing
room had a sculpted plaster ceiling and classic walnut paneling,
the dining room ceiling was covered in gold leaf and the solarium
was floored with terra cotta. Every modern convenience, from a
food-warming system to an intercom, was included. John Dodge
always bought quality.

Although no period pictures of the furnishings of the house have
survived, it seems fairly certain that they were both stylish and
attractive. Winifred and Isabel Dodge both grew up to be women
of great style and taste. They possessed a knowledge of the latest
fashions—Isabel was particularly likely to sport the most recent
European trends in clothes—and the aplomb to ignore them on
occasion. They were truly their father's daughters: intelligent, self-
willed and confident. Whatever the emotional scars of their childhood, they showed no sign of them to the world.

Just as John Dodge's first family was beginning to reach adulthood, he started a second one. And an interesting question—the
subject of much recent legal debate—is how many children that
new family really contained.

On November 27, 1914, Matilda gave birth to a baby girl, named
Frances Matilda. Almost seventy years later, in 1982, a Detroit
woman named Pat Mealbach filed suit against the Dodge estate,
claiming that she was the Siamese twin sister of Frances. It is her
contention that John Dodge, fearing the stigma that was attached
to such unusual births in that era, used his money and political
power to keep the birth of Siamese twins a secret. In the same
fashion, she charged, he arranged for a secret operation to separate
the two girls, and then put one of them up for adoption.

Pat Mealbach based her conclusions on the evidence she uncovered when trying to trace her past history. It was not until 1959 that she learned from the reading of her father's will that she was adopted into the Manzer family. When she tried to find out about the circumstances of her adoption, she came up against a wall of silence. Of course, such secrecy is not unusual in adoptions, but Pat felt that the people who arranged for her adoption were particularly effective at conspiring to keep the matter completely private. She dropped the matter for twenty years. Then she happened to pick up a book that contained pictures of the Dodge family and of John Dodge's house on Boston Boulevard. She immediately recognized the house as the one to which she had been taken one day when she was a child. "I remember as a young girl that a lady came to pick me up and my mother told me to go with her. She took me to a very beautiful house. We went up a great big staircase, she took me to a bedroom, and there was a lady in the bed. I remember the room, it was so beautiful, it was in pink and green with lace curtains. . . ." Pat was never given any explanation of where she had been taken, nor why she had gone there, but the visit made such a deep impression on the child that she had gone back home and tried to create her own lace curtains out of crepe paper. "I never forgot that day, or that lady, and then I opened up the book and saw it again." She also recognized the names of associates of the Dodges as lifelong friends of her own family, including Frank Upton, who handled many of the Dodges' affairs and was a steward at the same church as Pat's father was. Finally, Pat and her own daughters were struck by her resemblance to photographs of John Dodge. Pat Mealbach was determined to pursue the matter.

In the course of her investigations, she learned from one source that she had been born on November 24, 1914. She also obtained a birth certificate for Frances Dodge, born three days later. She was surprised to see that the certificate had been checked in the box for "Other" rather than for single, twin or triplet birth. Her suspicions thus aroused, she visited a doctor and asked him to examine old scars on her head and shoulder, near the back of the neck. The doctor gave the opinion that it was not inconsistent with the results of surgery to separate Siamese twins.

Putting all the evidence together, Pat Mealbach deduced that she was Frances Dodge's Siamese twin. At the urging of her daughters, she brought suit against the John Dodge estate to be publicly named one of his heirs. According to Mealbach, she simply wants to be recognized as who she is, to have her heritage officially established. There might, of course, also be the possibility of inheriting a part of the remaining Dodge fortune. The chances of such an inheritance, however, seem slim. Although the filing of the suit temporarily stopped the final distribution of the trust left by John Dodge, a judge ruled against Pat Mealbach in 1982, and the money was distributed. Mealbach appealed, and in 1986 a judge ruled that there was insufficient evidence to cause him to open the sealed records of her birth, and Mealbach's second appeal failed in 1988. As of this writing, Pat is involved in legal action to try to open sealed records relating to her birth and adoption that might shed additional light on the matter.

How likely *is* Pat Mealbach's story? Improbabilities abound in the Siamese-twin theory. It is hard to believe that even as rich and powerful a man as John Dodge could keep the titillating news of the birth and subsequent separation of Siamese twins a complete secret. Too many people would have had to know about it—doctors, nurses, hospital personnel, the skilled surgeons who performed the separation—and surely not all of them could be bought. The evidence of the birth certificate raises as many questions as it answers. If Pat was a Siamese twin, then can the fact that she was born three days before her sister be explained? And if the date on the certificate was altered, why not the other information as well?

One other compelling piece of evidence refuting the Siamese-twin theory is the physical presence of Pat Mealbach herself. Siamese twins are identical twins, the product of a single fertilized egg that divides in two but fails to divide completely. Identical twins not only look strikingly similar, but also have similar personalities, interests, habits and attitudes. Some twin studies indicate that even when identical twins are raised separately, they still exhibit amazing similarities. But Pat, although she does indeed bear a resemblance to John Dodge, is not so similar to Frances. Frances was unusual in the Dodge family in having an oval face and a pointed chin; Pat has the round face that is characteristic of most of the rest of the Dodges. Frances was always willow-slim, and was a lifelong athlete; Pat has ample proportions and little athletic inclination. Frances was the kind of person who radiated nervous energy, whereas Pat is cheerfully calm and relaxed. It is difficult to believe they could be identical twins.

But one need not believe in the Siamese-twin theory to conclude that Pat Mealbach might well be a member of the Dodge family. Remove the misleading evidence of the birth certificate, and some significant facts still remain: Pat's memory of the Boston Boulevard house; her strong Dodge family resemblance; her medical records that show she was hospitalized in Niles, Michigan, soon after her birth and remained there until her adoption; her adoptive parents' sudden prosperity after she joined the family (they paid off their mortgage in cash, her mother had a new fur coat and her father drove a new Dodge); and the high level of secrecy surrounding the adoption. One might speculate that Pat Mealbach was not one of a pair of Siamese twins, but nevertheless a Dodge child born out of wedlock.

If so, who were her parents? We can rule out the women of the Dodge family. Della was too old for childbearing and, moreover, was in the public eye through much of 1914 for her club activities. Matilda was already pregnant. Anna, Winifred and Isabel all had social activities that would have made a secret pregnancy impossible. But three men remain as potential fathers: John, Horace and sixteen-year-old John Duval. Horace is the least likely candidate. He was not much of a ladies' man, and, besides, the evidence of Pat's visit to the Boston Boulevard house points to the John Dodge side of the family. To judge by her memory, the visit probably took place in 1920, when Matilda was so seriously ill she thought she might be dying. And there would be no reason for Matilda to indulge in a deathbed visit with her brother-in-law Horace's child.

She might have been the product of a youthful indiscretion by John Duval Dodge. He was already a wild young man, and events of his later life make it all too easy to view him as a womanizer. The mother would probably have been a girl of lower social status than the Dodge family, such as a maid in the house, or someone John met while out carousing. If he went to his father about the problem, it would be totally in character for John Dodge to arrange a comfortable and secure future for the child while still protecting the family name and fortune from the child and/or the mother. A discreet adoption, coupled with a lump-sum payment to the adoptive parents, and possibly even some ongoing subsidy, would be a neat way to resolve matters.

Another possibility is that Pat Mealbach is the illegitimate daughter of John Dodge himself. With his own wife pregnant with their first child, he would certainly have good reason to keep the matter as quiet as he could, so the option of putting the child up for a carefully arranged adoption would have been appealing.

If John Dodge was the father, the intriguing question then arises of who the mother might have been. She could, of course, have been almost anyone. John spent most of his evenings away from home, and therefore had the opportunity for casual encounters with women whose names will never be known. But there is evidence that suggests he might have had a long-term affair closer to home—with his sister-in-law Amelia.

From the time Amelia first went to work at Dodge Brothers in 1904, there was an obvious attraction between the secretary and the boss. Although Amelia dutifully left the company when her sister told her to, she returned several years later, and she worked closely with John Dodge for a number of years. She finally left the company in June 1914, some five months before Pat Mealbach was born. The ostensible reason was that her father, George Rausch, had died (in a servant's bedroom at Meadow Brook Farm, attended only by his wife and younger daughter). Thereafter, Amelia supposedly decided to stay on at the farm and keep her mother company. So far as her actions can be traced, she did not leave the isolation of the country for the rest of the year. In fact, she never again returned to live in Detroit, despite the fact that she much preferred the city to the country.

So the chronology of 1914 supports the hypothesis that Amelia Rausch could be the mother of a child by John Dodge. And John's tenderness for Amelia certainly lends credence to the theory that the two had an affair. John was continually concerned with Amelia's welfare. Before her move to the country, he was the one who insisted that she be included in Matilda's social life, making sure she received invitations to the charity events the Dodge family was beginning to attend. After Amelia moved to Meadow Brook, John worried over her safety in such a remote spot, and bought her a revolver and taught her how to use it. He often gave her presents—so often that Matilda occasionally protested. And he also included Amelia in his will, leaving her a bequest plus a trust fund that provided an annual income.

Additional clues might be seen in the behavior of Amelia, a pretty and lively young woman who suddenly immured herself in the country. Thereafter, she seemed to take on the role of maiden aunt to John and Matilda's children, looking after them devotedly. She gave up the possibilities of an independent life to become a satellite in her sister's family. And she allowed her sister to dictate to her, often rather cruelly. Could this all be due to the fact that Amelia had been labeled, by herself and others, a fallen woman? Presumably, it would have been impossible to keep the fact of her pregnancy from Matilda, although the identity of the father of the baby might have been concealed. Matilda's disdainful treatment of Amelia could well have sprung from a respectable, church-going, married woman's view of an illegitimate pregnancy.

Or Matilda's attitude might have arisen simply from her resentment of her sister's importance in the eyes of John Dodge. There are not enough facts available to know whether Amelia might have been the mother of Pat Mealbach, but there seems to be good circumstantial evidence for concluding that Amelia and John Dodge had some sort of romantic attraction, which was suspected by Matilda—and avenged accordingly.

7

The Dodges Take On Henry Ford

"Someday," John Dodge once said, chuckling, "the people who own a Ford are going to want an automobile." When they did, the Dodge Brothers would be ready to sell it to them.

That the Dodges would sooner or later break with Henry Ford was a foregone conclusion. It was obvious that their interests conflicted. Dodge Brothers profited by Ford Motor Company's dependence on it as a supplier, but that dependence was threatening to the Ford company and to Henry Ford's ego, too.

As major stockholders, the Dodges profited from every cost-cutting move Ford made. But as suppliers whose business was contractually limited to Ford, they feared Ford's efforts to save money by manufacturing more and more of the Model T's parts at Ford's constantly expanding Highland Park plant. The situation that created undreamed-of wealth for all three men was too unstable to last for long. It was also apparent that Henry Ford wanted to take sole credit for the success of the Ford car, as he did for everything he had ever been involved in, ignoring the major contributions of his colleagues. As John Dodge commented, perhaps not as privately as he should have, "I am tired of being carried around in Henry Ford's vest pocket."

The Dodge-Ford conflict extended to the personal level as well. The Dodges did not trust Henry Ford, and he was suspicious of their hotheaded, combative temperaments. Dodges and Fords did somehow manage to maintain a cordial social relationship for a decade. Henry and Clara Ford were invited to Winifred's debut, for example, and John Dodge received a personal invitation to a dinner given by Henry Ford that included on the menu such dubious delights as "Gasoline Soup," "Magneto Salad," "Dividend Squab" and "Model T Dessert." But underneath the smiles and jovial inquiries about the family, the men were looking for ways to end their partnership.

As early as 1910, Dodge Brothers had brought up the idea that Ford might like to buy the entire company and run it as a subsidiary. It was a sensible solution. Ford would realize instant expansion and achieve self-sufficiency with a single signature in the checkbook. The Dodges would receive a fair profit on a decade of work and risk and have the capital to start some new enterprise. Negotiations for the sale began and led to a lease on the Dodge Brothers plant signed by Henry Ford. But eventually the Dodges realized that Henry Ford was stringing them along, with no intention of concluding the deal. Shortly thereafter he gave a final No to the purchase.

With the advantage of hindsight, it is easy to see that Henry Ford never intended to buy Dodge Brothers. For one thing, he was simultaneously negotiating to sell his own company. The interested buyer was William Crapo Durant, whose fortune came from carriage making. Durant had already bought Buick and REO, and now he had approached Henry Ford with an $8-million offer. According to a story told by Peter Collier and David Horowitz in *The Fords*, it was James Couzens who talked to Durant, downstairs at the Belmont Hotel, while Henry Ford lay upstairs on the tile floor of his bathroom trying to relieve his aching back. When Couzens relayed the offer to his boss, Ford said, "Tell him he can have it if the money's all cash. Tell him I'll even throw in my lumbago." Only the fact that Durant ultimately failed to raise that cash sum prevented the sale from being concluded.

Another indication that Ford was not really serious about buying the Dodge Brothers plant was that he was simultaneously planning his own expansion at the Highland Park plant, as well as the creation of a new division of Ford to manufacture tractors at a new site in River Rouge. Perhaps the real reason he didn't conclude the deal with the Dodges, though, was intelligent self-interest. However appealing he might initially have found the idea of acquiring Dodge Brothers, with its plant, machinery and workers all custom-tailored to the Ford operation, Henry Ford probably realized that any sale was simply putting capital into the hands of very able and knowledgeable competitors.

But the Dodge brothers could make their own car with or without the co-operation of Henry Ford. When the negotiations to sell their company fell through, they made alternate plans. On July 17, 1913, John Dodge wrote a formal letter to the Ford Motor Company, canceling the lease and ending the relationship with Ford Motor Company.

> On August Thirteenth, 1912, there was a certain lease entered into between the Ford Motor Company of Detroit and the copartnership of Dodge Brothers covering the business as existing between the two companies.
>
> One of the principal reasons for the making of this lease was to do away with the trouble arising annually when prices were agreed upon. Inasmuch as this lease has failed to overcome this trouble, we wish to exercise our right as given under clause ten of this lease permitting either party to cancel the same upon twelve months' notice. . . .

The initials at the bottom of the letter show it was dictated to and typed by Amelia Rausch, still John Dodge's confidential secretary. In a subsequent letter, John resigned his position as vicepresident and director of Ford. The Dodges would, however, continue to hold their Ford stock.

Shortly after the break came the expected announcement: Dodge Brothers would start to manufacture a car under its own name to join the more than three million cars already on the American road. The news aroused great excitement in the automotive world. According to *Automobile Topics*, it was "like the announcement of a new gold strike—another Comstock Lode or a second Klondike—that the famous Dodge engine builders were to have a car of their own." Immediately, more than 22,000 people applied for Dodge dealerships, hoping to share in the envisioned profits. As *Automobile Topics* confidently predicted,

> once the plant is released from contract work, the pulsations of engines, the hum of machine tools, the whir of belts, the shock of heavy steam hammers, the roar of heat-treating furnaces, the staccato of pneumatic devices, the rumble of overhead cranes, the hiss of molten metal, and the noise and bustle incident to manufacturing in the Dodge way, all will blend in a sound that tells of Dodge car production on a scale commensurate with the mammoth capacity of the organization.

Only one voice was heard to speak against it, the writer of a column in a magazine devoted to cars. He called the Dodge brothers "money mad" and inveighed, "Not once in 100 years does any success come to light in this world like the Ford Motor Company's success. . . . Dodge Brothers may have something new to spring on the public, but they are about as liable to make a loss of what they may have as a success."

The Dodge brothers could afford to take the gamble. By 1913,

At an early Dodge dealership in the town of Albany, Oregon, Dodge cars are lined up for the inspection of eager buyers. (Chrysler Historical Collection)

their combined worth was over $50 million. Annual sales of Ford parts brought in $10 million a year to Dodge Brothers, solely owned by Horace and John, and dividends on their Ford stock brought in several more million per year.

Throughout late 1913 and early 1914, John and Horace sweated over the details of the car that was to bear their name. John, Horace and a small team of workmen worked late into the night, got a few hours of sleep on wooden workbenches and then woke up to resume work at an early hour. Horace was primarily responsible for the design of the engine. Capable of developing thirty-five horsepower, the four-cylinder L-head engine was built of the most durable materials: gray iron pistons; cam, rods, crank and valve stems of drop-forged vanadium, a new alloy that was lighter than steel and possessed ten times its tensile strength; and timing gears

The 1914 ads for the new Dodge Brothers' car went into exhaustive technical detail about its mechanical and engineering superiority. (From the collection of Dick and Carl Perry)

of heavy steel. That four-cylinder engine was so well designed it was the only one they would make until 1928.

Every mechanical system in the car was planned to have similar durability. Gear-driven pumps circulated both oil and water. The twelve-volt electrical system was specially developed for Dodge by Northeast Electric. The starter was operated by a button on the floor, and Horace had designed it so that whenever the voltage generated by the engine fell below the voltage of the battery, the starter would automatically begin cranking the engine again. Thus the car could not stall, leading Dodge Brothers to promote it as "ideal for a woman." The three-speed transmission, with a leather-faced cone clutch, featured heat-treated vanadium-steel gears. As the *Michigan Manufacturer and Financial Record* confidently predicted, "When the Dodge Brothers new car comes out, there is no question that it will be the best thing on the market for the money. The Dodge brothers are the two best mechanics in Michigan. There is no operation in their own shop, from drop-forging to machining, from tool-making to micrometric measurement, that they can't do with their own hands."

But there was in fact one area of car manufacturing and design about which they knew little, and that was the body. Most car manufacturers used wood for their car bodies, a material with which the Dodges had scant experience. As former employee Ralph Vail recalled, "The Dodges did not understand wood, nor did they trust it." So when railroad-car manufacturer Edward Budd came to them with a proposal to manufacture an all-steel body, they quickly agreed. But they were not absolutely certain the bodies would be up to Dodge standards. At the Dodge factory, the welded bodies, made of 1,200 stampings, were reinforced by the addition of many rivets, "just in case." Budd kept assuring the Dodges that the rivets were totally unnecessary and offered to pay full costs if any of the welds broke. John Dodge conceded that the rivets were probably useless but kept right on adding them anyway. "They can do no damage," he pronounced.

The arrangement the Dodge brothers made with Edward Budd

was typical of the way they did business. Budd candidly admitted that he did not know how to estimate the costs of producing the steel car bodies in quantity. John Dodge solved the problem simply. He told Budd, "Go ahead and make this thing. Make as many as you can and ship them to us as fast as they come through. At the end of the year, show us your books. If you have made too much out of us, we'll yell; if you've lost your shirt, we'll lend you something on your cuff buttons."

The new Dodge Brothers Motor Car Company was incorporated in June 1914, with stock worth $5 million—all owned by John and Horace. John was the president, Horace vice president, and both men were directors of the corporation. The legal requirement dictating at least one outside director forced them to add employee A. L. McMeans to the roster as secretary. He was in fact John's private secretary and the office manager of the company, sure to function as a loyal yes man.

The existing factory, geared to turning out parts for Ford, had to be expanded and almost entirely retooled. The amount of work space was nearly tripled, from 500,000 square feet to 1.4 million. Among the new operations the expansion incorporated were a design department, an aluminum foundry, the press shop for stamping frames, a body assembly area, a trim and upholstery department, a radiator shop, a wheel shop and the first testing track in Detroit. In addition, the shipping platform and assembly areas were greatly expanded. All this new construction cost well over $1 million.

The retooling was probably nearly as expensive. According to industrial historian Charles Hyde, "The conversion was so massive that it swamped Dodge's tool-making force of 180 men, so they hired four other Detroit firms to produce the required fixtures and jigs." Hyde discovered that producing the Dodge engine cylinder block alone involved seventy-three different foundry operations and eighteen machine-shop operations, each of which required all new machines and tools.

The expansion created a huge number of additional jobs at Dodge

Brothers. The work force more than doubled, going from 3,500 employees at the height of the Ford contract work to 7,500 at the outset of independent manufacturing operations. "We are not going to try to build all the cars in the world," John Dodge said reassuringly, but it seemed obvious that they intended to have the capability of manufacturing a good share of them. And when some of the newly hired workers had nothing to do, because of the uneven pace of the expansion, the Dodges kept them on the payroll and gave them busywork to keep them occupied until the flow of manufacturing began.

The effect of the newly expanded plant on the visitor was enthusiastically recorded in a magazine article called "The Tremendous Plant Created by the Dodge Brothers." Opined the writer, "The first impression of the plant is an unusually pleasing one, a vista of green lawns, bright with flowers, in the midst of which an attractive brick office building rises. Like all other component parts of the Dodge Brothers' plant, the building is handsome without being ornate."

Fred Haynes said that the first Dodge was designed on honesty, built on honesty and marketed on honesty. What that meant was that the car was as good as John and Horace Dodge knew how to make it. One contemporary magazine article made the point succinctly: "The Dodge Brothers had decided between themselves that when the new car was actually disclosed they should be able to point to it with pride and say, 'That is the kind of car Dodge Brothers know how to make.' " Not only did they use the best materials on the market, but also they rigorously tested their final product to make sure it would perform as promised and endure longer than expected, driving the prototype secretly through the streets of Detroit in the dark of night. John personally tested the tires used on the Dodge by dropping them off the four-story plant to see how they fared. In an even more impressive display of dedication to the concept of personal testing, he drove the cars into a brick wall at a speed of 20 mph. "I might as well," John said,

John and Horace Dodge sit in the back seat of "Old Betsey," the first Dodge Brothers car off the assembly line, in the driveway of John's Boston Boulevard house. (Chrysler Historical Collection)

"because someone else is going to do it when these cars get on the road." On the wooden test track, each assembled car was driven up and down a steep grade to test the transmission and the brakes. Even years later, Horace always tested every changed design by putting it on his own car; for example, his last Dodge, made in November 1919, had an innovative rear axle, which did not make it into production until 1922.

The first Dodge rolled off the twelve-man assembly line on November 14, 1914, and was promptly given the nickname "Old Betsey." John and Horace got in the back seat and rode from

Hamtramck to John's Boston Boulevard house, where they posed for photographs in the high open car, which stood nearly seven feet tall and weighed more than 2,000 pounds. Like the Ford, it came in just one color, black. At first, it also came in just one model, the five-passenger open touring car. In 1915, a two-seater roadster was brought out. Every car proudly carried the Dodge Brothers emblem on the radiator: a turquoise-blue-and-white six-pointed star was superimposed on the globe; in the center were the interlocked initials DB. The symbol, sometimes called "Solomon's Seal," or "the Star of David," represented Greek deltas, and also was supposed to represent the mystical union of two opposing forces: the light and the dark, the mind and the body, the flesh and the spirit, or possibly Horace and John.

Only 249 Dodge cars had been made by the end of the year, but by 1915 the factory was up to speed, and more than 45,000 Dodges were manufactured. Initially, the company announced that there would be no model year. Improvements and changes would simply be made as soon as possible after they were designed. That concept proved to be an impractical marketing idea, and soon Dodge had model years like all other cars.

The new Dodge sold for $785, as compared with $450 for Ford's Model T. John and Horace understood that the Model T had a lock on the low end of the car market and did not attempt to compete with it. Although they were consistently fair in pointing out that the Model T was a good car for the money, their own preferences were for a heavier, sturdier car that would be utterly reliable and extremely durable—and, as always, what they wanted for themselves was what they made in their factory. It turned out that a sizable number of consumers wanted the same thing. A popular saying gave the public's verdict on Dodge dependability: "A Ford rattles, a Packard purrs, and a Dodge chugs."

The Dodge was one of 120 new makes of car introduced in 1914; others included such names as Allis-Chalmers, Arrow, Cort, Detroit Speedster, Hazard, Meteor, Michigan Hearse, O-We-Go,

Peter Pan, Playboy, Rex, Royal, Star, Tiger, Twombly, Vixen and Wizard. The Dodge shot ahead of most of its competitors, new or old. Figures indicate that the dependable Dodge lost money during its first year of manufacture, since start-up costs were so high, but then the wave of sales took the company back into the black. Sales of reliably chugging Dodge cars increased significantly every year. Here are the production figures:

1915	45,053	(worth $35 million)
1916	70,000	
1917	101,000	
1918	99,000	
1919	105,398	
1920	145,000	

By the time the company was five years old, it had moved into the number-three position among literally hundreds of car manufacturers, behind Ford and the new conglomerate, General Motors.

A large part of the Dodge success came from the fact that it was indeed a superior automobile. Another important ingredient, however, was the fact that it was built by Dodge Brothers. That, by the way, was how the brothers insisted on being addressed. Any correspondence received, even orders for new cars, was returned to the sender unless it bore the correct heading: "Dodge Brothers," with a capital *B*, if you please. As employers and businessmen, these two brothers—as inseparable as Tweedledum and Tweedledee, and bearing a striking physical resemblance to those egg-shaped twins—had created such a fund of goodwill that the car could be sold on their name alone. An early advertising slogan proclaimed that the Dodge car "Speaks For Itself," but what the slogan really meant was that the Dodge name spoke for the car. Consumers trusted the Dodge reputation to insure that the car would be well engineered, durably built and honestly priced. They were also impressed by the fact that the Dodge came with a sixty-one-page manual that told the owner everything necessary about

John and Horace Dodge (front row center) *gather with a group of Dodge Brothers executives in front of Horace's home, Rose Terrace.* (Chrysler Historical Collection)

care and maintenance of the car. Dodge Brothers would not let its car suffer at the hands of careless owners! The manual even told motorists how to reverse the head lamps, to provide light for changing a tire at night.

One other factor in the Dodge car's success was the astuteness with which the business was run by the two brothers. They were on top of every detail. They invented a system whereby every dealer wrote up a complete report of weekly sales and inventory on hand before locking up on Saturday night and put a copy in the mail on the way home. By Tuesday morning, the reports were on John Dodge's desk, and he was able to analyze the week's activity in all Dodge dealerships. Once a year, he took the records with him for a two-week stay at Meadow Brook, along with blueprints of the factory and designs for the cars, and tried to think of ways to improve the car, the manufacturing process and the level of sales.

The Dodges were smart enough to surround themselves with talented and able managers. Fred Haynes, who had left Franklin, in Syracuse, New York, and joined the company in 1912, enjoyed the full confidence of both brothers and held a number of different administrative posts before he eventually became the president of the company, after the deaths of the founders. Russell Huff, a fifteen-year veteran of Packard, became chief engineer at Dodge in 1915. A. Z. Mitchell took over as factory manager. Harrison Phelps was a brilliant sales manager, who built a strong sales organization on a firm no-discount policy. He also succeeded in exporting Dodge cars to forty-seven countries. Each car, with a manual in the appropriate language, was beautifully crated.

Phelps later recalled how hard it had been to persuade the Dodge brothers to spend money on advertising. John once told him, "Horace and I go out into the factory and sweat blood to save a tenth of a cent and you fellows turn right around and throw away ten percent." According to one newspaper article, John loathed the whole idea of advertising. Yet the early advertising for the Dodge car was brilliant in its simplicity. The ads showed just the name, *Dodge Brothers*, and the emblem, followed by three words: *Reliable. Dependable. Sound.* It was the perfect way to capitalize on the reputation Dodge Brothers had already created.

If the Dodge brothers had a weakness as businessmen, it was their financial conservatism. They were quite willing to spend their own money to expand as fast as possible, but they refused to borrow so much as a dime. Their capital was completely unleveraged; in fact, the company did not have a single credit line at any bank. Although they had amended the organization of Dodge Brothers Motor Car Company to double the total stock, issuing $10 million worth of shares, it was still wholly owned by the two brothers, and they still ran their multimillion-dollar empire as if it were a little mom-and-pop business. They never learned much about high finance, and the only way they ever juggled their books was to carry all their assets at the lowest possible valuation. For example, the goodwill that was such an important part of their business was valued in their books at the token price of $1.

News of the merits of the new Dodge cars spread far and wide. A fleet of five dependable Dodges was used by famed paleontologist Roy Chapman Andrews for his expeditions to the Gobi Desert. England's Prince of Wales (later King Edward VIII) ordered a Dodge touring car. Dodges were used in Mexico in 1916 by Lieutenant George S. Patton, Jr., in a daring raid on the headquarters of one of Pancho Villa's commanders. A news story filed on May 27, 1916, gives the details:

> Efforts to round up a bunch of bandits headed by Col. Julio Cardenas failed when cavalry was used. The bandits seemed to get word of the approach of the cavalry. The officers then decided to try a faster means of transportation for the attacking force and three Dodge cars were used by Lieut. Patton and 15 men in their attack on the Cardenas headquarters at daylight on May 14.
>
> The approach to the ranch was over an open stretch of a mile, but the Lieutenant had his machines ready for a speedy dash when they got in sight of the farmhouse where the bandits were believed to be making their headquarters. Shoving their gears into high, the chauffeurs cut open for high speed and the dash over the desert was made at better than 40 miles an hour. The machines were within a few yards of the ranch before they were detected and then half-clad bandits made their appearance through doors and windows as they streaked for some cover.
>
> "We couldn't have done it with horses," said Lieut. Patton. "The motor car is the modern war horse."

The success of Patton's motorized mission led his commanding officer, Brigadier General John J. "Blackjack" Pershing, to order 250 more Dodges for the Mexican campaign, and later to drive them on the battlefields of France.

The U.S. government, which had declared war on Germany in April 1917, wanted more from Dodge Brothers than just the dependable car for the army. It also wanted John and Horace to undertake the manufacture of the delicate recoil mechanism of a famous piece of artillery, the French 155 mm fieldpiece, which was jamming in use. John was invited to Washington to consult with army officials about the problem. The plainspoken John immediately rubbed Secretary of War Newton D. Baker the wrong way. When Baker said something John considered erroneous, John blurted out, "That's damned nonsense!" The surprised Baker indicated huffily that he was not used to being contradicted in that fashion. John retorted coolly, "Well, the country would be a lot better off if you were."

John returned to Detroit to talk the matter over with Horace. Then he breezily told the army, "We can build it; just tell us how many you want." Dodge Brothers would do the work without making a profit; the only condition was that the Dodges be allowed to do things in their own way, without government supervision or interference. This was a highly unusual proposition, but the need for the Dodges was desperate because two other plants had already tried and failed.

The army agreed to John's conditions on Saturday, October 27, 1917, and he immediately made a phone call to Horace to get things started. By six o'clock Monday morning, nearly 2,000 men were already at work building the new factory and designing the necessary tools. Throughout the cold Michigan winter, the managers slept in tents erected at the site to enable them to work around the clock. About 130 new machines were designed, most of them by Horace, who also spent time in the machine shop improving the design of the recoil mechanism itself. Specially tempered steel was ordered from the Bethlehem company furnaces. Four months later, on March 1, 1918, the new $10-million plant was in full operation, turning out twenty recoil mechanisms a day. The skeptical French were amazed by the speed, quality and efficiency of Dodge Brothers' work—so much so that after the war was over, the French commander Marshal Ferdinand Foch paid a visit to the Dodge plant to convey his nation's thanks in person.

The Dodges were patriotic Americans who were happy to do what they could to help the war effort. Horace made the great sacrifice of volunteering his yacht, the *Nokomis*, for naval service as a submarine chaser. On the day the ship was turned over, in May 1917, Horace and John drove to the pier in a 1914 Dodge touring car and boarded the *Nokomis* for a final farewell. Guests at the sentimental occasion were later given a souvenir booklet containing a photo of the brothers waving from the stern and the following poem, rumored to have been written by Delphine:

> The wind is lashing the somber lee,
>   And the foam-flecked waves roll high,
> And my heart is stirred like the stormy sea,
> As you sail from the shores of "Used-To-Be",
>   Goodby, Nokomis, goodby!
>
> You've served me well in days of yore,
>   When the sun shone bright on high,
> Go now and weather the storms of war,
> And make me proud of the name you bore.
>   Goodby, old friend, goodby!

The *Nokomis*, valued by the navy at the time of receipt at $200,000, was commissioned under the name *Kwasind* and converted into a submarine patrol boat carrying six officers and fifty-seven in crew. Its primary duties turned out to be transporting U.S. Marines to Guantánamo, in Cuba, and San Pedro de Macorís, in the Dominican Republic. It was decommissioned at the end of the war and sold to William H. Todd, the president of Todd Shipyards, who renamed it *Saelmo* and used it to host such notables as Charles Lindbergh, Richard E. Byrd and Wiley Post. After Todd's death, the ship was purchased by the state of Maryland and rechristened the SS *Dupont*. It saw service again in World War II as a Coast

Guard vessel. That was its last incarnation; it came through the war in such bad condition that it was finally scrapped in late 1945.

Horace had thought to console himself for the loss of the *Nokomis* by building a new and bigger version, the *Nokomis II*. It was almost identical in design to its predecessor, but measured 243 feet in length, rather than 180. The 582-ton steam yacht had steel bulwarks and deckhouse, and polished mahogany deck fittings. Accommodations were luxurious. Horace and Anna's stateroom had more than 300 square feet of space and its own private bathroom. The main lounge was twenty-four feet long, ending in a large lobby with stairs descending to guest staterooms. The ship had its own ice machine, barbershop, laundry room and not one, but two galleys, said to be the equal of any hotel kitchen in the United States. The *Nokomis II* carried its own fuel in bunkers that held 350 tons of coal. It was built at the Pusey & Jones shipyard in Wilmington, Delaware.

Poor Horace! Almost the moment he took delivery of his new pride and joy, it was requisitioned by the navy. He had just one excursion on his dream ship, the trip from Delaware up the Saint Lawrence and through two of the Great Lakes to its intended home at the dock in front of Rose Terrace, before it was enlisted in the war effort.

The success of their own car put the Dodges in the public eye. Their fame spread past the confines of Detroit and into the larger world. The Dodge factory was a stop on many distinguished visitors' itinerary. For example, presidential candidate Charles Evans Hughes paid a visit in 1916, and then wrote to the brothers, "I shall never forget my visit to the Dodge Brothers plant. . . . It was very gratifying to note the exceptionally cordial relationships which existed between you and your employees and the spirit that pervaded the meeting." The activities of all the Dodges were breathlessly reported in the press: the debuts and weddings, the lavish gowns and even more lavish charitable contributions. And, as is always the case with the rich and famous, there was a healthy appetite for every gossipy detail of the lives they led behind the doors of those ornate mansions.

So the press had a field day in the spring of 1918 when they discovered that John Duval Dodge had entered into a secret marriage. His bride was a pretty and personable young girl, Marie O'Connor, a classmate at Eastern High School. But her working-class Catholic family was apparently unacceptable to Dodge social ambitions. And, amusingly enough, John Dodge, himself the veteran of a secret marriage ended by an equally secret divorce, was incensed that his son had tried to sneak behind his back. Perhaps things would have gone better if John Duval had possessed his father's talent for concealment. But the news of his secret elopement to Maryland, which ended with both parties returning to the homes of their respective parents, leaked out when Marie became seriously ill with pneumonia several weeks later. The frightened young woman told her parents the news, and they summoned their new son-in-law to her bedside. The press got hold of this romantic story, with its happy ending of Marie's quick recovery, and John Dodge had the humiliation of reading all about his son's actions in his morning paper. He took immediate action of his own. John Duval was fired from his sinecure at the Dodge plant, where chief mechanic Fred Lamborn was training the young man in the business. He commented that his pupil "would do anything for you— he had the cleanest heart—but he was spoiled." Employees nicknamed him John Devil Dodge. After the break, John Duval and his wife were given enough money to move to faraway Texas to start a new life away from the eager newshounds—and the snickering socialites of Detroit. And four days after John had learned about his son's secret marriage, he executed a new will that would leave John Duval nothing more than an income of $150 a month.

John Dodge always held the concept of family in high esteem, so disinheriting his son was surely not a step he took lightly. But apparently he had for years considered the boy a disappointment to him (although it is clear that John himself was responsible for

This 1918 photo shows Matilda Dodge in a snazzy Dodge Brothers roadster, with four-year-old Frances. (Chrysler Historical Collection)

many of the problems in their relationship). When John attended the 1916 wedding of Henry Ford's handsome young son, Edsel, already a force in Ford Motor Company, to lovely young socialite Eleanor Clay, he told the father of the groom wistfully, "Henry, I don't envy you a damn thing except that boy of yours." It is not clear whether John really meant the disinheritance of his son to be permanent, or whether it was intended to be a form of discipline for John Duval.

Whatever John's intention, the result was the virtual disappearance of John Dodge's first family from his Boston Boulevard house by mid-1918. Winifred and her husband were living in Indian Village, and Isabel was living with them; John Duval was somewhere in Texas. John was free to concentrate on the children of his second marriage. There was Frances, born in 1914, and then there was Daniel George, born on July 23, 1917, and named after his two grandfathers. The family was completed the following summer with the birth of Anna Margaret, on June 14, 1919. Photos taken by professional photographers to memorialize Dodge family life show John doting on the beautifully dressed babies. He intended these children to have the best of everything.

He could well afford it. John and Horace's wealth had increased enormously, despite Henry Ford's best efforts to prevent that growth.

Back in 1916, Ford had taken a step that he thought would weaken the Dodge brothers financially and possibly even force them to quit the automobile business. He knew they were counting on their Ford dividends—paid to them at a rate of more than $1 million a year—to inject needed capital into their new car venture. Acting as majority stockholder, he made a decision aimed at shutting down their cash flow. In the past year, the Ford Motor Company had accumulated $58 million in profits, scheduled for distribution to stockholders. Early in 1916, Henry Ford and his engineer, C. Harold Wills, dropped by Dodge Brothers for a chat with John and Horace.

As John Dodge later recounted the story:

> the object of the interview in the first place was to discuss his tractor plant. There had been considerable talk about the forming of the tractor plant, and there had been some objection on the part of some of the stockholders of the Ford Motor Co. My understanding was that it was his purpose to use the engine of the Model T and the facilities and resources of the Ford Motor Company to produce this tractor and still own the tractor plant himself. . . .

John remembered the occasion as a pleasant afternoon, and the conversation a harmonious one: "We discussed Ford Motor conditions in general and finally drifted to the resignation of Mr. Couzens. . . . Spent most of the rest of the time telling about the shortcomings of Mr. Couzens. . . ." Then, as the visit was drawing to a close, Ford made a surprise announcement.

> He said he did not propose to pay any dividends except the nominal dividend; that the stockholders had already received a good deal more than they had put into the company, and he did not propose to pay any more. He was going to put the earnings of the company back into the business to expand it. He was going to double the size of his plant and double the number of cars produced and sell them at half price.

The Dodges naturally viewed this statement with alarm, and John told Ford that if he proposed to carry things to such an extreme, he should buy out the other stockholders so he could run the business as he saw fit. Ford said he already owned the majority of the stock and saw no need to buy more.

Ford's next step came on the last day of August 1917, when he released to the press a statement that the company would retain all of that accumulated $58-million profit "to re-invest for the growth of the company. This is Mr. Ford's policy at present and it is understood that the other stockholders cheerfully accede to this plan." Ford concluded piously, "My ambition is to employ still more men, to spread the benefits of this industrial system to the greatest possible number, to help them build up their lives and their homes."

At least two stockholders were anything but cheerful about this plan. Such high-handed behavior was guaranteed to enrage the volatile Dodge brothers. In November of the same year, they responded with a lawsuit to compel Henry Ford to pay out the retained profits in dividends.

As is so often the case with legal matters, the rush to court was followed by months of frustrating inactivity. Lawyers for both sides took depositions, searched for precedents and planned their lines of attack. The Dodge position was staked out early. A business organization should be run for the benefit of the stockholders, who were entitled to reap all they could from the risk of their capital. If Ford Motor Company was now paying off big, that was only fair: The initial risk had also been enormous.

Henry Ford's assertion was that the company should be run for the welfare of its customers. Workers of America, he proclaimed sanctimoniously, ought to be able to buy a good car at a low price— and that's what he could offer if he plowed his profits into improved production at his new River Rouge plant. He also sniffed at the notion that the stockholders *deserved* a single additional penny. Why, they hadn't contributed anything to the Ford Motor Company but a few thousand dollars, and they'd already been repaid millions. In questioning Ford, the lawyer for the Dodge side, Elliott G. Stevenson, began by dealing with the general problem of how the credit for the Ford company's success should be apportioned.

STEVENSON: What did you contribute to the company for your stock?

FORD: A working model, I guess, of the car.

S: You contributed no money or other property?

F: Fifteen or twenty years of experience.

S: I say, you contributed no money or other property?

F: I contributed the car.

S: Did you contribute any money or other property?

F: I put in a working model of a car, that I paid a lot of money for.

S: Did you contribute any other money or any other property?

F: Buying the stock with money, do you mean?

S: It seems to me that is quite plain, Mr. Ford. You say that your contribution was the model of the car?

F: Yes, sir.

S: Now I ask you if you contributed any other property or any other money in addition to that, for your stock.

F: No, sir, I don't think so.

S: What did Mr. Malcolmson contribute?

F: I don't know, it is all on the books, I guess.

S: You and he together took a majority of the stock, did you?

F: Yes, sir.

S: He had financed you to develop the model of the car, hadn't he?

F: Partly.

S: And for his financing you in developing the model of the car, he got the other 25 and one-half percent?

F: Yes, sir.

S: So that between you and Mr. Malcolmson, for the model of the car, you got 51 percent of the stock?

F: Yes, sir.

Later, in his cross examination of Ford, Stevenson returned to the same point.

S: You started out with a model of a car?

F: Yes, sir.

S: That is what you started with, wasn't it, Mr. Ford?

F: Yes, sir.

S: Yes, and a pretty poor model at that, wasn't it?

F: It seemed to sell alright; it would sell though.

S: Sold after it was made, but who made it?

F: We made the first model ourselves.

S: Who made the first cars that you sold?

F: Dodge Brothers made part of them.

S: Dodge Brothers made the car?

F: Made part of it.

S: What part of it did they make?

F: The motor.

S: What else?

F: The frame.

S: They made the whole thing, except the tires and the body, didn't they?

F: From our drawings, yes.

S: And they made a car that you were able to sell, too, didn't they?

F: From our drawings.

S: From your drawings they made a car that you were able to sell?

F: Yes, sir.

S: And where was your plant, your big plant, in those days?

F: Which days?

S: When you started the business in 1903?

F: On Mack Avenue.

S: What kind of a plant did you have?

F: A barn, I guess.

S: You had a barn. Mr. Strelow's carpenter shop, wasn't it?

F: I guess it was.

S: Mr. Strelow's carpenter shop. Dodge Brothers made the completed car, except the rubber tires and the body, and that was taken up to Mr. Strelow's carpenter shop and the body was put on the car, and then your selling agent sold it?

F: Yes, sir.

S: That was the history of it, wasn't it; and Dodge Brothers had to equip their plants to produce those cars, too, didn't they?

F: I guess they must have.

At this point in Ford's testimony, the lawyer switched to consider the question of risk, as it was borne by the various parties concerned.

> s: Dodge Brothers jeopardized everything they had in the world, in the start, to make those cars, didn't they?
>
> f: I don't know what they jeopardized.
>
> s: You didn't jeopardize anything, did you? Didn't have anything to jeopardize, did you?
>
> f: We had our drawings and plans to jeopardize.
>
> s: You did? How were you going to jeopardize those?
>
> f: We gave them up to be manufactured.
>
> s: Didn't they have to equip a machine shop to manufacture those cars?
>
> f: I guess they did.
>
> s: And they had to buy machinery?
>
> f: Yes.
>
> s: And wasn't the extent of the purchases they had to make on that account, in their situation, jeopardizing everything they had, if that had not been a success?
>
> f: You can find that all upon the records.
>
> s: You know what they did, don't you?
>
> f: I guess I did at the time.
>
> s: Have you forgotten what they did?
>
> f: Quite a lot of it, yes, sir.
>
> s: You have forgotten, have you, that they produced the cars that were sold, to bring the money to make the Ford Motor Company a success, have you?
>
> f: No, sir.
>
> s: There isn't any doubt about that, is there?
>
> f: No.

A final decision was reached by Michigan's Supreme Court on February 7, 1919. The Ford Motor Company lost the case. The judge was openly skeptical of Henry Ford's motivation:

Where a corporation with an unsatisfied demand for its cars and the output of 500,000 per annum deliberately makes a cut of $80 in the price of a car, and enters upon a duplication of its present enormous plant, not to speak of other large expenditures, suspicion will arise that its motives are not wholly philanthropic; domination quite as much as philanthropy comes to mind.

The judge ruled that Henry Ford's refusal to pay out the company's profits to its stockholders was both arbitrary and illegal. Ford was ordered to make immediate payment of $19,275,385, plus interest of about $1.5 million. The Dodge brothers' share of this payout amounted to more than $2 million.

An aggrieved Henry Ford immediately counterattacked. Less than a month later, he told reporters he was going to leave Ford Motor Company and start a new car company. When asked what would happen to the company that bore his name, he replied vaguely, "Why, I don't know exactly what will become of that." It was the same dirty trick he had used on Alex Malcolmson, and it had the same purpose: to force stockholders out of the company. The stock, which had been valued at $18,000 a share, immediately fell to just $12,500. Ford made the public announcement that he had no intention of spending money to buy out the minority stockholders, but at the same time he was employing agents to approach the Dodges and others and to purchase their shares. By the summer of 1919, an agreement was reached on the price of $12,500 a share. That gave John and Horace Dodge a total of $25 million, an enormous sum in those days, or even later. Of course, the big winner in the deal was Henry Ford, who was able to buy about 40 percent of his company for $100 million dollars. Two years later, he was offered $1 billion for the stock of Ford Motor Company.

The whole episode starkly illuminated two aspects of Henry Ford's character. One was his dislike of sharing credit with anyone else. One by one, the men who had collaborated with him in his achievements found themselves overshadowed and then el-bowed out of the way. First were Jim Bishop, the mechanic who helped him build the first car, in 1896, and Oliver Barthel, who helped him with the first race. Next came the turn of Tom Cooper, who financed the building of the Arrow and the 999, and Barney Oldfield, who drove the racer for him when he was afraid to drive it himself. Alex Malcolmson, the full partner who backed him when nobody else would and provided the business experience Ford lacked, was the next to get the treatment, and in 1915 James Couzens, the general manager of the Ford Motor Company, was maneuvered into resigning. Engineer Harold Wills, who eventu-ally grew to hate Ford, was pushed into the position of depending on Ford's generosity for both his credit for the design of the Ford cars and his compensation. And finally, of course, came the turn of the Dodge brothers, whose skills and capital got the Ford Mo-tor Company off the ground; how like Henry Ford to "forget" what their contribution had been!

The episode also shed light on Ford's odd dual character. He could be affable, genial, an innocent country boy, when the pose suited him, and that was the charm that drew people into working with him. But there was a dark side to his personality, a determi-nation to get the better of everyone no matter what it cost, which found frequent expression. His own pastor, the Reverend Samuel Marquis, summed it up: "There is a conflict that at times makes one feel that two personalities are striving within him for mas-tery."

The Dodges were among the few men who ever succeeded in besting Henry Ford. Although John and Horace intended to put most of the money they got from the enforced distribution of div-idends and the sale of their Ford stock to work in their own car company, they also enjoyed a spending spree. On the day the sale of the stock was concluded, John and Horace went to the Detroit Athletic Club and offered to treat the house—all four floors of it! When they got the tab for all that everyone in the building had

Horace and Anna Dodge pay a visit to the shipyard to celebrate the laying of the Delphine's *keel in 1920; Horace's pleasure in the event was overshadowed by the sorrow of his brother's death.* (Collection of David Agresta)

ordered to eat or drink that night, they tried to pay for it with the multimillion-dollar certified check from Ford Motor Company.

Horace dared to dream of a new steam yacht and commissioned the *Delphine*, to be designed by the same naval architects responsible for *Nokomis I* and *II*, and to be built by the Great Lakes Engineering Company, in Michigan. When John heard of it, he teased his brother affectionately, "Well, H. E., I see you have another seaman's boardinghouse." Horace defended himself by asking John how much he paid for the last bull he bought for

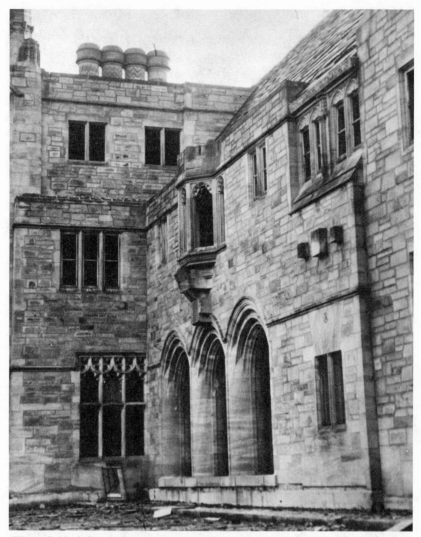

The unfinished Grosse Pointe mansion of John Dodge stood derelict for many years before it was razed, and in the summer of 1933 it was the site of a summer camp for future debutantes of Detroit. (Detroit Free Press)

Meadow Brook Farm. John then closed the argument by companionably ordering a 104-foot power cruiser.

John also embarked on the construction of a truly palatial home.

He bought a large site with water frontage in Grosse Pointe, to the north of Horace's Rose Terrace. The plans were drawn up by architects Smith, Hinchman & Grylls, and they clearly indicate that John Dodge intended his home to be the biggest and best in all Detroit. There were a total of 110 rooms, plus 24 bathrooms. The mansion was constructed of a varicolored granite quarried in Weymouth, Massachusetts, and carved by more than a hundred stonecutters imported from Scotland, where they had just finished working on Andrew Carnegie's Skibo Castle. John improved the site by creating a long peninsula that jutted out into Lake St. Clair, where he could build a dock for his cruiser and, of course, a berth for Horace's boat when he came visiting. Since the mansion would be separated from the dock by Lake Shore Drive, John also ordered a tunnel dug for easy access to the waterfront.

The house had a huge central hall, "covering the space of twenty ordinary rooms," according to an enthusiastic journalist. There were also a library, a solarium, a ballroom and a sixty-eight-foot swimming pool (in the basement). Stained-glass windows were commissioned from Tiffany Studios, and wood paneling by the acre arrived to be installed in the major reception rooms. There were eleven master bedrooms, a nursery and an upstairs kitchen to prepare meals that would be served in bed.

Matilda may have been consulted about some specifics, but the mansion was chiefly planned by John Dodge, who interested himself in every detail. Characteristically, no expense was spared. When he noticed that a beautiful old tree was located too near the site of the house, he had it dug up, its roots wrapped in a gigantic 125-ton bundle, and moved to another spot. He himself broke ground for the construction of the house, with a silver shovel, on July 29, 1918.

For Christmas of 1919, John gave Matilda a check for $1 million, and Horace told Anna she could have "any earthly thing" she wanted. A number of churches and charities also benefited from the Dodge brothers' additional wealth. John's charitable gifts in 1919 included:

Salvation Army	$137,400
Detroit Patriotic Fund	43,833
First Presbyterian Church	250,000
Hamtramck Polish Catholic Church	2,500
AME Church	7,500
Boy Scouts	500
Roosevelt Memorial (Teddy's, of course)	100
VFW	100
Little Sisters of the Poor	116.81
Detroit Women's Club	62,597
For child welfare	6,500

Horace's list of contributions had several of the same entries:

Detroit Patriotic Fund	$45,833
Eastminster Presbyterian Church	54,738
Hamtramck Polish Catholic Church	2,500
AME Church	7,500
Protestant Orphan Asylum	25,000
First Presbyterian Church	10,000
Boy Scouts	1,100
Roosevelt Memorial	100
Cottage Hospital	1,000
Children's Free Hospital	200

Another beneficiary was the Detroit Symphony. In the fall of 1919, the orchestra played its first concert in its new home, Orchestra Hall, which was built for them by the Dodges.

All in all, it was a good year for John and Horace. That New Year's Eve, they lingered together in the study of John's Boston Boulevard house even longer than usual, planning the glorious future. When they emerged, John said jovially to the assembled family, "This will be our last year in this house."

His words were sadly prophetic.

8

Death of the Dodge Brothers

On a cold January afternoon in New York City, John Dodge stood in his place at the head of a long table to make an address to the assembled Dodge Brothers dealers from the eastern region. As he waited for the applause to die down, the dealers were looking around the room for Horace. Everybody knew Horace did not like public speaking, the way John did, but wherever John went, Horace was sure to be nearby. Hundreds of pairs of eyes searched the shadowy corners of the room for the "other" brother.

John's first words put an end to the search. "Horace is pretty sick tonight," John announced somberly. Then he tried to put aside his visible distress and reassure the men in the room, whose futures depended on the Dodge brothers. "But I am healthy and strong," John boasted. "Nothing ever happens to me!" He emphasized his point by flexing the muscle of a still-brawny biceps and tapping it with a stubby forefinger. At fifty-six, John still showed traces of the physique that had kept him working long hard hours at Tom Murphy's boiler works.

John completed his speech, and stayed to shake hands and joke with the dealers who crowded round to meet him. He was, after all, there to take care of business. But as soon as the luncheon was over, he returned immediately to the Ritz Carlton Hotel, on Madison Avenue, in the midst of the most elegant shops and luxury restaurants the city could offer. He and Horace had traveled to New York in a private railroad car and taken a huge suite on their arrival at the exclusive hotel, planning to stay there nearly a week to attend a convention of car manufacturers and meet with their eastern dealers. During the first few days, they partied lavishly. When the public events of the convention were finished, they frequently adjourned to their suite and continued the festivities. The Prohibition Amendment was about to take effect, but they served a never-ending stream of drinks from the large private stock they had brought in a wooden trunk from the cellar of Rose Terrace. Then Horace fell ill, with what a doctor diagnosed as "grippe," a term used to mean a heavy cold or a respiratory virus, and the fun went out of everything for John.

On his return to the hotel that afternoon, John heard discouraging news. Doctors had been to look at Horace, and pronounced the illness grave. They were uncertain of the exact diagnosis, and made suggestions ranging from the grippe to influenza to pneumonia. The next morning, things looked even worse, and John decided to send for Horace's own doctor from Detroit, as well as for Anna, who was to be accompanied by Matilda. Yet the family still hoped that all would be well. Delphine had scheduled a party at Rose Terrace that Friday night for her young friends, and the party continued as planned, turning into a drunken spree, thanks to the huge supply of liquor in the basement storerooms.

Because the illness, whatever it was, was considered to be contagious, the doctors would not permit John to enter Horace's bedroom. So the anxious John had an armchair moved into the doorway between his room and Horace's, and a table placed in front of it. He would sit there, he said, to keep an eye on his brother. He asked the hotel to send him up some books to pass the tedious hours. "Bring me something light and happy," he commanded. He suggested Mark Twain, or that romance set in England, *Lorna Doone*.

All day Friday, all day Saturday, all day Sunday, John never moved far from the chair, watching his brother struggle for breath, listening as the doctors conferred in low voices at his bedside. Observers later remarked that John neither ate nor drank during his vigil. By Sunday, Horace seemed to be on the mend, and concern began to focus on John, who was showing definite signs of illness. Nevertheless, he insisted on maintaining his position at Horace's door for twenty-four more hours, until he was too weak to sit up any longer.

Once respiratory problems set in, John Dodge went downhill fast. His lungs, weakened perhaps by his earlier bout with tuberculosis, gave out quickly. He went into a coma on Tuesday. At 10:30 in the night of Wednesday, January 14, 1920, with his wife and two older daughters at his bedside, John Dodge died.

Horace was devastated by the terrible news. He wanted to return to Detroit on the train with his brother's body, but his doctors refused to let him out of bed for at least two more weeks. Anna stayed with him, as did the Dodge brothers' close friend, former mayor Oscar B. Marx, who had accompanied the Dodge brothers on their last trip together. Matilda, a very pregnant Winifred and Isabel accompanied John's body on the long and sad train trip home. Upon their arrival that Friday night, Matilda announced that she was too ill to carry on. She went directly home and upstairs to bed. John's body was taken to a Detroit funeral home, where it was placed in a bronze casket and returned to the living room of his Boston Boulevard home to await his funeral on Saturday afternoon.

That funeral was a great public event. The mayor of the city, who was none other than former Ford executive James Couzens, decreed that flags on city buildings be flown at half-mast during the ceremony; he also had the City Council draw up a resolution expressing the city's sorrow. The pallbearers were sixteen veteran employees of Dodge Brothers, and there were fifty-five honorary pallbearers as well, one for every full year of the dead man's life. They included Harold Wills and Henry Leland from the auto industry; former mayor Marx and present mayor Couzens; Dodge Brothers' attorney Howard Bloomer; the trial lawyer who had handled the case against Ford, Elliott Stevenson; and a host of men prominent in Detroit society and industry. The Dodge plant was closed the day of the funeral, and all the workers were invited to attend the funeral, which took place at John's home and was presided over by the minister of the First Presbyterian Church. Representing the family were Winifred and her husband, William Gray; Isabel; and John's sister Delphine Ashbaugh. Matilda remained prostrate upstairs. John Duval, the prodigal son, had not yet arrived from El Paso. And the person who loved John Dodge the most could do nothing but lie in his bed amid the splendor of the Ritz Carlton Hotel and grieve.

Tributes to John poured in from every quarter. One newspaper article summed up the impact of the man's personality:

> He was absolutely straightforward. He told the truth without quibbling. He always meant what he said, and mostly he said what he felt. He believed in fair dealing and practiced it. He also demanded fair dealing in others, and generally he obtained it. He was without fear, consequently he went to his objectives unhampered by many considerations that might have blocked a less forceful man. He was a dynamo of energy with a driving power that was tremendous.

John Dodge was buried in the imposing mausoleum he and Horace had commissioned back in 1913 in the Woodlawn Cemetery. It was a massive Egyptian temple of marble, the doorway framed with lotus-topped columns and guarded by a pair of long-

The Dodge mausoleum at Woodlawn Cemetery was obviously built for modern-day pharaohs. (Collection of David Agresta)

clawed sphinxes. When the mausoleum was finished in 1914, John had moved the body of Ivy, his first wife, from Lot 101, Section 13, into Crypt Number Five. Now he joined her on the west wall, protected by the symbols of ancient Egypt. If Horace and John saw themselves as the Pharaohs of Detroit, they were perhaps not far off the mark. Only Henry Ford had amassed a greater personal fortune from the city's automotive industry than the Dodge brothers had, and no one had enjoyed either the work or the money so much as they had.

On a gray February day, Horace came home from New York, looking thin and frail, without a trace of the robustness that had formerly characterized him. He was met at the station by his 1919 navy-blue Dodge sedan with the monogram HED on the side (now in the private collection of David Agresta), driven by long-time

employee Tom Parish, who was immediately instructed to drive
to the cemetery. Parish never forgot the naked grief Horace displayed that day at his brother's grave.

Horace stayed in Detroit only long enough to issue a statement
that Dodge Brothers would carry on as usual. Then he, Anna,
Delphine and Horace Junior took the train to Palm Beach, where
he could continue his convalescence in the sun, while Fred Haynes
looked after the day-to-day management of the company. Anna
had insisted on the southern vacation as vital to the continued
improvement of Horace's health. It was also vital to her own social
ambitions. She had concluded that the only way to get to the top
of Detroit society was to leapfrog right over it. If she could win
acceptance for the Dodges in Palm Beach, that playground of the
socially prominent rich, the first families of Detroit would simply
have to follow suit.

In her assault on Palm Beach society, Anna had a formidable
weapon: her two very attractive, very charming children. Delphine, with her piquant looks and her flapper personality, in particular was much sought after. Anna was thrilled by the prospect
of a well-connected son-in-law. Before the winter was over, she
had one in view. He was James H. R. Cromwell, the tall, dark
and dashing son of the queen of Palm Beach society, Eva Stotesbury. Eva's wealthy husband (her second) was Edward T. Stotesbury, of Philadelphia, a partner of J. P. Morgan. Although it was
whispered that the Stotesburys were not accepted in the top echelon of society in old Philadelphia, they were the undisputed
leaders of the Palm Beach set, and Eva was widely acclaimed for
her beauty, her taste, her style. From Anna's point of view, Delphine simply could not have done better than to land Eva's son
from her first marriage. The connection with the Stotesburys would
give the Dodges entrée into society in Palm Beach, Philadelphia,
New York—everywhere.

When Anna announced the news of Delphine's triumph to
Horace that April, and told him there would be an immediate
engagement, followed by a summer wedding, the poor man was

These pictures, printed from the family films of Delphine's wedding in the summer of 1920, show the bride; the groom, Jim Cromwell; and the bride's brother, Horace.
(Collection of David Agresta)

aghast. He was still racked with grief over his brother's death, still in the deepest mourning, had just returned from an extended stay in Good Samaritan Hospital. A big wedding wasn't possible, it wasn't right. . . .

As usual, the women of the family got what they wanted. Delphine married Jim Cromwell on June 17, 1920. Curious spectators lined up outside the Jefferson Avenue Presbyterian Church to see the lovely bride step out of a black Dodge and enter the church on her father's arm. After the ceremony, the wedding party motored out to Rose Terrace, where a lavish reception for more than 300 guests from Detroit, Philadelphia, New York, Chicago and Palm Beach was held. The family formed a receiving line along the terraced steps that gave the house its name. Delphine wore a gown of white satin and Belgian lace that looked deceptively simple, the sort of simplicity that only a great deal of money can produce; it had in fact come from New York couturière Lucille. Her new husband looked dashing in his cutaway and striped trousers.

The happy mother of the bride was resplendent in a fussy mauve taffeta creation and wore a big hat with purple ostrich feathers. She also wore an eye-popping string of pearls that were her husband's gift to her, the "any earthly thing" he'd promised her she could have when the money came in from the sale of the Ford stock. After meeting Eva Stotesbury, whose valuable pearls were renowned for their size and luster, Anna had decided she wanted something even more remarkable. Cartier found it for her: a five-strand necklace of 389 perfectly matched huge pearls that had once belonged to Empress Catherine the Great of Russia, as evidenced by the necklace's clasp, a jeweled miniature of the empress. Horace took Ned Stotesbury with him when he went to New York to look at the necklace in May, and Stotesbury pronounced the piece well worth the $825,000 purchase price. At the same time, Horace bought a smaller pearl necklace as a wedding present for his daughter. The necklaces were hand-delivered to the recipients in Detroit the day before the wedding and watched over by several burly detectives.

The mother of the groom, Eva Stotesbury, was wearing her own pearls, as well as a diamond collar said to have belonged to Queen Marie Antoinette and pearl-and-diamond earrings from the treasure chest of Queen Isabella of Spain. She wore apricot, carried a frilly parasol, and was followed everywhere by her conspicuously shorter husband. Horace looked subdued and went through his duties as host in a sort of daze. Matilda, who shared her brother-in-law's notion that it was too soon after John's death for a big family wedding, finally decided to accept the invitation, but she pointedly wore black and a mournful expression as she wandered through the reception. (Her sister, Amelia, had chosen not to attend.) Horace Junior was all charm and vivacity, cracking jokes, flirting and dancing with the bridesmaids and jumping in front of the camera to make silly faces.

No expense was spared to make the reception a party that Detroit would remember for years to come. Despite the fact that Prohibition was in effect, champagne and other liquor flowed freely. Home movies taken for the family showed guests fox-trotting on a specially built outdoor wooden floor to music played by the Detroit Symphony Orchestra. Massive tables of food were strategically placed around the grounds of the house, and of course the bounty of the wedding presents was on display upstairs. A man who worked at the wedding, helping the woman who had handled most of the arrangements, recollected:

> She and I were the only sober ones there. They had all the liquor stacked up in the garage with the local police protecting it. The police had their drinks, the staff in the house had theirs, and everyone else was having a fine time. Miss Burnham and I had to keep an eye on the entire party, because no one else was capable. That was quite a party.

When Delphine and Jim were ready to leave on their honeymoon, they simply walked down the steps of the Rose Terrace and boarded the waiting 243-foot *Delphine* (the former *Nokomis II*, which had finally been returned to Horace after World War I was over), with its crew of sixty, to embark on a long and leisurely cruise. After embracing their parents and thanking them profusely, the newlyweds waved their good-byes from the stern as a group of friends on the dock, spearheaded by Horace, playfully shot flares and rockets at the departing boat.

Anna was elated by the success of Delphine's wedding. She gaily traveled to Philadelphia later that year to attend a huge party the Stotesburys gave to introduce the newlyweds to society, and then she began to look forward to the next big social event, the wedding of her son. It was announced in November that he was engaged to marry Lois Knowlson, a local young woman with a fine background; Detroit society had finally opened its doors to at least one of the Dodge family. There was a lavish engagement party at Detroit's Statler Hotel, attended by most of the Dodges. Afterward, Horace and Anna were scheduled to go to Palm Beach to move into the comfortable oceanfront villa they had just purchased from New York theatrical magnate Charles B. Dillingham. When Anna headed south in late November, she was on the crest of a wave.

The only worry was Horace's health, which continued to deteriorate. Horace had taken a turn for the worse after the engagement party and had therefore traveled to Palm Beach with his Detroit medical man, Dr. E. W. Haase, who stayed a few days to see that Horace recovered from the rigors of the trip. Dr. Haase recommended complete rest and relaxation, but it seemed that even the sun at Villa Marina could not help Horace. By early December, Anna was sending a special train to New York for several highly respected doctors. But before they arrived, Horace began to hemorrhage badly. He died on the night of December 10, with his son and his wife at his bedside. Horace Junior had left Syracuse University, where his father had sent him to study business administration, and hurried to Palm Beach as soon as Anna became seriously alarmed.

The news was telegraphed to Hong Kong, where Delphine and her husband, Jim, were traveling; she of course was unable to get back to the States in time for the funeral. Anna immediately made arrangements to return to Detroit with Horace's body in a heavy coffin covered with roses and violets. It was agreed that Horace would lie in a funeral chapel in downtown Detroit for a day before returning to Rose Terrace, to allow factory workers who would be unable to make the long trip out to Grosse Pointe the chance to pay their respects. More than 14,000 of them came. That same day, the Detroit Symphony gave a special concert in Horace's honor, playing Beethoven's "Funeral March" in memory of their patron.

The official cause of Horace's death was listed as hemorrhaging, with the added complication of cirrhosis of the liver. Some friends felt his death was really due to grief: Horace never recovered from the blow of his brother's death. Without John, Horace had very little to live for.

There were those who believed that the death of the Dodge brothers was more than an unfortunate chain of events, but was actually due to foul play. Rumors flew throughout Detroit that they had both been served lethal liquor at that automotive convention, and it was noted that the symptoms of their illnesses were very similar to those caused by certain types of poison. The talk, especially after Horace's death, was so widespread that several newspaper articles were written to examine the facts in light of the rumors. *The New York Mirror* interviewed a doctor who had examined both brothers in New York. He resolutely stuck to his original diagnosis of influenza—what he called "a regular old-style case of Spanish influenza"—complicated by pneumonia. He went on to pooh-pooh the notion that there could have been any other cause of death. Other doctors, with their varying diagnoses, were silent on the subject.

Amateur detectives tried to figure out how or when the poison might have been administered, noting that the Dodges preferred to consume the liquor they had brought with them from Detroit, limiting the opportunity to slip them a poisoned drink. Still, it could have been done by any determined person, since there were public events at which John and Horace took whatever drinks were passed to them. In an interview on the subject in 1988, Detroit Medical Examiner Dr. Warner Spitz, a leading toxicologist and forensic medical expert, pointed out that small amounts of a poison like arsenic, for example, can be administered even in a glass of water. Anyone in the crowd could have managed the deed.

Perhaps the very difficulty in arriving at any firm conclusion was what kept the gossip alive so long. Right up to the present day, in fact, there are people in Detroit who are convinced that John and Horace Dodge were murdered. Perhaps also the gossip was kept alive by a feeling of animosity toward the putative arranger of the murder: none other than Henry Ford!

Certainly, the deaths could be viewed as fortuitous for Henry, constituting in one stroke a revenge for his loss in court the previous year and the removal of one of the most serious competitive threats to Ford's dominance of the auto market. That dominance had been eroding year by year, and the Dodge was one of the reasons. The Dodge car had zoomed to the number-three sales position in the industry within a few years, and most observers felt the Dodge brothers were ready to give Henry Ford a run for the lead. With the large amount of capital John and Horace had collected from the lawsuit and the sale of their Ford stock, they had plenty of funds to invest in a battle for the lead. The death of the Dodge brothers effectively eliminated their company as a competitive threat to take over the number-one position.

According to Dr. Spitz, exhumation and tests on the bodies of the Dodge brothers would today be able to answer the question of whether or not they were poisoned by arsenic, which possibly causes hemorrhaging in its victims. Even in the unlikely event that the family would agree to such a step, and the tests were positive, who might have been behind it would not be known. Certainly Henry Ford was a ruthless competitor, and just as certainly by 1920 he had reasons for hating the Dodge brothers. Yet the Dodge family apparently disregarded the rumors. Dodges and Fords continued to have a limited but amicable social relationship, and both Henry Ford and his son, Edsel, were asked to serve as honorary pallbearers at Horace's funeral—an unlikely honor if the family thought Henry was Horace's murderer.

On December 15, 1920, the coffin containing the body of Horace Elgin Dodge made the final trip from the funeral at Rose Terrace, past the Dodge plant, to Woodlawn Cemetery. Mourners included the Fords, the Leland brothers, Mayor Couzens, Harold Wills, Michigan's Senator Truman Newberry, and the conductor of the Detroit Symphony Orchestra, Ossip Gabrilowitsch. Horace then joined John in the Dodge mausoleum. As all the papers pointed out milking every drop of emotion from the situation, the two brothers were once again reunited before the year 1920 was over.

One of the most perspicacious editorial comments at the time of Horace's death focused on the legend already established around him in the automotive industry:

> He was constantly scheming improved details, new processes, new methods and always building new machinery. He never lost the touch of the craftsman, could never leave machinery alone. The atmosphere of the shop, as he entered it, would cause a noticeable change in his bearing.

Outside, in the offices, in the places where men gather, even at home, he was quiet, reticent, and could be termed shy. But within the four walls of the shop he was the taciturn yet unquestionable master of the business.

Another paper offered this comment on Horace's private life:

> Horace E. Dodge disliked society in the conventional sense. The making of new friends in a class other than that in which he was born and reared did not interest him. It was one of his very few boasts that the major portion of his friends were the people he had known for thirty years and the chief uses of his wealth were to share the pleasures it brought with those who were near and dear to him. He had a deep and abiding contempt for the inefficient and a horror of the liar.

The Dodge brothers were gone, and the widows and children were left to carry on as best they could. Not one of them was prepared to handle either the enormous amount of money the brothers had made or the responsibility of using it wisely. John and Horace had been strong men who followed the traditional code that husbands and fathers kept their business and money worries to themselves, protecting the "little woman" and the children. They had done nothing to train their children to take over the business, nor to teach them how to manage money. One veteran Dodge employee noted, "It was pretty much a case of John and Horace giving the kids cash and telling them to 'get.'" Another long-time Dodge coworker, Fred Lamborn, added, "The old boys didn't have time for their sons. Horace Junior and John Duval were both capable, but being rich men's sons, it just didn't work out." The Dodge brothers had delighted in their capacity to give their families everything they wanted; all anyone had to do was ask. That childish, essentially irresponsible approach to existence would continue throughout the lives of the next generation.

In fact, the wills of the fathers virtually guaranteed that the children would live out the rest of their lives on their dole. There were individual bequests: annuities to their sister, Della, to the aunts who had helped them in the early days, to their half-brother Charles. John Dodge had left $5,000 plus an income of $1,000 a year for life to his mother-in-law, Margaret Rausch, and there was that troubling bequest, so resented by Matilda, to Amelia. Horace's will left the boats—the *Delphine*, valued at $175,000, and the *Delphine II*, still under construction and valued at $922,729.69— to Anna outright. He left $1,500 a year to his wife's sisters, Mae and Catherine, and $2,400 to her father (her mother had died several years before Horace). John left Matilda his real estate, including Meadow Brook Farm and the still-unfinished house in Grosse Pointe.

Everything else that belonged to both brothers was put into two very conservatively managed trusts, each worth a minimum of $40 million. That included several hundred thousand dollars in cash, many shares of stock in banks and bonds of public utilities, mortgages they held for friends, the value of their other real estate and, of course, their stock in Dodge Brothers, of which they were the sole owners. The Dodge Brothers stock was given an extremely low value of $10 million, probably about 10 percent of its true value. The income from Horace's trust was to be paid to Anna, with the principal divided between Delphine and Horace Junior at her death. The income from John's trust was to be paid to his widow and five of his six children (John Duval having been cut out), but the principal was not to be divided until the death of all of John's children.

Matilda was the one who inaugurated what became a virtual Dodge tradition: going to court to break a will. She decided she was not satisfied with a mere one-fifth share of the income from the trust, as stipulated in her husband's will. Thus she petitioned the court to allow her to take, instead, the lump sum or "widow's share" that would have been hers had John Dodge died without a will. The case was decided in 1921, with Matilda receiving one-half of the amount she would have received if John had died intestate, and no further income from the trust. Her share amounted to about $5 million. She stretched her funds by having Frances, Danny and Anna Margaret pay the family's living expenses out of their share of the trust income.

Although they couldn't touch the principal, Winifred and Isabel at least received a regular income and could make their financial plans accordingly. But John Duval was to receive nothing more from the trust than a monthly stipend of $150; he had been well and truly disinherited. He, like his stepmother, refused to abide by the terms of the will. He was the second in the family to sue the estate for what he considered his rightful share. Winifred and Isabel were in favor of offering him a settlement. They agreed that he had been unfairly treated; if John Dodge had not died so suddenly, and so soon after John Duval's marriage, the two men might well have made up, and John Duval would have been reinstated as an heir. John Duval's sisters also assumed it would cost no more in the long run to make a settlement than it would to fight his lawsuits. Matilda eventually agreed with them, and in 1921 John Duval was offered a lump sum of about $1.6 million. He took the money and went on a belated honeymoon with Marie. When they returned, they moved into a big apartment in Grosse Pointe.

Delphine and Horace Junior were at once both richer and poorer than their cousins Winifred, Isabel and John. Eventually, they would inherit more money, since on their side of the family there were only two children, so their expectations made them among the richest people in the country. Yet they received no income of their own and had to ask Anna for everything, including an annual living allowance. One suspects that she enjoyed the power that gave her. Delphine and Horace would remain in a state of childlike dependence on their mother for the rest of their lives.

All the Dodge heirs proved to be much better at spending money than making it; virtually nothing was added to the fortune from the year of the brothers' deaths to the present. Perhaps it was a measure of the dominance of John and Horace that no one in the family seemed to take the slightest interest in the business the brothers had worked so hard to build, and had gotten so much pleasure from. John Duval was estranged from his family even after he returned to Detroit, and he never again set foot in the Dodge Brothers plant. Horace Junior, who never bothered to return to college to go on with his studies in business administration, apparently recognized that he could never fill his father's shoes. He tried working on the factory floor for a few weeks, but it was not a success; as he explained to the press, his hardest job was to manage to get up at 6:00 A.M. It was an attitude his mother tacitly encouraged. She wanted to see her son conquer high society, not follow in his father's footsteps and spend his life in a hot and greasy machine shop. The two widows made occasional appearances at the plant, more to demonstrate that there still was a Dodge family than to make any suggestions about managing the company. Fred Lamborn remembered that for the first few years, "Anna was there at the plant quite often, and Matilda, she got after Haynes once in a while."

There were rumors about what would happen next: John Duval would return to take over, Isabel and Delphine would jointly take control of the company, the business would be held in trust until Daniel came of age. But in fact what happened is that Fred Haynes was made president, and he ran the company by following the traditions and policies set by John and Horace. The Dodge car continued to sell well; it was so well built and so advanced in its design and engineering that it held its own in the market for quite a few years with only minimal changes. What was missing, of course, was the potential for future greatness. As long as Dodge Brothers was a family-owned business, even the best of managers would be little more than a caretaker, unable to introduce sweeping change when it would eventually be needed.

Various members of the family did make attempts at business ventures. One of the least successful was that of Della/Delphine Ashbaugh. Shortly before the death of her brother John, she had taken a job as superintendent of the Michigan Industrial Home for Girls. Her tenure was brief; within a year, she was censured by the Board of Trustees for her extravagance in instituting such things as French lessons and art classes. She abruptly moved to California with her companion, a spiritualist who was later to be Anna Dodge's secretary, and got involved in a speculative oil venture. The result was a mess that Anna Dodge had to rectify. (Matilda was no longer on speaking terms with Della.) Anna sent her son-in-law, Jim Cromwell, to investigate, and he reported:

> Mr. Hodge [an agent for the Dodge family] fears that should the attention of the Commissioner be drawn to the Dodge Syndicate an investigation might occur which would be very dangerous for Mrs. Ashbaugh. He does not mean that Mrs. Ashbaugh herself has had anything to do with the irregularities concerned, but these irregularities which he believes are very serious ones occurred when she was Trustee. In order to protect her name and your own, therefore, I would advise your borrowing the necessary funds from the bank until Dodge Brothers declares its 1923 dividend.

Anna followed his advice and spent nearly $100,000 to rescue Della, setting a pattern that was to be repeated many times, for many different relatives. It was in fact soon to be repeated to save Jim Cromwell. He had become involved in a company called Florananda that was hoping to profit from the Florida land boom, but, instead, became one of the first to go down in the collapse of the mid-1920s. Delphine and Jim begged Anna to help them save Jim's good name—and keep them personally from going bankrupt, despite the $3 to $4 million Anna had already given the young couple in the six years since their marriage. Anna wrote a somewhat indignant letter to Eva Stotesbury about the whole matter.

> As you know, Eva, it was not at my instigation that Jim got involved in this affair and it seems that I am being

asked to carry an altogether disproportionate part of the settlement. . . . Once or twice I have settled up Jim's debts to the extent of $100,000 or more. This I will not do again, nor will I participate in helping to settle them. If the children cannot live on an income of $200,000 a year with the gifts from me that I give them from time to time, then it is high time they began to learn to do so.

I suggest that this indebtedness, both personal and Florananda, be pooled; that you and I place in the bank, in equal parts, enough to pay these debts. Unless I have cooperation from you it will be impossible for me to continue further, and the whole affair will have to take its own course and work out its own solution.

Anna got the cooperation she sought, and all the society investors in Florananda got their money back, a total of $3 million. An editorial in a New York paper the following year commended the two women for their actions, saying they were to be applauded for their "humanitarianism and straightforward business methods."

Another business venture was undertaken by Horace Junior. He had inherited his father's interest in boats and had achieved some success as a racing-boat driver and sponsor. His immersion in the world of boating gave him the erroneous notion that there was a mass market for powerboats, just as there had been for automobiles. In early 1924, he introduced the Dodge Water Car—a boat by any other name. It was in fact a beautiful creation, elegantly streamlined and fitted with African mahogany trim. It could achieve a speed of twenty miles an hour and cost only $2,500. One newspaper article enthused, "It is said of Dodge that he is doing for motor boats what his father did for motor cars. He is placing within reach of the general public a form of sport that gives health as well as pleasure." Actually, it was immediately apparent that no mass market existed for such a pretty toy, but it was sold throughout the 1920s to the wealthy and was heavily advertised in such publications as *Palm Beach Life*.

Once the brothers were gone, there were no Dodges with a good head for business. They were better suited to making the headlines of the society pages. Isabel took the spotlight on Thanksgiving Day in 1920, when she became engaged to George Sloane, a New York broker and member of an eastern establishment family, who was interested in horse racing and other patrician sports. Since her stepmother was opposed to an engagement before two years of mourning for John Dodge were over, Isabel chose to be married from her sister's house in Detroit's Indian Village, rather than the Boston Boulevard house, which was now her stepmother's, a decided snub for Matilda. The wedding took place in February 1921, and all the details of the event showed signs of the taste and style for which the two sisters were becoming known. The bride wore a dramatic cornette of pearls and a sophisticated pearl-embroidered satin gown. Winifred was her matron of honor, and one of the bridesmaids (who were all dressed in cool gray satin) was Mrs. Edsel Ford. In the end, Matilda decided to attend the wedding, but once again she was dressed in somber black.

There was another Dodge wedding that year, when Horace Junior married Lois Knowlson. Horace's was a quiet and small wedding, appropriate for a family so recently bereaved. On June 21, the couple was married in the Knowlson's home on Jefferson Avenue.

When weddings come, can birth announcements be far behind? The next generation of Dodges had already begun to arrive. Winifred had two children: another Winifred, always called Peggy, and Suzanne, born only two months after the death of John Dodge. Horace and Lois had a daughter on March 30, 1922, named Delphine Ione after his sister, and on August 3 of the following year, a son they proudly named Horace Elgin Dodge III. Delphine's daughter Christine was born in Philadelphia on September 10, 1922. According to Jim Cromwell, Delphine had such a long and difficult ordeal during the birth that he nearly fainted himself before the instrument delivery. Delphine was severely disappointed that the baby was not a boy.

Horace Junior and his bride, Lois Knowlson, were married quietly at the home of her parents in 1921. (Collection of David Agresta)

Not all the events of the early 1920s were quite so wholesome. In the spring of 1922, Winifred announced that she was divorcing William Gray. That was scandal enough, but adding fire to the flame was the fact that the Grays' neighbors in Indian Village, Wesson and Gwen Seyburn, were also getting divorced, and that Winifred planned to marry handsome Wesson Seyburn, a banker from one of the oldest families of Detroit, as soon as they both were free. By modern standards, such conduct does not seem particularly remarkable, but in 1922 it was quite shocking. The public would have been even more shocked if the gossip in Indian Village had been made public. According to rumor, the strong-willed Winifred, truly her father's daughter, had openly approached the current Mrs. Seyburn—sister of Winifred's old beau Jack Currie—and offered her money if she would obtain a divorce. Rumor further had it that Gwen agreed, and subsequently used the windfall to make a comfortable home for herself and her new husband, Count Tolstoi, a nephew of the famous Russian writer. The Tolstois and the Seyburns continued to see one another socially, remaining the best of friends.

It sounds harmless enough, since even the principals were unoffended. But it was all too much for Matilda, who had somehow managed to develop finer sensibilities about these matters than she had had in the days when she was dating the married John Dodge and waiting for him to decide to get a divorce from Isabelle. She refused to countenance her stepdaughter's actions, and pointedly planned a trip to Europe for the time of Winifred's second wedding. Anna Dodge, always delighted to find an opportunity to spite her sister-in-law, just as pointedly invited Winifred to accompany her on a six-month tour of the Mediterranean while the divorce was pending. In the fall of that same year, after obtaining a divorce from Gray on the grounds of cruelty, and alimony set at one dollar a year, Winifred was married to Wesson Seyburn at her sister's home at Hewlitt, Long Island. The newlyweds then returned to Detroit and began building an elaborate mansion on the water in Grosse Pointe, less than a mile away from Anna at Rose

Terrace. The house was in the style of a French country château, with a long allée of sycamores leading up to the front door. The formal gardens were bordered by yews, lilacs and hundred-year-old elms. It was one of the most attractive and comfortable homes in all Detroit, until it was pulled down in the 1980s by developers, after Winifred's death. Winifred's taste was always impeccable.

Matilda and Winifred managed to patch up their relationship and remain on speaking terms, albeit not particularly cordial ones. But the rift between Anna and Matilda was never bridged. Each was offended anew by every little action of the other. Matilda wrote an icy letter to Anna in 1923, after they had both returned from Europe, and angrily demanded that Anna contribute the $100,000 she had promised to a charity project connected with the First Presbyterian Church that was to be called the Dodge Community House, or else drop out and let Matilda name the building after John alone. The tone of the letter speaks volumes about the women's relationship: she concluded, "This is the last time I wish to be annoyed about the affair. Except for an acceptance from you, I shall pay no attention to any letters."

At least the feud between Anna and Matilda could be kept hidden from the press. Unfortunately, the scandal of John Duval's behavior was very public. The young man resembled his father in his determination to do exactly what he wanted to, no matter who stood in his way. He inherited the destructive aspects of the Dodge temperament without the constructive talents that redeemed John Dodge. John Duval had a history of speeding tickets and driving offenses, most of which were settled with low fines and little publicity. But early in 1922, he went too far. While his wife sat at home, John Duval (then twenty-four) and a friend drove to Kalamazoo on a Saturday night, looking for fun and action. They found it by offering three coeds from Kalamazoo College a ride. They were cruising around the back roads at high speed, sharing drinks out of a flask, when John's passes at one young woman became too importunate. She threw herself out of the speeding car, and John drove on for miles before finally turning around to go back and look for her. As it turned out, another motorist had spotted her lying dazed by the roadside and had taken her to the hospital. Although John made a settlement with the young woman, there was no way to hush up the story. He was charged with drunken driving, and also with transporting and distributing liquor in a time of prohibition. He had to spend the weekend in jail, where he complained about the food and attempted to throw his weight around. His dutiful wife was there to stand by him when he was finally released to await trial. A pack of photographers snapped pictures of "the Dodge heir" as he emerged from the Station house. John Duval was not a handsome man, but he possessed some of his sister Isabel's dramatic flair, and there was a dashing quality about him that was attractive to women.

More pictures of John Duval Dodge in jail were to come. A speeding ticket in Detroit landed him with a five-day jail sentence, possibly in reaction to the publicity of the Kalamazoo case. He emerged the day before he had to face his trial in Kalamazoo. The county prosecutor's case against him for drunken driving failed because John had a good lawyer, and because the young women were reluctant to admit they had been silly enough to get into a car driven by a stranger who was clearly drunk. But, in a second trial, the state of Michigan was more successful and easily convinced the jury that John and his male companion did indeed transport liquor in the car and distribute it to the three coeds, all of whom testified to the fact in court. Both men were given suspended sentences, with one year's probation, during which they were to forswear liquor and report monthly to a probation officer. John was also required to find a job; perhaps that was the worst punishment the judge could think of for the young playboy.

Matilda by this time refused to do anything at all to help her stepson. It was his sister Isabel who took the responsibility for finding him a job and a sponsor, and she found the latter in an unexpected quarter. One of her closest friends was Edsel Ford's wife, Eleanor, so she and Eleanor jointly persuaded Henry Ford to serve as John's legal custodian, and to give him a job at the

Ford factory. Perhaps Henry enjoyed the irony of employing the son of his old rival, dead just two years, in a menial factory job.

By the time John Duval was punching a time clock at Ford, Matilda had sold the Boston Boulevard house and leased a villa on the Riviera for a year. She and her three children settled in Nice, and she entered a carriage in the carnival celebration in March 1923, winning a prize for its lavish decoration and her stylish costume. When she returned from this European fling, Matilda moved into an attractive three-story residence with a greenhouse, gatehouse, and big front yard on Lincoln Avenue in Grosse Pointe, just a few doors from Jefferson, the location of Rose Terrace.

The move may well have been a ploy in her struggle with her stepchildren over the unfinished house in Grosse Pointe. It had been Matilda's intention to complete the house John had started and to live there with Frances, Danny and Anna Margaret. But Winifred and Isabel were alarmed by the potential cost of finishing such an elaborate project, on which more than $2 million had already been spent. They, of course, would derive no benefit from the house, whatever its condition. So they went to court to enjoin Matilda from finishing the house. Thus her move to Lincoln Avenue was probably intended as a show of economizing, as well as an interim stopping point on what she hoped would be her eventual move to the Grosse Pointe mansion. But the move was not to be. Her stepdaughters won in court, and Matilda was forced to stop all work on the property. It remained in its ghostly state—the walls up, the roof on, the interior largely unfinished—for years. Only the greenhouse functioned, and it supplied Matilda with flowers for her house and all special occasions.

Poor Matilda! Her stepchildren were proving to be a trial. It is likely that they were against her from the moment they met her, before supper on the day of her marriage to their father. So long as John Dodge was alive, the warring factions managed at least a truce, if not a genuine peace. But once his commanding presence was removed, the feud found free expression.

Soon Matilda had more serious sorrow to contend with. In the spring of 1924, her four-year-old daughter, Anna Margaret, suddenly fell ill, and she died on April 13. For Matilda, losing her happy, smiling youngest, the one who looked most like John Dodge, was a terrible blow. And she was bitter because the rest of the family seemed to show so little compassion. Anna paid one condolence call, as form demanded, and never said another word about the subject. Her stepchildren responded with another lawsuit, to get Anna Margaret's share of the trust reabsorbed into the principal; it took Matilda several years in court to be declared her daughter's heir and add another $4 million to her own net worth. Horace Junior did not bother to postpone the huge Venetian Ball he and Lois planned to throw at Rose Terrace a few months later, for 500 guests, at a cost of $40,000. Lois was her usual pretty self in a daring short red ballet costume, and Horace chose to go as Mephistopheles, the man who sold his soul for riches. The young Dodges' Venetian Ball was one of the most memorable parties of the 1920s, and newspapers were filled with photos of hosts and guests.

Behind the façade of parties and carefully posed pictures on the society pages, both Delphine and Horace Junior were having their own troubles. Delphine's marriage to the tall, dark and handsome Jim Cromwell was stormy, their financial problems were constantly pressing and it was already obvious that one of the casualties of their extravagant life style was to be young Christine, who was largely cared for by the hired help. Despite the attempts by Anna Dodge and Eva Stotesbury to induce the young couple to settle down, the young Cromwells were spiraling out of control. Like Horace Junior and Lois, they seemed to be living embodiments of the gilded flappers Scott Fitzgerald was to write about. Both Horace and Delphine wanted to live in the fast lane. They loved speed, on the water and on the highway. Delphine was starting to drive racing boats, and Horace at the wheel of his car behaved like a test driver. Horace's car seemed to attract trouble even when he wasn't driving it. In 1923, an employee of Horace's boatworks borrowed his car and promptly got into an accident that crippled a five-year-old boy. Horace was sued and had to pay $10,000 to the boy's parents.

This generation of the Dodge family was beginning to be a source of concern. Flamboyant spending, speeding and traffic offenses, financial mismanagement, one scandalous divorce and a couple of stormy marriages, and already a few days in jail for one scion of the family: The problems were starting to accumulate.

Those problems were in large part caused by the existence of a fortune that the widows and children had not helped to make and knew little about managing. The problems were then magnified by the advent of even more money from the sale of Dodge Brothers Motor Car Company.

It might seem surprising that the family would consider selling the company that was the real meaning of existence for John and Horace Dodge. It was their finest legacy, their truest memorial. And beyond the sentimental aspects, it was a terrific moneymaker, raining cash on the whole family. But the heart and soul of the company had died with the brothers, and no one else cared in the same way. Eager buyers had begun sniffing around the company even before Horace died, and once the last Dodge brother was gone, Dodge Brothers was considered fair game by investors. Neither Anna nor Matilda was a sentimental woman, and both were quick to understand that the sale of the business would produce not only more capital, but also more liquid capital, in the trusts. Moreover, it would sever the tie between the two sisters-in-law, who rarely agreed on any course of action. So they were ready to entertain offers.

It was Anna's son-in-law, Jim Cromwell, who convinced the family to sell the company through competitive bidding. Fifteen years later, Eva Stotesbury, Cromwell's mother, wrote a complete account of the behind-the-scenes maneuvering in the affair.

As she told it, a certain Mr. Ballantyne, the Dodge trustee and a prominent Detroit banker, was anxious to establish relations with the prestigious firm of J.P. Morgan & Co. Ballantyne had persuaded Anna Dodge that the sale should be made through Morgan and no one else. Ballantyne and Jim Cromwell visited the Morgan offices and negotiated with Dwight Morrow, one of the partners. Morrow insisted the plant was not worth $95 million; Cromwell insisted that at that figure they might as well give the company away. Cromwell then decided that competitive bidding might bring a better price. He approach Dillon Read & Company, who became very interested in the sale and asked to meet with Anna Dodge. As Eva Stotesbury wrote about her son, Jim Cromwell:

> I can take my oath that this boy came to me and said, "Mother, what is my duty about the sale of the plant? If Mr. Ballantyne persuades Mother Dodge to make J.P. Morgan & Company her agents they will not get the price the plant is worth, but of course Father will be delighted to have been instrumental in bringing such a business to the firm. . . . So what do you think is my duty in the matter? Is it to my stepfather, who has been so kind to me for so many years, or is it to my wife and child to get as large a price for them as I can?" I said "Jim, there is no question but what your first duty is to Delphine and Christine, but of course Father will be very bitter about the embarrassment of your taking this sale away from J.P. Morgan & Co., in view of Mother Dodge's conversation with Mr. Morgan in which she agreed that his firm should be the agents."

When the envelopes were opened on the day of the bidding, the one from the investment banking firm of Dillon Read contained an offer of $146 million, the high bid. Interestingly, in Dillon Read's calculations, $50 million was attributed to the value of the firm's good will, which John and Horace had carried on the books at $1.

The check for the purchase was written in March 1925, and of course it made both widows considerably richer, since the trust had valued Dodge Brothers at only $50 million, about one-third the purchase price. Newspapers touted Anna Dodge as the richest woman in the world, and estimated her daily income at $40,000. In actual fact, the money, quickly invested in the same conservative trust, made no immediate difference to either woman. But the final step of severing the ties with Dodge Brothers, and the increased income available for satisfying any desire, did have an effect that was soon to change the lives of both Matilda and Anna.

9

Breaking the Ties with the Past

The sale of Dodge Brothers Motor Car Company not only provided more liquid—and therefore more readily spent—capital for the heirs of Horace and John, but also cut the emotional cord that bound the family to the past. The brothers were dead, and the company that was their finest achievement was in the hands of strangers, who proved to be unable to manage it well. The Dodge brothers had given their company such momentum that in 1921, a year after their deaths, it reached the number-two position in sales, but it did not take long for poor management to undermine this accomplishment.

Dillon Read knew a lot more about investment banking than it did about the car business. The firm brought in three brothers of the Graham family, truck manufacturers who had worked with the Dodges on their line of trucks, to run the company. The Dodge trucks were a great success, with more than 100,000 sold by the time Dillon Read bought the company. But the Grahams, at Dillon Read's urging, made a major marketing mistake by trying to price the dependable Dodge as a luxury car, making the lowest-priced model cost twice as much as the Model T, and tagging other models at prices as high as $2,000. The result was a marked decline in the sales of the Dodge.

By the spring of 1928, Dodge Brothers did not have enough income to meet its next payroll. The investment bankers were ready to sell, and they had an eager buyer in Walter P. Chrysler. Since Chrysler Corporation at that time was smaller than Dodge, Detroiters likened the sale to a minnow swallowing a whale. At that time, Dodge employed more than 20,000 workers in a plant that covered 58 acres. The final terms of the sale saw Chrysler paying Dillon Read $170 million of its own stock and assuming $60 million in debt previously contracted against the Dodge assets by Dillon Read. Acquisition of the Dodge name and manufacturing facilities instantly made Chrysler the third-largest auto maker in the country. Walter Chrysler later reflected, "Buying the Dodge Brothers Company was one of the soundest acts of my life. . . . We had, before the merger, an intensely sharp spearhead in the Chrysler Corporation, but when we put behind it all of Dodge, our spearhead had a weighty shaft and had become a potent thing." Chrysler zealously guarded the value of the Dodge name and its reputation for dependability, but gradually Dodge was subjugated to the Chrysler empire. Today, few people remember that there were once two Dodge brothers connected with the Dodge car; the name Dodge seems as impersonal as Dart or Ram.

For the family that had so quickly relinquished its legacy, it was time to forget about the past and look to the future.

Matilda's vision of the future seemed essentially domestic. Her chosen theme would be the joys of family life. Ironically, she had experienced few enough of them in her life to that point. Her role of stepmother to the three children of John and Ivy Dodge had been painfully unsuccessful from the moment of her wedding supper, which was her first meeting with them. She had completely washed her hands of John Duval, especially after he had the gall to go to court to try to establish a claim to one-fifth of the estate of his little half-sister Anna Margaret. With Winifred and Isabel she observed just enough of the social proprieties to prevent malicious gossip. She was not on speaking terms with her sister-in-law Delphine Ashbaugh, and her other sister-in-law, Anna Dodge, remained a thorn in her side.

Matilda's relationship with the Rausch family yielded little more gratification. Her marriage to John Dodge had created a gulf between her and her saloon-keeping parents that Matilda considered too great to try to bridge. Although they had lived in her home, the Rausches were not really part of the family, and Matilda had been little affected by the death of her father. She continued to provide a home for her mother until Margaret Rausch's death in 1928, but the two women were never emotionally close. Nor was Matilda close to her sister, Amelia, who had in the past seemed dangerously like a rival for the affections of John Dodge. As soon as John died, and Matilda learned that both her mother and Amelia would get lifetime annuities from his estate, she meanly cut off the salaries John had been paying them to look after Meadow Brook Farm.

Throughout the 1920s, Amelia was a shadowy figure in Matilda's life. The death of John Dodge had removed her protector and her leverage, and she sank to the status of poor relation. Amelia was kept busy looking after Matilda's children when it didn't suit Matilda to be with them, supervising daily activities at Meadow Brook Farm, caring for the ailing Margaret Rausch. Finally, in 1931, she made a stab at achieving some degree of independence by marrying John Cline, the workman in charge of the farm at Meadow Brook. Matilda could see in her sister's action nothing but a desire to embarrass *her* by a misalliance, and she promptly forced Amelia and John to leave the farm. They settled in nearby Rochester, but Amelia did not see her sister again for years.

Despite the fact that she had so far experienced very little joy through family life, Matilda chose to focus her energies in that direction. The death of Anna Margaret was a sad loss that seemed to intensify her determination to give Frances and Danny absolutely everything children could want or need. And in 1925, she provided the one thing that was missing from their young lives, the presence of a man around the house.

Matilda was a devoted churchwoman, still a member of the congregation of the First Presbyterian Church on Woodward Avenue that had been one of the major beneficiaries of John Dodge's charity. There she became acquainted with a man who was both a deacon of the church and a member of the choir. He was Alfred G. Wilson, a man her own age whose father was a Presbyterian minister. Alfred was moderately successful in his own right in the lumber business in Michigan's Upper Peninsula. He was tall, he was handsome, he was still unmarried. Best of all, the gentlemanly Alfred was quite willing to adapt himself to Matilda's scenario. He loved children and he wanted to be a good stepfather to Frances and Danny. Moreover, he did not seem to mind the prospect of living amidst reminders of John Dodge's glory. Small wonder that Matilda accepted his proposal immediately.

The wedding took place on June 19, 1925, in Matilda's home on Lincoln Avenue. The affair was so small and quiet that guests were invited by telephone. The bride wore a simple knee-length dress of cream colored chiffon and a smart plumed hat; she carried a big bouquet of white orchids. Photos show her literally dwarfed by the tall groom, and decidedly dumpy in her fitted dress, but looking quite radiant. Wedding guests included her children, her mother and her sister, Winifred and Wesson Seyburn, Isabel and George Sloane. The ceremony was conducted jointly by the minister of the First Presbyterian Church and the groom's father.

The newlyweds spent their honeymoon in England, turning the trip into a visit that lasted almost a year and allowed them to tour nearly every English Tudor house in the country. For Matilda had decided that she would build a grand house of her own. Her stepchildren might have blocked her completion of John Dodge's dream house, but she would retaliate by spending as much—or more—on a similar project.

Matilda's choice of a site was an interesting one: She would build her mansion at Meadow Brook Farm. It was a locale completely identified with John Dodge, a place where she had spent little time while he was living. She did not share John's love of rustic surroundings, nor was she at that date interested in agricultural matters. In a memo written during the 1950s to Chrysler officials who were researching the history of the Dodge family, Matilda revealed that she and John had once considered building at Meadow Brook, rather than Grosse Pointe. But, she said, they changed their minds because of the problem of finding schools and friends for the children. In 1925, when she decided to settle at Meadow Brook, Frances and Danny were both still school-age children, but somehow the problem of their education and their friends was not then important. When Matilda and Alfred returned from their honeymoon, they settled into the farmhouse on the property, to be able to supervise the construction of Meadow Brook Hall.

It may be that the chief advantage of the site in Matilda's eyes was that it was a good distance away from Detroit. Matilda Rausch Dodge Wilson had had her fill of that city, which held little promise of gratification. Many members of Detroit society still viewed her as "little Tillie Rausch" who used to come around with her mother to collect the washing. In her own efforts to compete socially, she was usually outdone by her rivals. Stepdaughter Winifred Seyburn was already widely known for her wonderful parties, especially her Sunday-night suppers, served informally in the kitchen by her butler (who was busily engaged in making his own fortune in the stock market). Anna Dodge did not entertain as frequently, but she flaunted her Palm Beach connections whenever possible and did her best to behave like a haughty society matron. Isabel visited Detroit often and talked grandly of the race horses she had purchased at Saratoga, of her Long Island estate, and of her New York society friends. For the socially isolated Matilda, there was much to be said for leaving Detroit as quickly as possible.

At Meadow Brook, Matilda could create a world of her own,

one in which she reigned supreme. She began with the house it-self. Meadow Brook Hall would be in the Tudor style, like the house John Dodge had started to build, and it would even use the same firm of architects: Smith, Hinchman & Grylls. But Meadow Brook Hall would not be just a great mansion; it would be a country manor, and she believed it would be particularly "authentic" because she would model it after the houses she had seen on her prolonged English honeymoon. Ground was broken in mid-1926, and Meadow Brook Hall was completed in 1929, at an estimated cost of $4 million. (That was one in the eye for those stepchildren!)

On November 19, 1929, the Wilsons had a huge housewarming party at Meadow Brook Hall, in the teeth of a sudden Michigan blizzard. One of the guests remembered the three-hour trip out to the country on roads so icy and slick that he carried long poles in anticipation of going into a ditch. But when he entered the great hall and saw the huge fire blazing in the stone fireplace and the profusion of flowers lining the main gallery, he knew the trip had been worth the effort. He strolled into the drawing room, where a receiving line had formed in front of the fireplace, over which was displayed Sir Joshua Reynolds's painting *The Strawberry Girl*, one of the most instantly recognizable works of art in that era. Matilda was wearing a richly decorated dress in her favorite color, purple, and a smile of triumph; her husband, tall, gray-haired and distinguished, was at her side. More than 400 guests drove out from Detroit to see her new showplace, and how she loved their dazzled expressions!

The astute and traveled guest touring the new creation would have noticed that Meadow Brook Hall was actually a pastiche of the Tudor houses Matilda had seen in England, and which her architect, William Kapp, had revisited to absorb the details. For example, the paneling in the drawing room was copied from Kensington Palace, while the pilasters around the fireplace were an imitation of those at Knole. The dining-room decor was copied from a Christopher Wren country house, and the Chinese breakfast room mimicked the octagon room at Chiswick House. The chimneys were like those at Hampton Court, and Matilda's study was from a design by Inigo Jones.

A number of the decorative elements at Meadow Brook Hall came from the John Dodge house in Grosse Pointe. Tiffany stained-glass windows, ornamental gutters, paneling, stone carvings on the façade and even the chimney capstones were ripped out of the unfinished shell and incorporated into Matilda's new house. Furniture from the Boston Boulevard house also made its way to Meadow Brook Hall. For example, the two overstuffed chairs in which John and Horace always sat when they came home for lunch mingled with the new pieces chosen by New York decorators: the Hampton Shop, Arden Studios and Hayden Company. The entire third floor was designed to look like the Boston Boulevard house, and contained many pieces of furniture and art that came from it, including the bed Matilda had slept in with John Dodge. Apparently, Alfred was a good sport about this particular kind of memorializing.

Most of the furnishings in Meadow Brook Hall were good-quality reproductions. Although the furniture was impressive, very little was genuinely antique. That choice was in keeping with Matilda's intention of making the place a real family home. Both children had their own suites, consisting of a large bedroom, dressing room and bath, and a second bedroom with bath for a guest. Frances's room was decorated with flowered wallpaper and white frilly curtains; in her dressing room was a bay with mullioned windows and a deep-cushioned window seat. Doorknobs and drawer pulls were flowered porcelain, and the furniture was feminine without being dainty. Danny's room had a desk in the bay window and the Dodge crest on the ceiling, where he would see it when he looked up. The hardware and fittings in his room depicted cars and planes, and the ornamental carving that highlighted the paneling featured characters out of his favorites stories, such as Robinson Crusoe.

The luxury provided for Frances and Danny was not limited to the inside of the house. Fifteen-year-old Frances had a playhouse that was a scale model of a cottage at Knole. The six-room toy contained working kitchen appliances and custom-made furniture. Matilda remarked sententiously that the cottage was "not only that Frances might have a place to play, but that she might learn from first-hand experience early in life the art of being a housekeeper." For her younger brother Danny, there was a log cabin that contained a fully equipped workshop, complete with tools that were scaled down to fit a boy's hands. That too was supposed to be educational as well as recreational.

Soon there were more children at Meadow Brook Hall. Although Alfred Wilson gave in to his wife on most things, he was unyieldingly determined that they should have children of their own. Matilda, already well into her forties, either could not or would not comply. The solution they finally agreed upon was to adopt two children from a Chicago orphanage, in 1930: Richard and Barbara Wilson. They were established in the nursery suite, which was fully independent of the rest of the house, with their own nurse, and later each was given a bedroom of his and her own. Compared with most children from an orphanage, Richard and Barbara were indeed lucky, but compared with Frances and Danny, they were second-class citizens. They were never permitted to go into either Frances's playhouse or Danny's workshop. Of course, they had no share in the huge Dodge inheritance, and that difference in their circumstances was never forgotten. Whatever the future might hold for them, they did not have the expectations of the Dodge children.

It was clear that Matilda intended Frances and Danny to be able to hold their own with the best of Detroit society. She worried that Danny seemed lacking in social aptitude. Thin and serious, he spent much time alone, often in his workshop. Frances seemed more promising. Her youthful interest in horses was greatly encouraged, since Matilda had observed that entrée into the horsy set would be a great social credential. When Frances went away to school—first to nearby Cranbrook and then to the Ward Belmont School in Nashville—she took her horse with her. She entered a number of horsemanship competitions, and Matilda made sure her ribbons and trophies were prominently displayed.

While Matilda was throwing herself into domesticity, posing for pictures on the society pages surrounded by her children, her sister-in-law was trying to turn herself into one of society's *grandes dames*. Although Anna continued to spend part of the year at Rose Terrace, the home that held so many memories of Horace Dodge, the center of her life was more and more in Palm Beach. It was there that her social ambitions were chiefly focused, thanks in great part to her connection with Eva Stotesbury.

Eva had everything that Anna wanted. Although she was six years older than Anna, Eva, with her perfect oval face and her sweet dimples, possessed a pink-and-white prettiness that seemed untouched by time. She was always impeccably dressed, and it was a rare occasion when she was seen publicly in a dress she had worn before. She was considered such an authority on correct behavior that in Palm Beach all matters of etiquette, including how to curtsy to visiting British nobility, were always referred to her. Her collection of jewelry was so fabulous that she was always accompanied by a private detective (he even went along on her honeymoon!), and her elderly doting husband added to the collection regularly.

Eva's marriage to Edward T. Stotesbury, twenty-six years her senior, remained truly romantic until the day he died. The small but dapper Ned, who was reported to be earning at least $40 million a year at J.P. Morgan, let his wife buy anything she wanted, and enjoyed seeing her bedecked with jewels and wearing the latest styles. She commissioned a fashion artist to sketch every new gown she bought, so she could file it in a reference directory she consulted before she dressed each day.

Eva in turn cosseted Ned. When she decided to redo the patio of their Palm Beach house, she arranged for scores of workmen to come in between midnight and dawn, so all the work could be completed in a single night and her husband would not be bothered for so much as a minute. Eva's most public expression of her

This formal portrait of Eva Stotesbury was taken during her reign as the queen of Palm Beach society. (Historical Society of Palm Beach County)

affection for her husband came every year on February 26, when she regularly threw the grandest party of the entire Palm Beach season to celebrate Ned's birthday. Well-known classical musicians were engaged to sing for him, and Meyer Davis brought his entire orchestra to Florida by train to lead the guests in singing "Happy Birthday." The musicians later accompanied Ned as he performed his annual ritual. He had been a little drummer boy during the Civil War, and every year he re-created his past by hauling out his drum to play, and sing, for his assembled guests. He knew two tunes: "The Old Oaken Bucket" and "The Old Family Toothbrush That Hangs by the Sink." After Ned's performance, Meyer Davis played other sings of the Civil War era. Then Ned cut his mammoth birthday cake as Eva watched adoringly, and 400 or 500 members of the *crème de la crème* of Palm Beach society applauded the whole performance.

This gala event took place at one of the first houses that famed architect Addison Mizner designed in Florida. After he finished the Everglades Club, on Worth Avenue, Eva was the first to commission him to build a private home. It was called El Mirasol, and it was located on a large parcel of property that stretched from the ocean to Lake Worth. Mizner said he patterned the house after an old Spanish convent, but most of the effects were pure Mizner. Guests entered El Mirasol through a Moorish-style gate that opened into a long corridor lined with marble statues. Periodically, openings in the corridor framed a vista of a cool stone patio where fountains sprayed and splashed. Once they reached the house proper, guests walked up a grand staircase to get to the main reception rooms, which were all decorated in an antique Spanish style and contained woodwork, chandeliers, paintings and furniture that Mizner had purchased on tours of decaying castles in Spain. The "private apartments" of Eva and Ned were on the top floor, and contained grilled windows in the ceilings to let the ocean breezes cool and ventilate the rooms. A separate tea house, in the Moorish style, was built on the lake side of the property, in case the Stotesburys felt they needed a change of scene.

Edward Stotesbury poses with a guest on the stone walk in front of El Mirasol, the first oceanfront mansion in Palm Beach designed by Addison Mizner. (Historical Society of Palm Beach County)

Eva and Ned lived at El Mirasol on a grand scale, arriving on their seventy-foot yacht, the *Nedeva*, in January, to stay until April 1. The cost of opening and operating the Palm Beach house was estimated to be a mere $12,500 a day—negligible for a man whose income was many million dollars a year. The twenty-five acres of green lawn required a staff of fifteen to twenty gardeners year-round and at least 120,000 gallons of water a day, pumped by a private system hidden on the grounds. There was an aviary, a collection of monkeys, and groves of orange, grapefruit, mango, avocado and banana trees that supplied fruit for the table. The fruit was even shipped to the Stotesburys' house in Philadelphia when they went there in the spring.

Eva of course had her own maid to keep her clothes in order and help her dress for her public appearances. The rest of the indoor staff, which numbered in the scores of people, was supervised by the butler and the housekeeper. Guests at El Mirasol were given blank menus every morning, so they could order any meal they wanted during the day (although one guest joked, "They must have asked out of curiosity, as I didn't get anything I ordered"). The desk drawer in every guest room was stuffed with Eva's own choice of stationery: thick white paper so heavy it had to be bent rather than folded, with "El Mirasol" embossed in white at the top.

Eva's behavior as hostess was described by a dazzled reporter in a 1929 newspaper article:

> Mrs. Stotesbury, always a gracious hostess, greeted everyone and gave them those little personal attentions which she always remembers to do, seeing that they were seated, received service from the buffets on either side of the arched loggia, where delicious tea, iced drinks, frozen eggnog, coconut cakes and other delicious things were served. . . .

A 1920 society columnist quoted an unnamed "matron" on the subject of Eva's manner: "With some people, one rather objects to a grand manner, but with Eva Stotesbury, it is so different; she is 'grand' in such a lovely way." Eva had the very attractive and human quality of openly enjoying the possessions her husband's wealth had brought her. According to an amusing bit of Palm Beach gossip, a guest at one of the birthday parties noted that Eva was wearing a whopping string of pearls with a simple cotton dress. "Pearls in the daytime?" asked the guest archly. Eva responded without a trace of irritation, "Yes, my dear. I used to feel that way too. But that was before I had the pearls."

One of Eva's very best parties was the Valentine's Day wedding of her daughter, Louise Cromwell, to a youthful brigadier general of the army, Douglas MacArthur, in 1922. Louise was widely hailed as "a reigning and noted beauty," "one of the most popular and sought-after debs of her season" and "one of the most beautiful women in America." It was in fact Louise's second marriage, her first having already ended in divorce (and the two children of that marriage remaining out of sight at her home in Washington). Thus, holding the wedding at El Mirasol seemed most appropriate. An aisle was created down the length of the huge living room and lined with red, white and blue ribbons. At the end was an improvised altar, covered with a fine antique prayer rug and banked with crimson American Beauty roses; on either side were the flags of the United States, West Point, the Rainbow Division (MacArthur's World War I command) and his personal brigadier general's flag. As one account of the event raved, "All of these patriotic colors together with the wonderful array of beautiful and odorous flowers, taken in conjunction with the assemblage of smartly gowned women, formed a scene of impressive beauty." The bride wore apricot, and Eva was splendid in orchid chiffon with a matching hat. Ned Stotesbury gave his stepdaughter away, and her brother, Jim Cromwell, acted as MacArthur's best man. Among the guests were the mayor of Palm Beach; the builder of El Mirasol, Addison Mizner; and Anna Dodge, who diligently observed every smallest detail.

Yes, Anna had found her role model at last. She copied Eva Stotesbury shamelessly, slavishly. Eva's husband gave a fully equipped laboratory to Good Samaritan Hospital in Palm Beach; Anna had her husband, Horace, donate a whole building for contagious diseases, named after their daughter, Delphine. Anna dressed to imitate Eva, although Eva's fashions were much less attractive on Anna's shapeless body. Eva had fabulous pearls; Anna must have fabulous pearls. Eva had an Addison Mizner oceanfront palace; Anna must have one too. The comfortable Villa Marina that Anna and Horace had bought just wouldn't do any longer, especially since (thanks to the example set by Eva) the social scene was moving away from the hotels and private clubs and into lavish mansions. Anna sold the Villa Marina and moved into a "cottage"—meaning a perfectly comfortable vacation house—she had bought for Horace Junior and Lois on Seaspray Avenue while she made her plans. She considered having Mizner design a new house for her, and bought a large parcel of land at the south end of Palm Beach, down by the Bath and Tennis Club, that she thought might be a good location. (It was. She later sold the lot to E. F. Hutton, and he and his wife, Marjorie Merriweather Post, built Mar-A-Lago on it.) But building could take a long time, and demand a great deal of the owner's attention. Buying an existing house was a better choice. Late in 1925, a suitable one came on the market.

It was a house that was built by Addison Mizner for colorful oil millionaire Joshua Cosden, founder of the DX refineries. According to legend, while Cosden was visiting Palm Beach in the winter of 1922, he made the serendipitous discovery that as he sat on the porch of the old Breakers Hotel for an afternoon of sunshine and cards, he had made $1 million speculating on the stock market. He demonstrated his pleasure by commissioning Mizner to design a Palm Beach house. Called Playa Riente, or "Laughing Sands," it was the largest and most expensive home Mizner ever designed. Many people thought it was the most impressive house built in the United States during the whole prosperous decade of the 1920s. Cosden and his wife, Nell, a Tulsa-born beauty, entertained lavishly at Playa Riente. Their guests included the American aristocracy of Vanderbilts and Phippses, Lord and Lady Mountbatten, famed beauty Lady Diana Duff Cooper, and several miscellaneous dukes and duchesses. At the huge Cosden estate on Long Island, Josh and Nell entertained the future King Edward VIII of Great Britain.

But Cosden, an inveterate speculator, lost his entire fortune through some unwise machinations in the cotton market in 1925 and had to put the Palm Beach showplace (and eventually all his other estates as well) on the market to pay his clamoring creditors. A few years later, he had made another fortune and was planning to build another Mizner mansion, and a few years after that, he was broke again. The price Cosden set on the Palm Beach house—

The side of Playa Riente that faced the ocean looked out on a broad green lawn dotted with royal palms. (Historical Society of Palm Beach County)

complete with furnishings selected by Mizner on a special trip to Spain, and even including the art on the walls—was $4 million. Many prospective buyers looked at Playa Riente, including the Huttons and Washington publisher Edward McLean. But only Anna Dodge was willing and able to pay the price. She paid $2.8 million in cash for the house and land, with the rest in a separate payment covering furniture, art and decorative objects. The Palm Beach newspaper of April 13, 1926, reported the transaction:

> It is said that Mrs. Dodge had also considered one or two other large houses in Palm Beach, but that none had pleased her like the Cosden house and she is very happy to have become its possessor. Mr. Dillman is to be congratulated

upon having consummated this sale, as he has been the intermediary ever since negotiations commenced a week ago and had personally directed all the matters connected with the sale, which is the largest one for a single piece of property ever made in Palm Beach.

Soon there was additional reason to congratulate the skillful Mr. Dillman. Hugh Dillman McCaughy, the son of an Ohio tailor, was a man of innate taste and elegance. He left Ohio behind at the first opportunity, and his awkwardly unpronounceable last name as well. Hugh had a brief career as an actor, but proved to be better at looking the part than he was at playing it. Through his theatrical connections, he met and married the actress Marjorie Rambeau, who divorced him in 1923; although she'd had her moments of success, her career at that time was at a low ebb, so Hugh received no financial settlement. After the divorce, he went to New York, ran up some large bills and dabbled in real estate, with his wealthy friends as clients. A few of those transactions generated enough money to allow him to travel to Palm Beach, where he could mingle with the rich and hope to improve his fortunes.

A romantic story much favored by the newspapers claimed that Anna Dodge first met Hugh Dillman in Venice, where he gallantly rescued her from a boating mishap. A close scrutiny of the schedules of both parties suggests that the story was a fabrication, whether by the principals or the press being unclear. It certainly makes a better story than the truth: that they met in the course of a real estate transaction that proved to be extremely profitable for Hugh Dillman and probably unnecessarily expensive for Anna Dodge. Hugh handled the sale of the Cosden estate, got an incredibly generous commission of $1 million from the buyer—and in the process found a wealthy wife.

The courtship was a speedy one, carried on under the camouflage of the sale of Playa Riente. To the great surprise of everyone except her immediate family, Anna married Hugh on May 8, 1926.

The ceremony took place at the home she had recently bought for her son in Detroit. It was a Tudor-style mansion built by Albert Kahn in 1903 on the seven-and-a-half-acre site next to Rose Terrace. The owner, Charles Swift, had hanged himself in one of the closets, and the house went on the market in 1925. Anna "lent" Horace the money to purchase and redecorate it, so he could settle down next door, under her watchful eye.

Anna and Hugh were married by the pastor of the Jefferson Avenue Presbyterian Church. She wore a mid-calf, beige lace dress trimmed with coral, and a big picture hat made from the same lace. She carried white orchids and of course wore pearls. (They were not, however, the Catherine the Great pearls, which she announced she had given to Delphine.) The attendants were Hugh's brother and sister from Ohio. Horace Junior was the beaming host, unassisted by his wife, who was "vacationing" in France. The guests included Delphine and Jim Cromwell, the Stotesburys—even, for form's sake, Matilda and Alfred Wilson. Anna, who was born in 1871, gave her age on the marriage license as forty-nine, although she was actually fifty-five. A rather snide article in *American Weekly* pounced on the lie:

> Although Mrs. Dodge gave her age as 49 when she married Mr. Dillman, Mr. Dodge, before he died in 1920, said that they had been married for 30 years. There must be some discrepancy here, because if Mrs. Dodge is 49, this would make her only 13 years old when she married Mr. Dodge, and this is not likely. Mr. Dillman gave his age as 43, but friends say he can't be more than 40.

After the wedding, the Dillmans boarded the *Berengaria* to start a prolonged honeymoon, scheduled to take them all over Europe and America. In a cable to her lawyer, Anna said, THANKS FOR BEAUTIFUL FLOWERS AND NOTE LOVE FROM BOTH VERY HAPPY. This period of bliss ended rather abruptly on September 22, when the *Delphine*, on which they were by then traveling, put in for a stopover at New York and mysteriously burned and sank at the pier:

At the time of her marriage to Hugh Dillman, Anna looked youthful in her flapper-style dress. (Historical Society of Palm Beach County)

an evil omen for the beginning of their married life. The day after it happened, Hugh Dillman described the extent of the disaster to Anna's lawyer:

We are slowly coming back from the shock of the fire. We have no idea of how it started but we do know she is lying almost completely under water at the foot of 94th St. The insurance inspectors think the insurance will more than put her back in shape, but they can not be certain. Everything I had, except the suit I had on, was lost, and nearly everything of Mrs. Dillman's. All papers were on board. . . . We want to find out as near as possible what the furnishings cost: carpets, drapes, furniture, organ, piano, silver, linen, etc. I sent you a wire to this effect. Mrs. Dillman thinks these bills are in the Dodge Brothers personal files.

Although it took several years to do it, the *Delphine* was eventually raised and refitted. All the lost items were replaced, even though it turned out that the insurance did not really cover the entire cost.

The fact that it was Hugh Dillman, and not Anna, who was writing to the family lawyer about the business end of the affair indicates the relationship that was being developed in the marriage. Hugh was taking over the management of Anna's life—and, to a great extent, her checkbook. As he put it tactfully to Frank Upton, "I don't want Mrs. Dillman to have the bother of any correspondence." Anna was determined to look up to her husband, even though he was younger and considerably poorer. He would be the man of the house, no matter that it was paid for by Dodge money. Anna, poor thing, seemed very much in love with her handsome young husband, and as certain as mortals can be that he returned her affection. She believed she had found the right man—and in a sense, she had. Grievous problems lay ahead in the marriage, but Anna nevertheless had much to thank Hugh Dillman for.

At the time of their marriage, Anna was an aging and not particularly attractive matron: tall, overweight, neither pretty nor youthful in looks. She might have been able to fool the people at

The house that Albert Kahn designed for Detroit businessman Charles Swift in 1903 was bought by Anna Dodge for her son; the family always called it "the gray house."
(Albert Kahn Associates, Architects and Engineers)

the license bureau about her age, but she couldn't fool Mother Nature. Anna looked her age, and, what's worse, she also felt it. She suffered from a variety of chronic complaints, and before she had been married six months, she had to have all her front teeth pulled. Aside from Eva Stotesbury, she had few social connections and fewer friends. Even her intimate relationships with her family were not characterized by genuine warmth or closeness. Aside from a strong will and a burning desire to make herself into a pillar of society, Anna Dodge in 1926 had nothing but money. Hugh Dillman, on the other hand, unquestionably had the taste, the style, the social poise and the energy to create for his new wife the lifestyle she wanted.

Hugh was the one who planned all of Anna's parties. He masterminded the guest list, chose the entertainment, taught Anna how to select the menu. He thought up Anna's trademark as a hostess, a carved ice swan filled with the biggest and best beluga

Hugh Dillman, photographed in the early 1930s, strikes an elegantly theatrical pose.
(Historical Society of Palm Beach County)

caviar. He knew instinctively how to please and flatter all visitors and make them have a good time, and he tried to teach that knowledge to Anna. With his impeccable taste, he chose her stationery, her jewelry, even many of her clothes. All in all, he was a patient and willing Pygmalion to his rather dour and cold Galatea.

Thanks to Hugh, Anna was, in the 1920s and '30s, a noted Palm Beach hostess, able on occasion to rival even her idol, Eva Stotesbury. The extent to which she succeeded can be measured by a note Eva wrote after she had been entertained by the Dillmans at Playa Riente for the first time:

> Dearest Anna
>
> I feel I must write you this little note to tell you that your dinner last night was simply a waking dream of perfection and beauty. It will live in my memory *always*. There was not a flaw from beginning to end. I had not been in the house at night for many years, and of course the Cosdens never really finished it. Miss Winslow [another guest] said it was too exquisite to be real! The few moments alone with the music I shall never forget. Best of all, dear Anna, was that I sat by you and felt so welcome. We must never be parted again.
>
> Devotedly,
> Eva

Eva's comment about not being parted was a reference to the fact that Delphine and Jim Cromwell had gone through an acrimonious divorce, complete with a highly publicized custody fight over poor little Christine. Delphine got her divorce in Reno in September 1928. She testified that Jim Cromwell made sarcastic remarks about her large allowance from her mother and also spoke of Anna Dodge Dillman in a "contemptuous" manner. Moreover, he forced her to write a letter to her mother that created a temporary estrangement. Three months after the divorce was final,

Delphine married again. Jim Cromwell did not remarry until 1934; his next wife was tobacco heiress Doris Duke.

Delphine's second husband was Raymond Baker, former director of the Mint. Ray Baker was considerably older than Delphine, old enough to be a sort of father figure, and the family hoped he would help settle Delphine down. Exactly why they had such expectations is not very clear. Baker had gained notoriety as the "friend" of the novelist, Elinor Glynn, whose books and personal life personified the "Flaming Twenties," hardly an ideal credential for a settled life. Ray Baker had money of his own, and was extremely touchy about accepting financial assistance from Delphine's mother. He seems to have caused a number of rows about money, including making a fuss over Anna's paying them an allowance of $25,000 a year for seven-year-old Christine's support—for "school, clothes, and the many things that are required by her"—and Jim Cromwell's wanting to foot the bill for the governess's salary.

Delphine was married to Ray Baker on December 4, 1928, in her mother's fifteenth-floor apartment in New York's Ambassador Hotel. She wore a romantic gown of pink chiffon and carried a spray of lavender orchids. The wedding luncheon was hosted by Anna and Hugh, and then the newlyweds left for a honeymoon at Playa Riente.

Horace Junior attended his sister's wedding—with his new wife. His divorce from Lois Knowlson and subsequent marriage to Muriel Sisman contained a number of comic elements. As early as 1925, it was clear that all was not well between Horace and Lois. She made headlines during the Christmas season of that year when she suffered a broken nose while riding in a car involved in a Palm Beach accident that killed the driver, the thirty-five-year-old manager of Dodge. (Ironically, he was driving a Rolls-Royce; the car that killed him was a Dodge.) Some four months later, on May 1, 1926, Lois was involved in another accident, while she was a passenger in a car driven in France by New Yorker Alton A. Brody. Driving slowly through Boulogne, Brody's car struck a little girl;

when he was arrested hours later he gave his name to the French police as Horace Dodge. Only after Horace himself returned to France did he learn he had been convicted by default. He had to go to court to prove he had been in Detroit at the time, hosting his mother's wedding.

In January of 1927, Lois filed for divorce. Horace told curious reporters in Paris that he was returning to the States immediately and added, "Frankly, I am puzzled and cannot understand why she has not informed me. She has been in communication with me several times since the reported divorce action but made no mention of it. I cannot believe it is true." Although the marriage had been a stormy one, both parties seemed curiously reluctant to see it end. Lois went to Hawaii in the spring, and soon thereafter Horace followed her in a blaze of publicity over their impending reconciliation. Both returned to San Francisco on the same ship (with Horace using an assumed name), and other passengers claimed the two were together constantly. But when the ship arrived, and the Dodges were met at the pier by a gang of reporters and photographers, they denied that any reconciliation had taken place. When the press continued to clamor for more concrete information, Horace responded by knocking down several reporters, breaking some cameras and then losing a fistfight with another member of the press. He was immediately arrested and taken to the city jail. Later he apologized to all concerned and paid damages.

Whatever the truth of the reconciliation attempt, Lois went ahead and obtained her divorce in May. In court she testified that "Mr. Dodge and I were very happy in the first year of our marriage, but in the second year Mr. Dodge's attitude seemed to change." Lois added, "He indulged in fits of temper and used abusive language. And he would go away without saying where he was going or why. Sometimes he was away like that for two or three weeks." She concluded, "I told him I wished he would spend less time on his speed boats and more time at home." On September 2, she remarried, choosing as her second husband a handsome pilot,

Lieutenant Ben Manning. Horace, who had irrationally expected his own love story to have a happy ending, attended her wedding and waved her a fond farewell. He seemed crushed—but not too crushed to find his own new love.

She was a Detroit society woman named Muriel Sisman. Horace's courtship began almost immediately. Its speed is indicated by a cable he sent Muriel on February 9, 1928, while she was traveling in England: LOVED TALKING TO YOU ON THE PHONE TODAY THE ONLY WAY THAT I WOULD RATHER TALK TO YOU IS BEING WITH YOU AND SEEING YOU ALL MY LOVE TO YOU SWEETHEART HORACE. And his romantic style of courtship can be seen in one of his love letters to "Dearest Muriel," written in his unformed, childish hand:

> I love you more every day. When you arrive in the morning, it is just like a nice sunny day and when you leave at night, it's just like Mr. Gloom walking in. Your smile in the morning is something that I like to see, it cheers me up for a whole day long. Your kiss is heaven because I know that it is given from your heart. So dearest please come down every morning and keep that smile because I love you more every day in every way. All my love to you sweetheart.

They were married in England on May 17, 1928, at the Westbourne Grove Presbyterian Church in Bayswater, with a gala reception afterward at the Mayfair Hotel. Hugh Dillman was Horace's best man, and his children, Horace III and Delphine, were attendants. Muriel wore a white satin gown cut in a Victorian style, and had three friends from home come over to act as bridesmaids.

Both Horace Junior and his sister Delphine inherited the Dodge penchant for unrestrained enjoyment of life, and displayed the family traits of love of speed and hard liquor. But, unlike Horace and John, they had nothing to balance these tendencies. Delphine was too dynamic a woman, too young and too "modern" to be content with a society matron's life like the one her mother was busily creating. Horace Junior clearly suffered from having to follow in his father's footsteps. Both of them tried to find something to give their lives meaning and purpose.

Delphine, in looks the epitome of the boyish flapper, mourned the fact that she had not been more serious about her music. So she took piano lessons in the hope of belatedly achieving a concert career. At the same time, she threw herself into speedboat racing and did her best to compete with her brother (who was still trying to compete with his father). She searched for love, which she thought she had found with party-loving Jim Cromwell, but whom she soon outgrew; and she searched for a father figure, which she thought she had found in Ray Baker, but faced yet another disappointment. Motherhood was not any more satisfying. Christine had become a pawn in the argument between her parents, as she would later be in fights between Jim Cromwell and Ray Baker and, in a more covert struggle, between Delphine and her mother, who took care to point out Delphine's deficiencies as a mother. Delphine's second child, a daughter born on February 15, 1933, from her marriage to Ray Baker, was named Anna Ray. By that time, it was probably too late for Delphine to change the self-destructive pattern of her existence.

Horace also tried hard to give his life some purpose. The Dodge water cars were an effort in that direction, but he had guessed wrong about the public's interest in owning a boat and he was chagrined that he could not create a corporate giant. He became involved in the world of speedboat racing, with some notable successes. It was the speed he loved, and the personal triumph when he drove a winning boat: That was an accomplishment of his very own. But to be a top driver required the commitment of an athlete in training, and there was too much fun to be found in other things. After a few years, Horace retreated to the role of wealthy patron of a racing team. He took pleasure in his wins, but in his heart he suspected they were due primarily to the money he had inherited rather than to any action of his own. Like his sister, Horace had looked for love, and it seemed at first that he had found it with the demure Lois Knowlson, a nice and pretty girl from a good family. But things went wrong, perhaps just because there were too many opportunities for them to do so. Horace could not quite settle down; Lois resented his escapades, and eventually began to have some of her own. Horace clung to that marriage, which symbolized his hope that somehow he would be able to lead a life of accomplishment and commitment, with his wife and children at his side. When Lois went ahead with the divorce, Horace lost most of his illusions.

Yet whatever their emotional scars, all the members of the Dodge family continued their flamboyant life style. They had not yet been disillusioned of the hope that the perfect house, the right possessions, the life-style that other people envied, would bring them the security and peace of mind they sought.

10

The Search for Happiness

If money could buy happiness, the Dodges should have been the happiest people in the world.

They all spent freely, even the members of the younger generation who had little money of their own. They grabbed at everything they wanted. Was it a mansion in Detroit, a stately home in jolly old England, a horse farm in Kentucky? How about a new spouse? Another lover? A pet of a kind never before seen in this country? A long line of silver trophies for the mantel? Anything, everything . . . it could all be theirs.

The Dodge belief that happiness was available on the open market may have reached its zenith at Frances's debut, on October 21, 1933. It was the depths of the Depression, and Frances told a reporter from a Toronto paper that her coming-out would be a relatively quiet event: "People in Detroit haven't much money these days." The people she was referring to obviously were not the

Dodges, for Frances's debut was probably the most lavish and elegant such party in the annals of the family.

The place was the main ballroom of the Book Cadillac Hotel in downtown Detroit; the theme was a "Bal Moderne," very much in the high style of Art Deco. The ballroom floor had been striped in black and silver, and silver balloons floated festively above the room. Tables were covered with silver cloths under a layer of crackly black cellophane. The focal point of the decor was a life-size bronze statue of a horse, a valuable piece of art, that had been covered with a silver wash. Ice sculptures of horses on each table carried out the equestrian theme appropriate to Frances's interests. The chic debutante was wearing a dream of a dress, pure 1930s slink in silver lamé, very striking and quite a radical departure from the traditional girlish organza most debs selected. She had ordered a black orchid, as a final Art Deco touch, but the florist let her down and failed to get the rare orchid there on time. The resourceful Frances decided to improvise by painting a white orchid black.

As glamorous as any movie star, the young Frances Dodge had everything an eighteen-year-old girl could ask for. A year after her debut, some newspaper obtained and published an accounting of the way Frances spent her $250,000-a-year allowance during the Depression. This was the breakdown of her budget:

Stables with 70 horses	$100,000
Clothes	25,000
Railroad & steamship tickets	10,000
Entertainment	10,000
Car & driver	7,000
Dog kennels	25,000
Pool house construction	5,000
Fees at interior decorating school	5,000
Share of Meadow Brook Hall upkeep	25,000
Incidentals	20,000

Frances had decided to enroll in an interior-decorating school, in New York, because she was building a pool house and planned to do the decorating herself. After a few months of study, she selected a tropical theme. It was not unusual for her to have fifty or sixty guests out to Meadow Brook on Sunday to frolic in the pool, many of them wearing one of the fifty guest bathing suits imported from Paris that were hanging in the pool-house dressing room. After a poolside luncheon, they might all go to inspect her kennels, which housed a rare breed of white Pekinese that she had brought back from a trip abroad. The dogs had their own English kennel maid to look after their welfare, engaged by Frances on one of her frequent trips to London.

Frances who felt there was no acceptable substitute for a well-tailored English riding habit, was as skillful as she was stylish in the saddle. The brown-haired young woman with the heart-shaped face was a familiar figure in the show ring, her small, slender figure bolt upright as her impeccably gloved hands held her horse on a tight rein. She was in fact a serious amateur athlete who never let her social pleasures undermine her fitness for dressage competition. In addition to competing with her saddle horses, she also excelled in carriage driving, sitting atop a light landau that was beautifully made and fitted out. She might be wearing a pretty print dress, leather pumps and a jaunty hat tilted over one eye, but her strong wrists and arms had her horse under sure control. The long string of trophies in her room at Meadow Brook Hall attested to her skill, and to the fact that she was more than just a rich girl who could afford good horses.

There was gossip in Detroit that Frances was somewhat at odds with her mother. Matilda was said to disapprove of her daughter's sophisticated social milieu, with its smoking and drinking, and to have urged her to adopt a simpler life. There were stories about outrageous behavior that resembled her hard-drinking father's habits, and one man who dated Frances in those days recalled that Matilda sent a bodyguard along to watch over her daughter; this man was prepared to sling the young woman over his back and haul her out of bars if she got too obstreperous. But on that night of Frances's debut, Matilda seemed proud as she stood beside Alfred Wilson in the receiving line in the ballroom and introduced her daughter to 700 members of Detroit society (or, to be more accurate, shook the hands of Frances's society friends). Not even Frances had been able to transform Matilda into an embodiment of Art Deco chic for this occasion. She was, as usual, looking short and sallow and overwhelmed by her dress, black velvet with silver spangles. But her heavy face was radiant with happiness over her daughter's social success, and she loved hearing the oohs and ahs over the Bal Moderne theme. That evening, Matilda was still able to believe in a happy future for her family.

Although Matilda enjoyed basking in the glamour of her daughter's debut, she was showing herself to be less and less inclined to participate in such events. Most of the time, she lived quietly at Meadow Brook Hall in the company of her husband, Alfred. He was essentially a homebody, who enjoyed being with their adopted children and planning little improvements to the family home. He also took over the management of Meadow Brook Farm, with its pigs, cows and sheep. By the time of her daughter's debut, Matilda seemed ready to relinquish the attempt to make her own mark in the world and to join Alfred in the peace and solitude of Meadow Brook. Part of the reason was that she felt the necessity of cutting back her expenses. She had suffered unexpected heavy financial losses in the early 1930s.

The losses were largely the result of Matilda's involvement in the banking industry. She happened to be a major stockholder of the Fidelity Bank, located in downtown Detroit. In the spring of 1931, she was asked by the bank's board to take over the position of president. Claiming "my heart is really in the business world," Matilda made it a habit to be driven in to her office every morning and to spend a few hours going through the papers on her desk. It was not until some months later that the poor woman understood why she had been offered the job. In October 1931, the bank failed.

Bank failures were not uncommon in those dark days, but the implied backing of the bank by the Dodge fortune had made depositors trusting, as had the fact that (at the urging of the members of the board who had put her at the president's desk) Matilda had shored up the price of the bank stock by buying the shares that came on the market. The distressed Matilda initially announced that she would use her own fortune to pay back savings-account depositors who had lost their money. But when the totals were made, she realized she would have to pay $6.5 million to make good her promise. This came on top of the multimillion-dollar loss she had suffered through her investments in the now worthless stock of the bank—which, she learned, had been sold through middlemen by those very board members who had told her she had a duty to buy it. The idea of repaying the depositors was quietly dropped, and at the same time Matilda gave up the notion that she was cut out for a role in the business world.

She retreated into the quiet luxury of Meadow Book Hall, where there were still many projects to be undertaken. One of the most elaborate was the riding ring for Frances—still the largest indoor ring in Michigan. At one end of the building, Matilda had her own stables, with a playroom for Danny on the second floor, overlooking the ring. Frances's stables for her show horses were at the other end of the building, and her private dressing room was on the second floor. It was painted maroon and gray, the colors she had chosen for her stable, and the custom-made maroon-and-gray rug had a horse's head in the center. The bathroom, where Frances showered after a workout in the ring, was papered in silver foil with a unicorn pattern and was luxuriously appointed.

Matilda and Frances joined together to breed and show beautiful big gray draft horses from Belgium. Those horses had their own stables on another part of the estate, and the trophies they won were duly added to the growing collection. Matilda also had a herd of prize-winning guernseys, which she showed at fairs and agricultural competitions.

Danny joined his mother and sister at Meadow Brook Hall only during the summers. He had been sent to Choate, in Massachusetts, where he struggled to keep up his grades in literature and history; only his hobbies of mechanics and shopwork came easy to him. He remained a serious, skinny boy, looking young for his years. But he was a boy who had wonderful toys. Fast cars and fast boats were his birthright, and he even had his own small plane. At parties like his sister's debut, Danny was shy and uncomfortable, an awkward mixer. But he already felt right at home behind the wheel of a powerful vehicle. In his own way, Danny too shared the Dodge appetite for immediate gratification of the senses.

The adopted Wilson children, Richard and Barbara, were of course too young to attend Frances's debut party. They were at home with their nurse, out of sight and largely out of mind. Matilda was simply not able to regard these children as truly her own; she treated them more like wards than offspring. Frances had much the same attitude as her mother. It was only Alfred Wilson, and Danny when he was home from school, who seemed to enjoy the company of Richard and Barbara.

Nor was Frances's half-brother John Duval in attendance at her debut. In Matilda's eyes, his behavior remained as scandalous as ever. John had a brief fling in the automobile business, investing money and acting as a front man for a proposed company to manufacture a car called the Dodgeson, which went broke in record time. Next, he'd tried various other get-rich-quick schemes. The year of Frances's debut, he divorced the loyal and long-suffering Marie, who was given a property settlement of $325,000, plus custody of their nine-year-old daughter, Mary Ann, and a trust fund for her totaling $108,000. Almost immediately, John married an attractive blonde from Indiana named Dora Kline. They moved into an apartment in the swank Detroit Towers, located on the riverfront only a few blocks from Indian Village, and John tried to start a company to manufacture oil burners.

Isabel Dodge Sloan's house, Concha Marina, was the Palm Beach home Addison Mizner built for himself. (Historical Society of Palm Beach County)

The other two children of John and Ivy Dodge did attend their half-sister Frances's debut. On this occasion, Isabel Dodge Sloane was her usual stylish self. She had divorced George Sloane in 1929 (an action Matilda took as another blow to the family reputation) and seemed all the happier for it. Still an avid horsewoman, she owned a highly regarded racing stable, called Brookmeade Farm, in Upperville, Virginia. The year after Frances's debut, one of Isabel's 140 thoroughbreds, a brown colt named Cavalcade, won the Kentucky Derby; a month later her horse High Quest won the Preakness. Brookmeade Farm won more than a quarter of a million dollars in 1934, making it the top stable in the country.

In addition to her Virginia estate, Isabel also owned a charming house in Palm Beach that Addison Mizner had built for himself in

Isabel Dodge Sloane attends a race during the 1938 season when her horse Cavalcade won the Kentucky Derby. (Detroit Free Press)

1921 but decided to sell after occupying for only a single season. Concha Marina wasn't nearly as big as El Mirasol or Playa Riente, but that made it easier to live in. Located south of the town of Palm Beach on a site that gave ocean views without danger of salt-water damage, Concha Marina was actually three separate build-ings: a two-story bedroom section overlooking the still-untamed lushness along Jungle Road, a one-story section with living room, dining room and loggia overlooking the ocean, and a rear building for the servants' quarters. The three sections framed a secluded patio, where Isabel placed a pool. Another of Isabel's additions was a sliding wall that covered the bar (an idea sparked by the necessities of Prohibition). An underground tunnel connected the house to the waterfront.

Newspapers always referred to Isabel as a "sportswoman," a reference not only to her love of horse racing but also to her deportment. Isabel resembled her father in being a hard drinker, but a cheerful one. When distinguished Madame Jacques Balsan (the Vanderbilt daughter who had been married off as a girl to the Duke of Marlborough) came to call and asked the butler where Isabel was, he replied, "At the pool-house bar, madam, as usual." Heavy drinking was an integral part of Isabel's daily schedule, but it was a brand of high-spirited drinking that had few dark overtones. She drank because she enjoyed it, because it made her feel happy, because it made lunch or a game of cards or an afternoon at the races even more fun. She was never pretty: her face had the typical Dodge fleshiness, and her figure had long since lost its youthful svelteness. But many people found Isabel Sloane attractive, with her stylish attire (she was usually the first in Palm Beach to appear in a new fashion), her salty language, her expertise in horseflesh, and her wholehearted dedication to her own pleasure. Her house was usually full of friends, most of them women.

Isabel attended Frances's debut in the company of her sister, Winifred, and Winnie's husband, Wesson Seyburn. By this time, the Seyburns had two children of their own, Edith and Isabel, in addition to the two Gray children from Winifred's first marriage. Wesson, the scion of an old banking family in Detroit, was a banker as well as a real estate developer who turned the site of his grandmother's house into a luxury apartment building. At the house in Grosse Point, Winifred and Wesson entertained lavishly. Winifred Seyburn, with her neatly coiffed brown hair and her conservatively fashionable wardrobe, had become a pillar of the very best Detroit society.

When it got too cold in Detroit, the Seyburn family could spend time in Palm Beach, where they had bought a cozy home called Casa Giravente. At the time of Frances's debut, they had just finished building a third house, one to be used for country weekends. It was located on a corner of the Meadow Brook estate. Matilda had continuously expanded the acreage of Meadow Brook Farm, using a variety of stratagems to get her neighbors to sell to her. One holdout changed his mind when Matilda placed a large pig barn on the abutting edge of her land, just upwind of the man's house. She then agreed to let Winifred build on that very tract. Winifred's house there, called Plumbury, was intelligently designed as a weekend house: a sprawling white frame building that made the most of the natural setting and the views. It wasn't exactly tiny, but it was small enough to require little maintenance and few servants to keep it always ready for use. Later, Winifred added a pool for the kids and a big kennel for her German shepherds—many of whom are buried in a touching pet cemetery on the property. It was a pleasant country retreat for the Seyburns.

Custom dictated that the other side of the Dodge family should also be invited to Frances's debut, and despite her distaste for Anna Dodge, Matilda was not one to make a public point of their rift. Anna's daughter, Delphine Dodge Baker, was the mother of a new baby, Anna Ray, but that had not slowed her down. Her marriage to Ray Baker was showing signs of stress, and by the end of the following year, Ray Baker would be going to Reno to establish residence for the purposes of obtaining a divorce. As luck would have it, he died of a sudden heart attack before the divorce action was officially filed. Very soon thereafter, the widowed Delphine took her third husband, import agent Timothy Godde—but not before her mother had to settle a suit in which Delphine was charged with alienation of affections by Godde's wife.

The wedding was held on August 25, 1935, at an English registry office. (Anna Dodge Dillman, who was in England earlier in the summer, pointedly boarded a ship for America shortly before the ceremony.) The thirty-six-year-old bride, still as lithe as a young girl, was sophisticated in a black-and-white dress and with a chic little black hat on her dark curls; she carried a huge spray of red carnations. Afterward, the wedding party drove to St. Leonard's, the country home of Horace and Muriel Dodge for the reception.

Horace, with his mother's help, had bought St. Leonard's Castle in 1930, at a bargain price. It was an ancient building located on the edge of Ascot Park, quite near Windsor Castle. It had in fact formerly belonged to the Crown, and there was rumored to be an underground passageway from St. Leonard's to Windsor Castle. Horace told a reporter in the mid-1930s that his gardener had recently found what appeared to be a part of the old passageway while digging on the grounds, but it was filled with water. Joked Horace, "Gee, I'm going to have that water pumped out and maybe I'll be able to call on the king."

Horace was not actually acquainted with his royal neighbors, King George V and Queen Mary, but he had attracted their attention one year with his $2,500 fireworks display on the Fourth of July. "I wonder what those are about," the King was quoted as saying. "I do not know," replied the Queen, "but they certainly are very striking." In addition to his patriotic fireworks, Horace also emphasized his American heritage at the dinner table, where his American cook served such hearty fare as navy-bean soup, and where Horace was renowned for making good hot toast with an American toaster his mother had brought over and established as a fixture in the ancient dining room. (This was a novelty in England, where toast was made in the kitchen and stood around in silver toast racks until it was stone cold, when it was ceremoniously served.) At St. Leonard's, Horace could play on his own private golf course or one of several tennis courts. He and Muriel lived there for much of the year, and both their children were born in England: David, on April 1, 1930, and Diana, on April 6, 1932. At one time Horace even discussed with his Detroit lawyers the possibility of becoming a legal resident of England.

Horace's children from his first marriage only occasionally visited him in England. They spent most of their time with their mother and their grandparents. Not long after Horace and Muriel's wedding, Anna and Hugh had Horace III (called Bud) and young Delphine with them for a while at their suite in London's posh Berkeley Hotel. Anna wrote to Horace and Muriel about the visit:

> We just got back from a motor ride to Hampton Court with the kiddies, we had them out on the Thames in a motor boat so we all had a lovely time together. Bud is playing the phonograph and Delphine is in the bedroom. It is impossible to write collectedly with the children asking questions and the victrola going. . . . Beside the children interrupting, I have Hugh, he is trying on his new clothes and every minute, 'How do you like this?'

By the time of Frances's debut, Horace and Muriel were already separated. The marriage had begun to disintegrate almost as soon as the couple had shaken the rice out of their shoes. They indulged in epic quarrels, for which Muriel had the appropriately stormy temper. After the birth of Diana in the spring of 1932, Horace pressed for an official separation. Muriel responded by suing for the return of some jewelry Horace had used as collateral for a loan. Horace contended that she had told him years earlier it would be all right to use the jewelry as collateral if the need ever arose; and Horace's lawyers made the point that the jewelry was never officially given to Muriel anyway. But Muriel insisted that the jewelry was her property, and she wanted it back. Horace seemed to be reluctant to press the issue of the jewelry, apparently in the hope that Muriel would agree to a quiet, and inexpensive, divorce. Anna's lawyer became involved in the situation and opined, "From an inspection of the affidavits taken in England I believe that they create an uncomfortable situation for the wife. . . . It would seem as if a sensible woman who has been as indiscreet as the one under discussion would be strongly impelled to seek an adjustment privately rather than to have a public contest over matters of such a delicate nature." With her "indiscretions" held over her head, Muriel did agree to a separation. Reportedly, she was given an income of $30,000 and the guarantee of a multimillion-dollar trust fund when Horace was able to set it up (which meant when his mother died). Horace returned to Detroit in time for the boat-racing season.

Susceptible as he was to pretty, high-spirited women, it did not take long for Horace to fall in love again. His new girlfriend was New York chorus girl Martha "Mickey" Devine. Mickey looked like a cross between Clara Bow and Marlene Dietrich, and was prominently displayed in Earl Carroll's revue *The Vanities*. She had made headlines a few years earlier when she met boxer Primo Carnera at a Paris nightclub. In trying to explain to him what he did wrong in his last fight, the diminutive Mickey landed a punch on his chin that knocked him to the floor.

Horace, mindful of the fact that an open liaison would probably drive up the price of a divorce from Muriel, tried to keep the romance a secret. But it was the kind of story the newspapers loved, and there were constant headlines throughout the five years of their romance.

There were also headlines about Horace and Muriel. In 1934, the two met in a hotel in New York for a reconciliation. That brief idyll was abruptly terminated by an argument that ended with Horace walking out the door to take a boat back to England, and the angry Muriel throwing her diamond ring out the window after him. They had reached what one newspaper called "the cash-in and carry-on stage of separation."

In 1936, Horace took Mickey on a cruise with his mother. Anna had been opposed to the romance, but Horace thought if his mother could get to know the girl he loved, she would love her too. Mickey was, in fact, very easy to like. She was down-to-earth, genuine, without pretense. She didn't try to conceal her humble origins, or pretend that she'd been anything other than a chorus girl. She spoke frankly and she was warm-hearted. Anna probably realized that her son could do a lot worse. But Horace didn't seem anxious to commit himself to another matrimonial venture, and he dreaded the scandal of another divorce.

Horace's matrimonial difficulties were a source of real irritation to his mother. She had opposed the divorce from Lois, and punished her son for going ahead with it by taking back the deed to his house in Grosse Pointe and threatening to cut off her support for his boat-racing ventures. Although she had no warm feelings for Muriel, she counseled against divorce. In reality, she had no time to worry about Horace's marriage; she had enough trouble with her own.

At the time of Frances's debut in late 1933, it seemed as if her aunt Anna was on top of the world. She and Hugh Dillman had just returned from a trip to Russia with famed art dealer Joseph Duveen, having bought quantities of furniture, paintings and fabulous decorative *objets* that had once belonged to the Russian royal family and were being sold by the financially strapped Communist government at distress prices. These purchases were destined to fill Anna's new mansion in Detroit.

Over the years, Anna had many times visited the Philadelphia estate of Eva Stotesbury, with whom she remained on good terms despite their children's acrimonious divorce. Whitemarsh Hall, finished in 1916, was a monument to Eva's personal taste and inclinations, and some architectural historians have classed it as one of the greatest private homes ever built in the United States. Designed in the classical French style and bearing a marked resemblance to the Trianon of Louis XIV, Whitemarsh Hall was Eva's greatest achievement, a vision of elegant splendor both inside and out. Naturally, Anna wanted something just like it. It was not long after her second marriage that she hired Eva's architect, Easterner Horace Trumbauer, and began to plan her dream house.

Anna already owned one of the choicest sites in Grosse Pointe, the waterfront lot on which Horace Dodge had built Rose Terrace. Her son lived on one side of her, in the Tudor-style house designed by Albert Kahn. In the late 1920s, she was able to add to the property when the land and building on the other side, belonging to the Grosse Pointe Country Club, came on the market. She bought it from the club, which was moving to a site with a golf course, and then allowed herself the enormous satisfaction of tearing down the clubhouse of the society snobs who had not let Horace Dodge and his family become members.

Her next step was unusually unsentimental. She had the wreckers tear down the home her husband Horace built for their family. All trace of the Albert Kahn home where the Dodges had lived for so many years vanished in a matter of weeks. All that remained when the wreckers left were the steps leading to the terraced rose garden that had given the house its name. Even the furniture disappeared, since it would not fit the style of the new house Anna planned to build. Although she still spoke of Horace as "my dear one who has gone on before," she apparently did not feel the need to encumber herself with mementos of their shared past. The beautiful, comfortable, architecturally significant Kahn house was swept away, along with its memories.

The new house would be built in the center of the 8.8-acre site that Anna had thus created, approached by a long winding drive from Jefferson Avenue. Like its predecessor, it would also be called Rose Terrace. The exterior would be a close copy of the Hamilton Rice estate in Newport that Trumbauer had designed a few years earlier, patterning it after the Petit Trianon at Versailles. But the interior detail would be chosen by Anna and Hugh. While the house was being built, Anna and her husband could get a head start on the problem of filling up such a large and elaborate house through ceaseless travel in search of furnishings and decor. Once the Kahn house was gone, they would simply live on the yacht *Delphine* whenever they went to Detroit to inspect the house's progress.

Rose Terrace II was an imposing three-story residence. In the Midwestern tradition of building a house like a fortress, it had a steel frame, a reinforced-concrete foundation and exterior walls of fire-resistant brick faced with carved gray-white Indiana limestone. First-floor public rooms included a high-ceilinged reception hall, separate reception rooms for ladies and gentlemen (complete with lavatories), a sixty-foot-long music room that could also serve

The façade of Rose Terrace II was designed by Horace Trumbauer in the style of an eighteenth-century French château. (Collection of David Agresta)

as a ballroom, a dining room and a more intimate breakfast room, two cozy sitting rooms, a library, and a card room and a bar conveniently connected to the men's reception room. The second floor had eight principal bedrooms, eight baths, several sitting rooms, an office for Anna and another one for her secretary. Nineteen staff rooms, assorted cedar closets and pressing rooms, and a comfortable living room for the housekeeper occupied the top floor. The basement housed a gym, one room devoted entirely to the making of ice cream (one of Anna's favorite foods) and another for storing bottled water, a 150-gallon hot-water heater, and a row of vaults for the storage of silver, rugs and furs. The kitchen, also in the basement, was fitted out with heavy-duty restaurant equipment and could easily produce dinner for 100 people.

This is the "informal" breakfast room at Rose Terrace, where the family ate when there were no guests. (Collection of David Agresta)

Ground for the new Rose Terrace was broken in 1931, and the proud owners held their housewarming party three years later, for 1,500 guests. Although the inspiration for Anna's new mansion came from her continued slavish imitation of Eva Stotesbury, there is no question but that Hugh Dillman played a huge role in the building and furnishing of Anna's French-style château. Much of the correspondence with the architect about changes to the plans is in Hugh's handwriting. A letter written in 1932 to Horace Trumbauer addressed a myriad of the Dillmans' concerns after a look at the latest revision of the blueprints:

> What is the space in East End of main hall that looks like a fireplace? If a fireplace, think it advisable to eliminate. . . . Eliminate partition in closet in reception room, making one big closet of it. . . . In place of having door into Mrs. Dillman's bath from hall, close that door and make

space into closet with door only from hall, thus eliminat-
ing any entrance to her bath other than from bedroom
and dressing room. . . . The refrigerator space is not
sufficient. . . . Think it advisable to put door from bar
thru into men's room. . . . I want to talk over some details with you regarding my valet's room and pressing
room. . . .

Anna benefited greatly from Hugh's knowledge and taste when
it came to making choices about the house and its decor, and he
also contributed a lot of sheer hard work. Building and furnishing
Rose Terrace II was a major undertaking that must have given
employment to scores of people. Forty years later, when the executors of Anna's estate started to look through her papers, they
found an entire wall of filing cabinets that were full of nothing but
documents relating to the years she spent purchasing all the things
needed for a great mansion, from tablecloths made of priceless
antique lace to gold-plated holders for toilet paper. Dealers, decorators, antique shops, galleries, artists' agents, firms of crafts-
men—literally hundreds of different businesses were at work in
finding more and more things for Anna to buy. She obligingly
gave them all her attention, and bought and bought and bought.
What couldn't fit at Rose Terrace was shipped to Palm Beach to
squeeze into Playa Riente. When that house was first built, a
newspaper article rhapsodized that it was "a house that must be
furnished slowly, for only over the years would one be lucky enough
to find the right things for it." The writer didn't know Anna's
ability to shop! Soon Playa Riente too became overcrowded with
fine things. Some of the overflow was placed on board Anna's
floating palace, the *Delphine*, and other things were given to "the
children" to fill up their houses.

The whole process of frenzied acquisition began even before
ground was broken for the new house. In 1929, Anna and Hugh
went on a buying trip around the world. Both of them wrote about

it copiously, in letters back home and in their diaries. They did manage to stop shopping long enough to see some of the tourist sights: Anna pronounced the Taj Mahal "too beautiful" and the Ming emperors' tombs and Peking's Forbidden City "in good condition."

But mostly they shopped, and they worked hard at it. They bought rugs in Peshawar, old snuffboxes and antique kimonos in Japan, furs for lap robes and bedspreads at the foot of Mount Everest. Sample entries from Anna's diary of the trip, made on their arrival in Peking are typical:

> *May 19* Up late, lunch in sitting room. Took a ride down Jade St—bought 1 pr of jade trees for us & one pair for Horace. Dinner & bridge.
>
> *May 20* All Jade St in our sitting room this morning when I went in—couldn't find Hugh. Very tired. Bed.
>
> *May 21* Jade St again in the morning, bought many things. Bed.
>
> *May 22* We still have Jade St with us and still we buy— lovely things. Bed.

Every year they made another trip, and every year the loot poured back to Detroit: several hundred old barns from Greece, which were cannibalized for their aged cypress, to be used as paneling in the reception room; a French silver coffeepot made in 1787 by a famous silversmith; an antique mahogany backgammon table bought in London for £240; an entire French inn, which provided for the bar floorboards picturesquely marked by the hooves of horses that might have been ridden by Napoleon; fragile porcelains from Vienna. Anna's business manager was kept busy clearing the shipments through customs and arranging to get everything out to Rose Terrace. The task which that overworked man faced can be seen in one single letter Hugh wrote him from China, not long after the marathon encounter with the merchants of Jade Street:

We are sending home many things. The first to arrive will
be some old silk. If the customs think it looks new, it is
because it has been kept in chests as the Chinese do here.
There is thousands of yards coming out of hiding, some of
it loot from the Boxer uprising. . . . After the silk there
will be quite a big shipment of jade and some ivory and a
screen. These are very fine things and jade most delicate.
I would suggest having the customs send it all directly to
the red house [the Kahn Rose Terrace I—the year was
1930 and it had not yet been pulled down] and open it
there, for it must be opened with untold care. You be there
and look after it in person, for I know from past experience how they go after things. Tom [Parish] can get a drink
out for them and if they are careful etc. you might give
them each a bottle. . . .

But simply acquiring some pieces of furniture and a few knick-
knacks was only the beginning. The New York firm of L. Ala-
voine & Co., known for its lavish French period interiors, was
engaged to do the decorating; by no coincidence, they had also
decorated several of Eva Stotesbury's houses. Correspondence flowed
back and forth between Detroit and New York, as well as endless
checks one way, to cover all the work. Even the minutiae of Rose
Terrace's interior were time-consuming and expensive: $4,010 for
turning some of those jade statues and vases into lamps, $2,500
for Shawnee Polished Gray Granite for the main entrance, $9,385
for the wrought-iron grilles on the balconies. Every little detail
was specified; for example, the tub in Anna's bathroom was to be
"royal porcelain enclosed in marble . . . hot and cold control valves
with Louis XV flanges for valve stems, with bath-size hand chased
Dolphin handles."

Luckily for Anna, the trouble Hugh was willing to take over
such details was endless. He made a special trip, for instance, just
to see some rugs that were being custom-made for the house and
then wrote indignantly to the decorator in charge:

I was amazed to find the one for the library had a green-brown background. How has such an error ever happened? They claim that it has been done under your supervision but I feel confident this is not the case, for no one knew better than you that the carpet was to be with a black background as per the drawing submitted.

There was only one relationship into which Hugh did not interject himself as Anna's helper, and that was with the wily art dealer Sir Joseph Duveen. Anna became involved with Duveen because he had worked with Eva Stotesbury to find museum-quality furniture and Old Masters for Whitemarsh Hall; and, as usual, whatever Eva had, Anna had to have too—preferably in greater quantity. Duveen was a master of the craft of selling fine art, who had already succeeded in gently fleecing such builder/collectors as Andrew Mellon, Henry Clay Frick and Archer Huntington. He immediately recognized Anna as a prime prospect and took pains to keep her husband at some distance.

Duveen's technique was to send titillating lists of the items he was prepared to "sacrifice" to help Anna build her dream house. Each piece of art was lovingly described, with any slightest association with royalty of any kind played up. The typed prices accompanying the items were ridiculously high, but they had been lightly crossed out with the finest of lead pencils, and only slightly less ridiculous figures inserted. The trick worked with Anna, who thrilled to the thought that she was getting every one of the overpriced works of art at a real bargain. Since everything she bought was a "one-of-a-kind" masterpiece, only an expert in the field of art and antiques could estimate the true value of the purchases. And Duveen, in working with his other wealthy clients, had perfected a way of appearing to believe that any question about the price meant the prospective purchaser was unable to afford to buy so exquisite a piece. After Anna had made a significant number of purchases, Duveen flatteringly created for her a "catalogue" of her collection—or at least the part of it he had sold her—with the

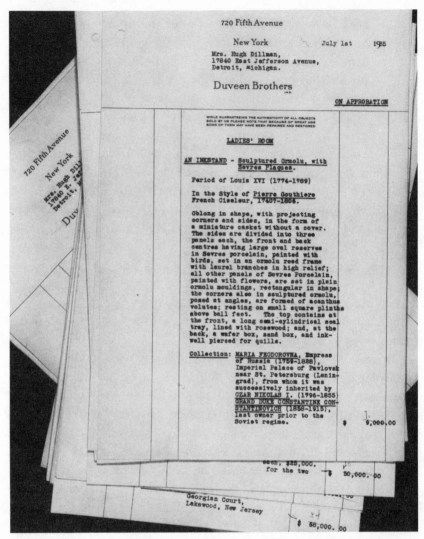

Some sample pages of correspondence to Anna Dodge Dillman from art dealer Joseph Duveen display his finely tuned sales technique. (Collection of David Agresta)

same florid descriptions of the items printed on heavy vellum. Handsome photographs of the works were pasted in by hand, and the whole thing was bound in several volumes covered in red morocco. As Anna's spending spree neared its close, Duveen issued a public statement announcing his "expert" opinion of Anna's collection:

> It is both a pleasure and a privilege to speak of the achievement of Mrs. Dillman in assembling such a magnificent collection of works of art of the Eighteenth Century. The greatest patience and finest taste have been required in order to select only the most perfect works. Necessarily, therefore, Mrs. Dillman has been obliged to spend several years in her search, devoting to it a considerable part of her time on each of her visits to Europe. . . . In my opinion, the house and its contents are unsurpassed as an expression of French Eighteenth Century achievement. What is so extraordinary is the combination of beauty and comfort—one rarely found and so difficult to achieve.

Duveen certainly fooled Anna Dodge Dillman about the value of her purchases, because the prices she paid for old French furniture, bronzes, tapestries and Sèvres were much too high, especially since she was buying in the depths of the Depression. In fact, when her estate was auctioned off by Christie's about forty years later, in the inflationary economy of the early 1970s, most of those pieces brought less than she had paid Duveen for them. But if Duveen cheated her in price, he never cheated her in quality. Everything he sold her was beautiful, and most of it was of museum quality. For example, a tulipwood table made by one of the foremost names in French furniture, Martin Carlin, was sold in 1971 by Anna's estate for $415,800 and sold again fifteen years later for more than $2 million, making it the most expensive piece of furniture in the world at that time.

The most impressive result of the collaboration between Duveen and Anna can be seen in the Detroit Institute of Arts, to which she left all the furnishings of one of the loveliest rooms of Rose Terrace, the music room. The Institute spoke thankfully of

The music room of Rose Terrace, with the jewel casket of Empress Maria Feodorovna in the foreground, is today installed in the Detroit Institute of Arts. (Collection of David Agresta)

the bequest: "We have to be pleased for the people of Detroit. The precious antique furniture and decorative arts now belong to all of us. . . . It will recall her taste and magnanimity." The display at the museum shows everything just as it was, with one exception. At Rose Terrace, the music room contained a portrait of Anna Dodge, painted in the early 1930s by English society artist Gerald Kelly. The painting is in the style of Boucher, and represents Anna as Madame de Pompadour. She is wearing eighteenth-century dress, a confection of sky-blue satin trimmed with innumerable bows, and powdered hair arranged in the sweet style favored by the king's mistress, the adorable and charming "Reinette," who captivated Louis XV and his court at Versailles. Alas, the aesthetic dissonance is so great that the painting borders on the comic. Anna was no Reinette. She hadn't an ounce of charm or gaiety, nor did she possess any of the prettiness of Pompadour. The portrait succeeds only in making her look far too much like her real self: a stolid, disapproving lump. When faced with this odd relic of the owner of Rose Terrace, the Institute diplomatically "forgot" to take the painting along with the priceless art and antiques; the family promptly sent it, heavily insured. To this day, the Institute has not found space for it. So visitors to the museum today will see the room without its presiding patroness.

The focal point of the music room was a jewel casket that had once stood in the bedroom of Russian Empress Maria Feodorovna. It was the work of Martin Carlin, and was covered with plaques from the Sèvres factory (patronized by Madame de Pompadour) and ormolu mounts. Four other pieces of similar design are known to have been produced, all now in major museums. The music room also contained a rosewood writing table by Jean Henri Riesener, usually considered the greatest cabinetmaker of his time. Another significant piece was a lyre-back chair that had belonged to Marie Antoinette. The walls of the room were decorated with a set of tapestries woven at the royal factory at Beauvais (also patronized by Madame de Pompadour), based on drawings by Boucher. Bronze and marble sculptures by the French artist called Clodion were placed strategically on and around the furniture. And several fine display cabinets held pieces of Royal Sèvres marked with Louis XV's monogram, painted with rural scenes and gilded and glazed with consummate craft. (Many such pieces were created at the behest of Madame de Pompadour.)

Today the room is enjoyed by thousands of visitors to the Detroit Institute of Arts, which has recently published a book on the furnishings. Every individual piece is impressive. How much more impressive it must have been in its original setting at Rose Terrace! Instead of the bare plaster walls of the museum, there was elaborately carved paneling in the style of eighteenth-century France. And through the doorways to the reception hall and the small sitting rooms at either side could be seen glimpses of other rooms full of fabulous furniture set atop glowing carpets. The tall French doors on the lakefront side of the room framed views of the terrace, with thousands of roses in bloom during the summer and the blue water beyond.

A guest at one of Anna Dodge Dillman's entertainments in the music room would have been met at the door by a footman wearing a dark-blue jacket embellished with silver buttons bearing a *D*. The music might have been provided by one of the concert stars of the day, and fellow guests would be not only members of Detroit society, but also the cream of visiting socialites from New York and Europe. One such party was held at Rose Terrace on December 6, 1935. According to the notebook kept by Anna's social secretary, there were fifty-five guests, invited to listen to Negro spirituals at nine o'clock, followed by a midnight supper laid out on the immense dining table. The menu (all of it turned out in Rose Terrace's kitchen) included lobster Newburg, chicken à la king, galantine of turkey, cold tongue, various aspics and salads and, of course, Anna's signature, the carved ice swan filled with beluga, which even in the depths of the Depression cost several hundred dollars. Dessert was ice cream and cake, and the entire meal was accompanied by champagne. Other drinks, including Pabst, Heineken and Schlitz beer, were available, as were Chesterfields, Camels, Lucky Strikes, Old Golds and Philip Morris cigarettes, along with a humidor of Coran cigars. The hostess wore a white satin dress with emerald-green sleeves, and an emerald-and-diamond necklace she had purchased earlier that year from the estate of Edith Rockefeller McCormick.

Standing at Anna's side throughout the evening was Hugh Dillman, to all appearances the very model of a devoted husband. Only a few weeks earlier, he had thrown a surprise cocktail party for his wife (among the guests were Winnie and Wesson Seyburn) as another token of his affection. And when they had been parted for a short time, he sent her an affectionate telegram:

DEAREST JUST TO SAY GOODNIGHT WON'T BE ABLE TO REACH YOU AGAIN UNTIL YOU REACH LOS ANGELES WHERE I WANT TO HAVE LETTER AWAITING YOU WIRE ME HAZEL'S ADDRESS SO I CAN SEND AIRMAIL ALWAYS MY DEEPEST LOVE HUGH

The reality was that even before Rose Terrace was finished, the marriage had gone sour. For her part, Anna felt she had done everything she could to make Hugh Dillman happy. She gave him, first, an annual allowance of $100,000, in addition to lavish gifts, and then she arranged for him to have his own trust fund, $6 million worth of the very soundest municipal bonds. He would enjoy a share of the income for life, and then the principal would pass to Anna's children, who also got shares of the income. The trust was established on April 1, 1932, but his gratitude was short-lived. A year later, Hugh (one of the trustees) was trying to break the terms of the trust and invade the principal. It appears he was so successful that Anna's lawyer and the other trustees began to worry about how long the principal in the trust would last.

By the spring of 1934, Anna and Hugh had effected a de facto separation when Hugh moved into the enlarged and redecorated house on a farm he had bought in West Palm Beach, called Sandy Loam Farm. Sandy Loam had 380 acres, which Hugh turned into a horticultural showplace. The grounds were lushly planted with specimen trees and shrubs, and eventually he also operated a wholesale nursery there, as well as a model dairy farm (not an easy feat in the heat and sandy soil of southern Florida). One newspaper story described Sandy Loam as "an enchanting place, like a stage set," with its handsome antique furniture in the low-key country setting. Until he sold it in 1942, Sandy Loam Farm was Hugh Dillman's chief residence, and he entered Playa Riente only to play the part of host on rare occasions. Hugh held one of his first big parties at Sandy Loam Farm on March 31, 1935, and it

Sandy Loam Farm was Hugh Dillman's private domain; the master bedroom was fit for an English squire. (Historical Society of Palm Beach County)

was duly reported in the Palm Beach newspaper—with no mention of Anna, wintering quietly only a few miles away at Playa Riente.

When Hugh moved out, Anna immediately took action to get Hugh's income from the trust reduced and to force him to resign as trustee. Hugh pressed for an undiminished income and claimed that Horace and Delphine supported the request, a claim they subsequently denied. Anna asked her lawyer in Detroit to talk to Hugh about the situation, and the lawyer wrote her an account of the meeting, with special emphasis on Hugh's view of his position:

> Hugh rather emphasized his earning capacity had he remained in business (he estimates this at the neighborhood of $20,000 per annum) and also stresses, that as a result of the marriage, he had to change his position in life from the standpoint of a more luxurious scale of expenditures. He also refers to the fact that he has his mother and other members of his family dependent upon him. He stoutly avers that his personal estate has shrunken to relatively small dimensions—not in excess of $400,000. He points out that he received a $100,000 per annum for services until the separation. . . . He denies that was in any way responsible for the drafting of the Trust in such a manner as to permit the eating up and consumption of portions of the principal. Hugh is extremely sensitive on the alleged attack upon his honor involved in our position.

What was the reason for all this unpleasantness? It seemed that Hugh had at last tired of meeting Anna's demands and finally dropped the mask. Her travel diaries indicate how fatiguing those demands could be. She was often unwell for weeks at a time, and during those periods, the ailing, aging Anna demanded that her husband be with her constantly, reading to her, rubbing her feet, fetching special delicacies. Lacking conversational abilities and social graces herself, she demanded that Hugh fill the void. Really, it is not surprising that he would eventually begin to find it all tiresome and try to arrange to slip away whenever possible. Anna, who still loved her husband and clung to a traditional view of marriage, had worried that her age and infirmities might cause him to turn to younger women. Then she discovered that his real preference was not for women at all, but for handsome young men. Twenty years later, Anna told her daughter-in-law (Gregg Dodge) that she had found Hugh in bed with one of the crew members on the yacht *Delphine*. For the strait-laced Anna, it was a devastating blow.

She considered divorce, and it appears that she spoke to her lawyer about using Hugh's homosexual activity as legal grounds. He anxiously counseled his client to abandon the idea: "There are so many reasons why the introduction of such a factor would have a prejudicial reaction that I am convinced that you will see that it is a matter which should be left most severely alone." He pointed out that "in the event of a contest, we should have to prove our allegations by a preponderance of evidence," and cautioned, "we ought to avoid if possible having the issue turn upon merely your testimony on the one side and his denial on the other." The lawyer concluded by urging Anna to try to come to some amicable arrangement with Hugh "without the occasion for a public contest in the courts."

When Hugh saw that Anna was really in earnest about divorce, he turned the charm on full force. The last thing he wanted was a social scandal. He was living the life he'd been born for, with the Dodge fortune at his disposal and high-society friends at his doorstep. A sign of his elevated social standing was the fact that in 1935 he became the president of Palm Beach's exclusive Everglades Club, housed on Worth Avenue in a building designed by Addison Mizner.

When Mizner built the Everglades Club in 1919, it was supposedly going to be a convalescent home for U.S. Army officers who had been wounded in World War I. But since the building contained only eleven bedrooms, it was obviously not well suited to such a purpose. It soon became a club (although there was initially some difficulty in catering elegant meals for 300 people out of a tiny diet kitchen), and, at the behest of its members, Mizner added to it throughout the 1920s: a ballroom; a wonderful outdoor marble patio; an orange garden, with a sliding roof that could be closed in case of inclement weather; and a row of "maisonettes" that could be rented by members who did not want to bother opening their grand houses. Then a golf course was added, docking facilities on Lake Worth, a picturesque lagoon for moonlit walks and five clay courts for tennis players.

Hugh's selection as president surely owed something to Anna's willingness to invest heavily in a bond issue needed to keep the club afloat during the financial troubles of the Depression. But it was also a tribute to Hugh's social talents, the same talents he had devoted to the service of Anna's social climb. Hugh supervised the final redecoration of the club, and he oversaw all the entertainments there. A history of the Everglades Club noted that the fabulous costume parties, which were the focus of the Palm Beach social season, "were usually master-minded by Hugh Dillman, who once having been a professional actor, had a theatrical flair which set The Everglades Club parties apart from anything else that occurred in the resort." Hugh instituted Barn Dance Night, when Palm Beach came out in blue jeans to stamp their feet. He was the inspiration behind the Hawaiian Night Party, and the party featuring the "Everglades Special," for which the entrance to the club was decorated to look like a railway station, with a newsstand and piles of schedules; food was served as if on a dining car, and admission was by invitations that looked exactly like train tickets. One of his most outrageous ideas was the Afromobile race on the grounds of the club. "Afromobile" was the old Palm Beach nickname for an early mode of transport along the palm-shaded walks, a sort of tricycle with a sizable wicker chair on the front. Passengers rode in the chair, and locomotive power was supplied by black workers, thus giving the conveyance its name. Hugh's Afromobile races had the women members of the club pedaled around a course by the males, who rolled up their pant legs (to keep them out of the bicycle chain) and displayed their socks and garters—all quite titillating behavior at the Everglades Club.

A divorce would be very inconvenient for Hugh Dillman, especially if the divorce started talk about his parties at Sandy Loam with an all-male guest list. So he wooed Anna all over again. It seems likely that this time she was not really taken in by his show of interest and affection. But she didn't really want the scandal of a divorce either. They would try to make the best of it when they had to be together, and they would be apart more and more frequently.

If Frances Dodge's debut makes a good place to start looking at the Dodge search for happiness, her wedding is a logical place to draw it to a close. Frances was married at Meadow Brook Hall on July 1, 1938. The groom was James Johnson, from New Jersey, a young man with more energy than resources, more charm than background. Like Frances, he was interested in horses; she had met him at a riding competition. He was also interested in popular music, and was just starting a magazine about swing music called *The Cat's Meow*. Perhaps he was not the ideal choice, but Matilda was glad just to see her daughter looking happy, and she hoped marriage would help to settle her down and stop her heavy drinking.

If Jimmy Johnson was not the perfect groom, Frances was certainly the perfect bride, and Meadow Brook Hall the perfect place for a wedding. The organ resounded throughout the house as Frances, elegant in ice-blue satin cut to cling and reveal, walked down the grand staircase of the house and into the living room, where the improvised altar stood. Frances's dramatic taste had made everything beautiful and unusual. The invitations to the 900 guests were printed on pale-blue paper, and all the engagement and wedding photos were covered with a pale-blue wash. The wedding cake was four feet high, and the buffet table groaned under the weight of an incredible variety of food.

The receiving line formed in front of a portrait showing the round face and rotund figure of John Dodge, Frances's father and the one who had provided all the bounty of the wedding. There Frances stood to smile and shake hands with the guests. They included her half-sisters Winifred and Isabel; her cousins Horace and Delphine; her aunt Anna Dillman. The guest on whom most of the press cameras were trained was none other than John Dodge's old business partner Henry Ford, as skinny as ever and in good health for his age.

It was a great moment for the Dodge family. It also marked the beginning of its downward spiral.

11

The Downward Spiral

The rustic hunting lodge on Manitoulin Island was a perfect honeymoon spot. The nearest town, Gore Bay, was twenty miles away, on a narrow twisting road that took an hour to drive. The lodge was not fancy but it was quite comfortable, and all around was the natural splendor of the northern Ontario woods. Although it was only the second week in August, in that northern climate there were already harbingers of the coming change of season. The leaves were starting to turn, and the wind sometimes whipped up the waters of Gore Bay. With the hint of fall in the air, there were long afternoons in the slanting sunshine when the newlyweds could go hiking hand in hand through the crunchy leaves, take a speedboat ride to buy their groceries, lazily fish the clear waters.

The honeymooners enjoying this remote and blissful spot were not Frances and Jimmy Johnson, who had opted for weeks of the high life in London. No. They were Matilda's other child, Daniel Dodge, who was the groom, and his bride, a young telephone operator from Gore Bay, daughter of a Great Lakes tugboat captain there. The story of their love appeared to be a romantic one.

Although he was only twenty at the time he took on the responsibility of a wife, Daniel was already in the habit of asserting himself. Photos show him looking old for his age, perhaps due to the Dodge round face, the Rausch heavy jaw, and the thick wire-rimmed spectacles. As a boy, he had been his mother's favorite— the serious dark-eyed child who liked to be with her and who embodied her hopes for the Dodge family in the future. But even then he spent long hours by himself, shut away in his workshop or reading in his room. When there was a party at Meadow Brook Hall, Danny didn't bother to argue about whether or not he would be there; he simply disappeared. He perfected the skill of quietly doing as he pleased, without antagonizing anyone.

Something of the odd quality of the young man's life can be seen in his purchase of Kagawong Lodge in Ontario. He bought the property in 1935, when he was a student at Choate and only seventeen years old. All he had to do was write a check out of the income from his share of the trust his father left. Other boys went home for the summer holidays; Danny Dodge flew his own amphibious plane up to his own hunting lodge, to be alone in the woods and work on some marine engine that needed his attention.

Of all his generation of the Dodge family, the boy who bore his grandfather Dodge's name was probably the one with whom John and Horace would have felt most comfortable. Like them, he had a passion for machinery, an ability to become totally absorbed in the problems of making an engine run quietly and efficiently. Of course, there was no longer a family business for this Daniel Dodge to enter; by the time the prep-school student bought his hunting lodge, Dodge Brothers Motor Car Company had been gone for a decade. But he was working steadily on the development of a diesel engine that might be commercially feasible. Perhaps he was dreaming of a new company that would take the Dodge name and reputation into the future. . . .

There was no telephone at the lodge, so when Danny needed to communicate with the outer world, he took the car or the boat to Gore Bay, a small town of 700 residents, and made his calls from the square brick telephone exchange there. That was how he met Annie Laurine MacDonald, the operator at the exchange. She was a small-town girl whom early photographs show to have been rather plain. Two years younger than Danny, she shared his interests in hiking, swimming and fishing. He taught her how to drive a car and lent her his big roadster; later he also taught her how to drive a speedboat. Of course she knew that Dan Dodge was rich. But in Gore Bay that really only meant having a nice hunting lodge and a good speedboat. At the time of her girlish romance, the full meaning of the Dodge wealth and social status was probably beyond Annie Laurine's power to imagine.

The romance was common knowledge in Gore Bay, and eventually Danny also made it public at Meadow Brook Hall. Matilda was totally opposed to the match. A mere telephone operator was no fit match for the heir to the Dodge name and fortune. According to Matilda, Annie Laurine would never be able to hold her own in society, and probably she was a fortune hunter anyway. From the way Matilda talked about the disgrace of the mismatch, it would seem she had forgotten all about the young secretary at Dodge Brothers who had aspired to marry the boss. Interestingly, Annie Laurine's parents were also opposed, perhaps because they too feared that the gulf between the Dodge heir and a backwoods telephone operator was too great.

Despite parental opposition, Danny and Annie Laurine became engaged. The new Dodge fiancée was introduced to Detroit society at a double engagement party, held on May 22, 1938, for Frances and Danny. There was on this occasion much talk about the plans for Frances's wedding, scheduled to take place just six weeks in the future, but silence on the subject of Danny's marital plans. The question came up again at Frances's wedding, when her younger brother gave her away. When would his own wedding take place? Matilda evaded all such questions, and Danny was no more forthcoming.

In fact, Danny's wedding was held with no advance announcement on August 2, at Meadow Brook Hall. The contrast with Frances's elaborate nuptials one month earlier could not have been greater. The simple ceremony was attended by only seven guests (the bride's parents not among them). The minister, Dr. Joseph Vance, from Matilda's church, told reporters, "We three men moved a few chairs around in the living room before the ceremony. Those were the only arrangements there were." The bride's youth was her chief ornament. Her wedding dress was plain, ivory lace over ivory satin, and she wore only one small jeweled brooch, a gift from the groom. Instead of the traditional veil, she wore a broad-brimmed ivory hat. After the ceremony, she quickly changed into a traveling dress, and the newlyweds left in Dan's car for an undisclosed location, which turned out to be the Ontario hunting lodge.

Thirteen days later, Daniel Dodge was dead.

His death was both a tragedy and a mystery. People are still puzzling over the peculiar circumstances of the young bridegroom's death. On the afternoon of August 15, Dan was working outside on the property with his caretaker, Lloyd Bryant, and another employee, Frank Valiquette, both men of his own age. A local reporter dropped by to interview the Dodge heir, and Dan told him, "My wife and I are happy. What more is there to be said?" He then excused himself on the grounds that he had work to do and rejoined Bryant and Valiquette. The three of them then decided to set off some old dynamite they had found on the place. As they were conferring in the garage, Annie Laurine walked over to call her husband for dinner. Suddenly there was an explosion. Valiquette later told the press, "While Dodge was holding the dynamite in his hand, it exploded. It shattered his arm and struck the side of his face and head. Mrs. Dodge was hit in the legs. Bryant was badly hurt. He was hit on the side." Bryant was unconscious. Dan was in great pain. Frank Valiquette was only mildly injured.

Annie Laurine knew it was imperative to get the injured men

to medical help. The boat trip to Gore Bay would be the fastest way. Although her arm was broken and her legs were severely burned, Annie Laurine helped load the injured men into Dan's speedboat. She sat in the cockpit and drove while young Mrs. Bryant tried to minister to the wounded in the rear. Midway through the rough trip, Annie Laurine called out to the others that she was too weak to go on driving. Valiquette, who had been trying to put a tourniquet on Dan's mangled arm, climbed up front to help her. She moved to the rear.

Then, inexplicably, Daniel Dodge went overboard. The others caught a quick glimpse of him in the water and then he disappeared without a struggle. They circled the spot where he'd gone overboard (during which time Annie Laurine fainted and was rudely revived by the icy waters splashing into the boat), searching the choppy lake, but saw nothing more of Dan. Badly wounded, bleeding heavily, with one arm useless, Dan could not possibly, it seemed, have survived in the cold and rough waters. After ten or fifteen minutes, the boat resumed its course, to get help for the others.

As soon as they landed, other boats were dispatched to continue the search for Dan, but no trace of him could be found. A doctor who tended Annie Laurine upon her arrival put her in the hospital, but said she would recover in a few weeks. He added that she had talked about the tragedy but "I was really too busy dressing her wounds, and, too, I am a little bit deaf so I didn't understand all the details." The doctor's considered opinion was that the pain of his injuries had driven Dan out of his mind, causing him to leap out of the boat.

The sad news was telephoned to Meadow Brook Hall. The only thing the Dodge money could do for Danny now was to send up sophisticated diving equipment, including a small submarine, to help in the search for his body.

That search took nearly three weeks, and, in the end, success happened by accident when a couple of fisherman noticed a screaming pack of gulls over a dark spot near the shore. Alfred

Wilson accompanied his stepson's body back to Meadow Brook Hall, where the simple funeral service was held by the same minister who had married the young man only weeks earlier. On September 9, 1938, Daniel Dodge was laid to rest in the family mausoleum.

The event was only the beginning of the pain caused by Dan's death. As soon as the young widow left Detroit after the funeral, she retained a smart lawyer and demanded a satisfactory settlement of her husband's estate.

It was revealed that Annie Laurine, at the urging of Matilda, had agreed to sign a prenuptial agreement limiting her claim on Daniel Dodge's estate to a maximum of $250,000. Now her lawyer said she acquiesced only because she had no idea at the time how large his estate really was. She was stunned to learn that it amounted to nearly $11 million. She was also surprised to learn who would benefit the most from her husband's death. According to the will Dan left, after Annie Laurine took her share (she got the Ontario hunting lodge in addition to the $250,000) and other small bequests were paid, the residue of the estate, more than $10 million, would go to Matilda. Annie Laurine took immediate steps to contest the will.

The biography of the Dodge family points out one moral, over and over: The presence of a large fortune tends to bring out the worst in people. Annie Laurine, who, only months before, had stepped away from her switchboard in Gore Bay, must at the time of her marriage have considered the claim to an eventual inheritance of $250,000 a piece of rare good fortune. It took only a few months—and a few trips to Meadow Brook Hall, with its stables, kennels, large staff and luxurious atmosphere—to make her see the situation quite differently. Her expectations had already been raised. While she was in Michigan for her engagement party in May, Dan had shown her the place he and his mother had decided Mr. and Mrs. Daniel Dodge would live. It was an eight-bedroom house on the estate that had originally been built for Alfred Wilson's nephew. Work to get the house refurbished and ready to be the home of a Dodge heir was going forward when he died. He and Annie Laurine must have talked about their future in that house and their other plans as well. It did not take long for her to realize that $250,000 and the hunting lodge in Ontario were definitely second best.

On the other hand, there is the spectacle of Matilda Rausch Dodge Wilson fighting hard to hang on to the $10 million she suddenly found herself in line to inherit. The saloon-keeper's daughter already had millions of dollars, and she was surrounded by all the luxury that money could buy. Yet not even grief over her beloved son's death could make her behave generously toward his widow and persuade her to offer some kind of settlement. Matilda was determined to keep every penny that her son's will left her.

The determination of Danny's widow to get her fair share of his estate hardened into feelings of enmity for the whole family. (The fact that they treated her like a second-class citizen probably didn't help either.) With no support from them, she managed to endure the ordeal of the coroner's inquest, which determined Dan's death to have been accidental, even though his injuries from the explosion were definitely not fatal, and even though no one could understand why the injured man had not been wearing one of the life belts with which the boat was equipped. Once that unpleasantness was behind her, she petitioned the court to grant her a monthly allowance of $33,000, an amount she deemed necessary to continue living in the style to which her thirteen-day marriage had accustomed her. She was initially granted $5,000, and then the amount was increased to $7,500. While the fight over Dan's estate dragged on, she was able to live in comfort. She tried going to college—taking a commercial course, she told the press, to enable her "to better handle her business affairs." But she couldn't seem to settle down to her schoolwork, and left after part of a semester.

In the summer of 1940, Annie Laurine agreed to a settlement of her suit to break her husband's will. She got about $2.5 million in cash, in return for giving up all further claim to the estate of Daniel Dodge or to the trust fund left to Dodge heirs by John Dodge. Six months after the settlement, Annie Laurine remarried. Her second husband, Dr. Lange, was the Detroit plastic surgeon who had treated the scars left on her face by the explosion that killed Dan. Lange was a strong personality, who seemed to offer some stability in her life. Ironically, he turned out to be an unstable person himself, given to violent outbursts and particularly resentful of the fact that many people assumed he married Annie Laurine for her money. Two years later, she was in a divorce court, testifying about her husband's strange ways, which included "discipline" of his young wife. Ten days after the divorce, she married her third husband, a young army officer stationed in Detroit.

Annie Laurine's was only one of the many lawsuits that were filed as the family squabbled over the inheritance of the huge trust fund left by John Dodge. When Winifred, Isabel and Frances learned that the bulk of their brother's estate would go to his mother and his widow, they jumped in with suits of their own. They claimed that Danny's trust should not be regarded as his own personal property to be willed as he chose, but as an integral part of the original trust set up by John Dodge, and thus should be divided in the same way as the original trust. They were so sure of the validity of their claim that they shared in the out-of-pocket expense involved in Annie Laurine's settlement. At almost the same time the sisters filed their suits, John Duval entered the fray with his own suit to try to claim a larger share of the estate of John Dodge. If everyone else in the family, including a widow of thirteen days of marriage, was getting more money, why shouldn't he?

Matilda must have felt as though she was under siege. In addition to her stepchildren, even her own daughter was trying to snatch from her the money to which she considered herself legally entitled. Perhaps it was an instinctive need to tighten defenses on her perimeter that made Matilda decide at this moment to tear down the dream house John Dodge had almost finished building in Grosse

Pointe. It had been on the market for years without finding a prospective buyer; her lawyers told her the property would probably be more marketable when the house was pulled down and the ground cleared, so someone else could begin building his own dream house. Allowing it to remain standing brought nothing but an annual tax bill of $7,387. Eventually the property was sold to developers, who tore it down and constructed a dozen "executive homes" on the property. The demolition of John Dodge's "castle" made the front page of both Detroit papers when it was begun in September 1941. It was news because it was the definitive end of an era, a tacit recognition that the twenty-one years that had passed since John Dodge's death had so altered the circumstances of the family as to make his hopes and dreams for the future irrelevant. Soon the tree that he had spent so much money and care in moving to a new location died, and then the tunnel to the water, simply closed at both ends, filled with gas and caused an explosion in one of the newly built houses (which happened to belong to a member of the Ford family). Today all that is discernible of John Dodge's grand design is the peninsula he constructed to provide a good place for Horace to dock his boat when he came to visit.

John's son John Duval was another failed hope. After his half-brother's death, John Duval's lawyers came up with a number of hair-splitting reasons why the settlement he had received when he initially contested the will in 1921 was invalid. But this time around, he got no support from his sisters, and the court eventually decided that the 1921 agreement was watertight. The disappointment soured John Duval's already uncertain temper, and his erratic behavior—usually under the influence of alcohol—increased.

John Duval Dodge was well known to the local police department, so perhaps they were not terribly surprised when a complaint they received on the night of August 12, 1942, turned out to involve him. Residents of a house on Van Dyke Place, a quiet middle-class street on the edge of Indian Village, called to say they had seen a man apparently trying to break into a house there. When the squad car arrived on the scene, the cops met John Duval, then in his mid-forties, in the doorway of the house in question, drunk and abusive. Lying dazed on the living-room floor was his wife, Dora. The side of her face was bloody, and there were fragments of a cut-glass bowl in her hand. John Duval belligerently refused to identify himself, refused to identify the owners of the house in which he and his wife were found, refused to explain what had happened. The police put him in the car and took him down to the station.

Later investigation established some facts. After a night of carousing in bars, John had decided to go visiting. He arrived at the house on Van Dyke Place, on the doorstep of a woman identified by the newspapers as an "unemployed interior decorator who called herself Mignon Fontaine." The woman let him into the house, where she rented rooms on the second floor. But then, for reasons that were never specified, she asked him to leave. What ensued was a scene of tragicomedy. John Duval left and then tried to climb in a second-floor window as Mignon fled out the front door; when he found the house empty and left again, she tried to return. This ludicrous chase was still going on when Dora arrived. As it happened, she was spending the evening with friends who lived next door. It is not clear whether she realized what was happening at Mignon's house before she went there. According to her version of the story, she simply went next door with a glass bowl to fetch some more ice cubes, found her husband in the house, and was attacked by him because he thought she had followed him there. Mignon later claimed she was unable to say what happened between John and Dora, because she was hiding in the bushes outside the house (and resolutely stayed there during the visit by the police).

But the real mystery was not what happened in the house on Van Dyke Place, but what happened at the police station after John Duval was brought in. The police said Dodge was so drunk and disorderly that, while resisting an attempt by several officers to move him from one room to another, he fell backward onto the terrazzo floor and hit his head. Others suspected that he might have fallen while alone, due to his drunken condition. Still other, darker, suspicions, fanned by varying accounts by other prisoners, focused on the question of police brutality. Whatever the cause of Dodge's fall, the result was a skull fracture, and John Duval instantly lapsed into unconsciousness. He was taken to a nearby hospital, and his wife was notified. At first the doctors mistakenly assumed that his was a simple case of drinking to excess, but soon they realized the full seriousness of John Duval's condition and did all they could to save him. Nevertheless, he died in less than twenty-four hours, without ever regaining consciousness. Only Dora was at his side.

It took many weeks of sifting through the evidence to try to find answers to the question of how John Duval died. There was a lengthy formal inquest that concluded by labeling his death accidental. A later police department investigation failed to find any evidence of wrongdoing by the police who arrested and restrained him.

John Duval Dodge's sordid death was sadly in keeping with his troubled life. He was given the funeral of a black sheep: a brief service at a funeral chapel, attended by a small crowd, many of them reporters. His first and second wives and his sisters, Winifred and Isabel, were the chief mourners, although other members of the family sent flowers. Matilda Wilson was conspicuous by her absence. She was unable to forgive her stepson, even in death, for his scandalous behavior. At the insistence of his sisters, John Duval was finally reunited with his father in the family mausoleum. His first wife, Marie, settled down quietly in Grosse Pointe, remarried, and raised their daughter, Mary Ann. His second wife sank out of sight until her death made headlines in 1950. She was in a car parked on the railroad tracks that was hit by a train; Dora was killed instantly. It was not clear whether she had intended suicide, or had had too much to drink and fell asleep without realizing where she was parked, or had been attacked and left there purposely. No firm answers to these questions were ever established.

In life and in death, the Dodge family was constantly in the news. Matilda, who liked to believe that the divorces in the Dodge family were all on the other side, was chagrined in 1948 to find that her daughter's divorce was a hot new item. Frances and Jimmy Johnson had been separated for much of the war, but when he got out of the service they returned to Meadow Brook Hall together along with their daughter, Judith, who was born in 1941. Frances also owned a country place in South Carolina, and after the war, she purchased a large horse farm in Kentucky as a headquarters for breeding and training her harness horses. Her horses continued to triumph, but she and her husband could not seem to find a way to coexist. They were divorced in 1948. Matilda, to whom the evils of divorce were becoming an obsession, was angry over that event, and even angrier when she discovered that Frances was planning to remarry soon, and that her new husband was also a divorced man. When Frances married Frederick Van Lennep, there was an open breach between mother and daughter, and Frances moved out of Meadow Brook Hall, never again to live there.

Matilda might cringe to see how frequently the children of John Dodge were in the headlines, but their publicity was probably exceeded by that of the children of Horace Dodge, who came in for their own share of attention and unflattering headlines.

A case in point was the publicity surrounding the filing of a $2-million lawsuit that charged Delphine Dodge Godde with alienating the affections of Irish boxer and would-be crooner Jack Doyle from his former wife, an actress named Judith Allen. According to the complaint by Allen, she and Doyle had planned to reverse their recent divorce with a full reconciliation. But in the fall of 1937, Delphine had completely destroyed that optimistic possibility "by offering him several hundred thousand dollars for the purpose of creating a life of luxury for him, and by giving him many gifts amounting to many thousands of dollars." Delphine had met Doyle when she was in Reno, establishing residence in order to obtain a divorce from Tim Godde. Lawyers retained by Anna after the filing of the Allen suit quickly learned that Delphine and Jack Doyle had definitely been intimately involved, a fact they discovered when Doyle was pursued by bill collectors for the unpaid rental of the secluded cabin he and Delphine had occupied at Lake Tahoe, plus his gambling debts while they stayed there.

After Judith Allen filed her suit, with maximum publicity, Doyle left Delphine and headed for New York. It appears that she was sorry to see him go. The lawyers wrote Anna dryly, "In view of the fact that Mr. Doyle does not know the exact whereabouts of Mrs. Godde, I urged her not to make any attempt to contact him, on the grounds that his conduct towards her did not warrant her pursuing him any further."

The press soon got hold of the story, perhaps through Doyle himself, since he was hoping to generate enough publicity to allow him to embark on a national tour with his new singing act. The beleaguered Anna sent Hugh Dillman out to the West Coast to keep Delphine under wraps—and away from Jack Doyle. She then urged her lawyers to settle the suit with all due haste. Anna must have been a trying legal client. One day she wrote a letter suggesting they try to get Judith Allen to make a statement to the papers that she and Delphine had both been taken advantage of by Doyle, who had played on their sympathy, a story Anna seemed to think would clear Delphine entirely. The next day brought a letter from her in an entirely different tone, complaining that "you evidently do not realize that I wish this case settled—definitely— once and for all—immediately." She went on to threaten, "If you cannot do this, then we must find someone else who can." Her lawyers wrote their fractious client soothing letters and continued to negotiate quietly with the actress's lawyer to get her to drop the suit in return for a reasonable out-of-court settlement. Their success was demonstrated by the fact that, in May, Judith Allen's complaint was withdrawn. Her lawyer told reporters she "had made up her mind she would not marry Jack Doyle again if he was the last man in the world."

The settlement the actress got for dropping the suit of course came straight out of the pocket of Anna Dodge Dillman. Her control over the Dodge fortune translated into perpetual control over the lives of her children, who seemed willing to give up their autonomy in return for all the financial blessings she could bestow on them. They kept acting out the role of naughty children, and she reciprocated by playing the disappointed parent each time they sinned anew. Back in the early 1920s, when Delphine and Horace *were* young, the psychodynamics of this role playing was relatively harmless. The "children" overspent their allowances, they asked for more money, they got it with a little lecture on the need for economizing. As these two naughty children aged, the scenario took on darker overtones. They weren't just careless; they were destructive. They left behind them a trail of broken marriages, lonesome children, shattered dreams and promises that cost other people a high emotional price. Most of all, they were self-destructive. Unable to discipline their desires for instant gratification, and, all too frequently it seems, gratified by their own abasement, they drank to forget, and the drinking caused more behavior that needed to be forgotten.

Delphine succumbed to her self-destructive urges with the speed she had always loved.

As soon as the Judith Allen suit was settled, Anna took Delphine on a trip to Europe, hoping that time and distance would allow her present notoriety to die down. As it turned out, the Doyle escapade was really the last act of defiance or will that Delphine was allowed. Anna promptly engineered a reconciliation between Delphine and Tim Godde, although there is evidence to suggest that the relationship was never very warm thereafter. Delphine spent her remaining years virtually shut up on her estate, Deltim Farms, in Rye, New York, isolated and unhappy. With little to do but brood over the past, it was inevitable that she would drink even more heavily. The alcoholism led to frequent illnesses, which became more and more severe. There seemed no way to save her from her downward course.

Due to the physical ravages of acute alcoholism, Delphine's sad story came to an end on June 18, 1943, when she died in New York. Her husband was with her; her mother, who had been there earlier, had left to go try to solve some problem of her son's. At the time of her death, Delphine was only forty-three years old, still reed slim and small-boned, with a beautiful face. She was an accomplished pianist, good enough to have soloed with small local orchestras, and an expert driver of cars and boats. Her possessions were enough to make any woman envious: the estate in New York, beautiful furnishings (many of them gifts from her mother), a fashionable wardrobe that was continually restocked from a Detroit store that kept a mannequin with Delphine's measurements, so new clothes could be perfectly fitted before they were sent to her, and a jewelry collection that included the pearl necklace of Catherine the Great that Horace Dodge bought Anna back in 1920, as well as a very expensive diamond necklace and more than fifty other significant pieces incorporating diamonds and pearls. But none of it had been enough to diminish Delphine's pain, and in the end the only thing she really wanted was oblivion . . . which she found in alcohol.

Delphine's body was taken "home" to Rose Terrace—a home she had never lived in—for the funeral. After the service, the heavy bronze casket, completely covered with a blanket of white orchids, was carefully slid into another niche in the Dodge mausoleum. Four members of the younger generation had now joined John and Horace there; half of the hope for the future of the Dodge family had already gone. Anna had only Horace Junior left; Matilda had Frances; Winifred and Isabel had one another.

Delphine's will made her mother the executor of her estate. That was certainly reasonable, since most of her estate consisted of debts to her mother. The debts were incurred in the natural assumption that Anna would die before Delphine. The money that Delphine had been advanced would then simply be deducted from her share of the Dodge estate. Now that the natural order had been reversed, Anna had to sell most of Delphine's property in order to repay herself. Some personal items were kept for the children, but

After the death of her daughter, Delphine, Anna Dodge established herself in the role of family matriarch. (Historical Society of Palm Beach County)

everything else was dispersed. Delphine's widower, Tim Godde, was persuaded to drop his claims to anything from the estate by a promise of a lifetime income of $4,000 a month, paid to him by Anna. He married again, his choice of a wife being Delphine's maid. The daughter of long-time Dodge employee Tom Parish still remembers the sad spectacle of seeing little Anna Ray Baker clinging to this unlikely pair and calling them "Mommy and Daddy."

Years before she died, Delphine had ceased to be an effective parent to her two daughters, Christine Cromwell and Anna Ray Baker. Like most children of the rich, they were away at school a great deal of the time. Even their vacations were not spent with their mother, but with other relatives. Christine saw her father, Jim Cromwell, frequently, even during the period of his marriage to Doris Duke. He remained concerned about her welfare, but he could not see her regularly, since he had embarked on a career in politics that took him away for months at a time. (He eventually was named U.S. Ambassador to Canada.) Christine's grandmother Eva Stotesbury sometimes took her during vacations. A letter she wrote to Anna in the spring of 1938, while Christine was staying at the Duke house in Hawaii, is typical of the way the young teenager's life was arranged, often at the last minute, by her parents and grandparents:

> I am particularly anxious to talk to you about our dear Christine, to learn what your plans and Delphine's may be regarding her for the summer months. . . .
> Christine seems to adore her Honolulu life, the riding, swimming and outdoor existence they all live there evidently suits her active temperament. She has just persuaded her father to give her a pair of horses for her own use and that of a groom or a friend. I am sure she would be perfectly willing to stay in Honolulu, if your plans are such that it would be inconvenient for you to keep her, or she could come to me for half the summer at Bar Harbor, provided she had a companion. . . .
> Perhaps you have already decided what you wish to do with her and will be good enough to let me know what, if anything, I can do to help.

As Eva's letter makes clear, even as early as 1938, Anna Dodge acted *in loco parentis* for Delphine's daughters. It was to her that their schools wrote to ask about holiday plans and changed sched-

Cousins Diana Dodge (left) *and Anna Ray Baker pose on the staircase at Rose Terrace, allowed for this one occasion to stand on the marble treads.* (Detroit Free Press)

ules. It was also to Anna that the girls wrote about all the things that happened at school. Christine's letters, first from Cranbrook, in Michigan, and then from the Fermata School, in Aiken, South

Carolina (where Frances Dodge Johnson had a country estate), were jolly, chatty, always amusing. She told her grandmother about the funny things that happened with her friends at school, about going skiing and discovering that snow wasn't as soft as it looked, about her difficulties in learning to live on her allowance, which she illustrated as flying away on wings! "Cece," as she was nicknamed, was a bright and charming young girl—and also a lonely one. Her letters always concluded with pleas for more correspondence, with hopes for seeing someone from the family soon, with an outpouring of love. Sadly, one recognizes that her letters were rarely answered, and never in the same tone of open-hearted affection.

It must be admitted that at least Anna did her duty, not only for Christine and Anna Ray, but for the children of Horace Junior's two marriages as well. All four had become casualties of their father's repeated marital problems.

Horace finally filed for divorce from Muriel in April 1938. He charged her with cruelty, instancing that she had made disparaging remarks about him in front of other people. It was actually a passionless divorce; the two of them had long since vented the real fury of their wrath in their fights and a previous spate of lawsuits that were all settled before going to trial. When the principals finally appeared in divorce court, the newspapers noted that Muriel testified "in a marked British accent." The terms of the divorce were essentially the terms of the separation in 1932. Muriel was to continue to get $30,000 a year, and she was also to be the beneficiary of a $1-million trust fund Horace would set up for her at the time in the future when he received his own inheritance.

Their children, David and Diana, remained in school in England until the end of the term. Thereafter they lived at Rose Terrace with their grandmother, who to all intents and purposes raised them. It was an obligation she took on dutifully, if not joyfully, and she succeeded in providing them with a sense of stability and showed concern for their well-being. David and Diana

A romantic Horace Junior holds hands with his third wife, attractive chorus girl Mickey Devine. (Detroit Free Press)

responded by treating her with respect and some measure of affection.

Despite his frequent protestations that he would never do any such thing, Horace married Mickey Devine the following year. They eloped to Maryland, where they were married in a small ceremony with only the officiating minister and the required witnesses in attendance. One year later, their relationship still a happy one, Horace and Mickey returned to the "scene of the crime" and were married all over again, in a religious ceremony aboard Horace's yacht, named *Vanities* after the show in which Mickey had once appeared.

Delphine Della Dodge had her debut at Rose Terrace, her grandmother's house, in 1939.
(Detroit Free Press)

Life with Mickey seemed to absorb all of Horace's energies. Thus it was Anna who gave Horace's daughter Delphine her coming-out party during the Christmas holidays of 1939. Delphine's

debut was one of the most lavish parties ever given at Rose Terrace. There were about 700 guests, dozens of the trademark ice
swans filled with caviar, an orchestra so the young people could
dance. The thousands of fresh tropical flowers had been flown in
from Sandy Loam Farm, and its owner, Hugh Dillman, was invited to join the combination Christmas/debut celebration, along
with his sister Mary, who had stayed in touch with Anna. Mary
wrote to Anna afterward:

> Oh! Anna I just can't get over thinking about our good
> time at Christmas and wasn't it grand that we have it to
> think about. To think that we could all be together and be
> there for Delphine's party was just too wonderful. Hugh
> had such a good time and did so thoroughly enjoy it.

Christine Cromwell's debut the following summer was almost a
carbon copy of Delphine's, with the deb in demure white organdy
and Anna encased in heavy brocade with a massive pearl necklace
to set it off (another purchase from the estate of Edith Rockefeller
McCormick). Horace took advantage of the occasion to introduce
Mickey to the rest of the family. Pictures show her impeccably
dressed and quite beautiful, but according to eyewitness accounts,
she was very nervous throughout the entire party, fearing that she
would be harshly judged by what she referred to as Horace's society friends.

For the sake of her grandchildren and their entrée into society,
Anna entertained lavishly at Rose Terrace that entire summer, in-
viting guests from her regular list and her new "Young People"
list as well. A sample menu, from a dinner for twenty-two guests
on June 27, 1940, included not only the usual fresh beluga caviar,
but also green-turtle soup, poached salmon, chicken breasts on
slices of Virginia ham, avocado-and-grapefruit salad, and homemade vanilla ice cream with fresh strawberry sauce.

Perhaps Anna's finest hour as a hostess came the following spring,
when the Duke and Duchess of Windsor made their first visit to

Christine Cromwell's debut at Rose Terrace was one of the biggest parties ever given by Anna Dodge. (Detroit Free Press)

Palm Beach. The Duke was at that time governor-general of the Bahamas, and the glamour of his brief rein as King Edward VIII of England and the romance that led to his abdication in 1936 had not yet worn off. The Duke and Duchess were guests at several

The patio at Playa Riente was the scene of Anna's greatest triumph as a hostess, her reception for the Duke and Duchess of Windsor on their first trip to the United States after their marriage. (Historical Society of Palm Beach County)

intimate dinners (including one for twenty-four guests given by Winifred and Wesson Seyburn) but the largest party given in their honor was held at Playa Riente. The honor was probably due at least as much to Hugh Dillman's prestige as president of the Everglades Club as it was to Anna's wealth or social standing, but the combination put them ahead in the social sweepstakes.

A long line of limousines began to arrive at Playa Riente promptly at 5:45 P.M., and the 500 guests were cordially greeted by Anna, Hugh and Captain Alastaire Mackintosh, a personal friend of the Duke who had left England to become the owner of a cocktail lounge on Worth Avenue called "The Alibi." When everyone was assembled, the royal couple was formally escorted out on the patio and thence to one of the loggias, where "tea" was served. (The menu consisted chiefly of cocktails and countless pounds of beluga caviar.) A newspaper account of the great event said, "The honor guests remained on the loggia until 7 o'clock, when they retired briefly with their hosts to a small room off the west loggia, then left quietly to get ready for dinner at the home of Herbert Pulitzer." To her chagrin, Anna was not invited. The snub increased a feeling of bitterness about the whole occasion. Ten years later, she told her son's wife (Gregg Dodge) that the Windsors had been rude guests, with their staff interfering with all Anna's arrangements and their little dogs yapping at everyone's feet.

Horace was proud of his mother's triumph, but she saw little of him during this period. His happiness was proving to be as evanescent as his previous wedded bliss. By March 28, 1944, Mickey had filed for divorce. Her complaint charged that Horace had forcibly taken jewelry from her person, that he had hurled a typewriter at her head and that he had openly lived in London with an English actress. Horace fought back, alleging that Mickey was frequently abusive to him. Mickey's response was to hire a private detective to follow Horace to gather more information about his activities and to increase the amount of the settlement she was asking. A brief attempt at a reconciliation ended, Mickey said, when Horace assaulted her in his Park Avenue home.

The fight over the divorce grew progressively more bitter. Mickey was seeking alimony of $100,000 a year, plus $90,000 to cover her legal expenses in obtaining the divorce. (Her actual costs eventually totaled $103,123, making hers the most expensive divorce action on record at the time in Manhattan's courts.) Mickey climaxed her disparagement of Horace by saying that he had been perpetually drunk from the day of his induction into the army, and added that he was nothing but a detriment to America's war effort. Within days, it was announced that Horace would be retired from active duty. It seemed that the army more or less agreed with Mickey.

Horace's entry into the army was a blatant example of the power of money and influence even during wartime. With no military experience whatsoever and few skills useful to an army, Horace managed to enter the United States Army in July 1942 with the rank of major. There was soon such a deluge of protest over this show of string-pulling that the army was compelled to issue a statement about why Horace had been given a commission.

> Mr. Dodge was recommended for appointment by the commanding general of the Army Air Forces on July 22, after a board of officers had passed upon his qualifications and found him to possess qualifications as a well-known expert and exponent of speedy small craft used extensively by the Army in landing and other coastwise operations, which make his services desirable.

In actual fact, Horace spent most of his time providing R & R for his commanding officers. He maintained a suite in a Washington hotel, and took with him an employee who regularly mixed his drinks and tasted his food. Horace entertained lavishly at the hotel, and on occasion also on the Dodge yacht. The *Delphine* had entered the war, having been commandeered for service with the navy; for the duration, it was used by Admiral Ernest J. King. There was, however, a tacit agreement that when the *Delphine* was not in use, it could be "borrowed" by Horace, who invited the top brass from his outfit to join him in long days of heavy drinking. Rumors flew around Washington about the wild parties Horace was supposedly involved in, and no doubt that gossip was one of the reasons the army began to regard him as an embarrassment. At the time of Mickey's divorce action, Horace entered an army hospital, where he stayed for several months, being treated for the tactful complaint of "exhaustion." The army was thankful to find a reason to remove Horace from active duty, and after a time, he was discharged. For the rest of his life, Horace enjoyed being called "the major."

Mickey got her divorce in early 1945, along with a million-dollar settlement, some of it so secretly arranged by Anna's lawyers that

Horace's home in England, St. Leonard's Castle, sustained extensive damage from bombing raids in World War II because it was so close to Windsor Castle. (Collection of David Agresta)

not even Horace knew about it. But Horace had not given up on the noble institution of matrimony; he promptly married wife number four. Her name was Clara Mae Tinsley, and she had been a nurse during the war. She was not an actress, nor was she a beauty. She was a jolly person, who liked to have a good time; she could match Horace drink for drink. Later, Horace would say she was his favorite among all his wives, but his mother did not share that feeling. She refused to have any sort of relationship with her new daughter-in-law, which made the propinquity of "the gray house," as the family called the house next door, too great for anyone's comfort. So when the war was over, Clara and Horace went back to England, to live in St. Leonard's Castle. Because of its proximity to Windsor, a target for German bombers, it had suffered several direct hits. St. Leonard's had also suffered from being turned over to the United States Embassy for official use during the war. Much renovation and redecoration had to be undertaken to turn the castle back into the residence of a rich American.

By all accounts, the years of hard drinking and emotional disappointment had not diminished Horace's charm, when he wanted

Boat racing was the one arena in which Horace Junior could boast of genuine accomplishment. Here he accepts a trophy from President Harry S Truman. (Collection of David Agresta)

to display it. In the hospital at the time of his divorce from Mickey, for example, he was a popular figure because he tried to cheer up the other patients. (One of his efforts was a turkey-roasting competition between himself and the hospital chef, with everyone on the floor getting to sample the results.) Tom Parish's daughter remembers how he insisted on buying her trousseau when she got married in the 1940s. Big cardboard boxes kept arriving from the most prestigious stores in Detroit, and one of her new dresses was so expensively exquisite that it made her mother cry when comparing it with the wedding dress she had so lovingly made by hand for her daughter.

But the charm could vanish as rapidly as it appeared, to be replaced by an aggressive and abusive hostility. He made scenes, called people names, threatened and bullied. He was, in fact, very much a Dodge. The problem was that he was a Dodge without a goal, without the spur of need to drive him into constructive accomplishments. And he was a Dodge whose mother juvenilized him by keeping him dependent on her. She hushed up his indiscretions, bought off the consequences of his careless actions. As time went by, mother and son became locked in their *folie à deux*.

Anna and Horace became noticeably more dependent on one another after the death of Delphine in 1943, and that dependence increased further with Anna's deepening estrangement from Hugh Dillman. Their reconciliation had not lasted very long, or gone very deep. Hugh could be called upon for such duties as rescuing Delphine, or receiving the Windsors, but, by mutual preference, most of his time was spent at Sandy Loam, playing the role of the country squire. He claimed that it had all started as an experiment for the benefit of the poor: "I planned to try to prove whether or not an average negro could make a living off of a three-acre farm, if he were industrious and really worked at it. I found it couldn't be done. . . ." After the experimental farm came the flower business, then the herd of Jersey cows, and some Black Angus for beef. A 1941 article in a Palm Beach newspaper described Sandy Loam at that time: "Today it is 380 acres, a model community with curving, tree-shaded drives; beautifully landscaped grounds; a master's log cabin house that resembles a beautiful stage setting; cottages housing seven families and a staff of from 30 to 40 employees; greenhouses, a dairy, an airport and subsidiary buildings." Hugh told the reporter that he had given up his night life in favor of the fun of "poking around the farm in old clothes and a big hat." Local gossip suggested that the quiet life at the farm had other attractions; as one long-time resident put it, the fun out there was "on the gay side." In the Palm Beach gossip, Hugh's homosexuality was an open secret.

Hugh treated Anna correctly but distantly. For instance, he wrote her a lovely letter in early 1942 (on Sandy Loam Farm stationery, imprinted with a trio of green palm trees), when his benefits from the Dillman trust, set up a decade earlier, finally terminated. "I want to tell you how much I have enjoyed and appreciated all of the benefits derived from the trust and how generous I think you have been with me." An amicable divorce finally came in 1947 on the innocuous grounds of abandonment. Anna testified in court that they had lived apart for seven years and that Hugh no longer spoke to her. After the divorce, Anna took back the name of her previous husband, and spent the rest of her days as Mrs. Dodge. Hugh sold the farm and moved into an apartment in Palm Beach, continuing to serve as president of the Everglades Club until 1950. Shortly thereafter, he returned to Ohio to live near his sister. He died there, far from the wealth and glamour he had once enjoyed, in 1956.

At about the same time that Anna parted company with the man who had helped her create her life-style, she also lost the model upon whom the life-style was patterned. Eva Stotesbury had begun to have problems of her own when Edward Stotesbury died in May 1938, just a little over two months after his eighty-ninth birthday (celebrated with the usual party). Only a few weeks earlier, Eva had written to Anna, "Ned is improving beyond our fondest hopes. He lunched . . . at the Everglades Club today and got a silver vase as a prize for the 'best dressed and most popular man in Palm Beach.' This did him more good than a dozen doctors and nurses." His death was a sorrow to her. Moreover, it came as a nasty surprise to discover that the estate he left was relatively small and not at all liquid. Eva inherited the three great houses—El Mirasol, in Palm Beach, Whitemarsh Hall, in Philadelphia, and an oceanfront house in Maine—but she had no money with which to keep them up.

Eva faced her situation gallantly. She put all three houses on the market, but buyers for such great mansions were few and far between in 1938. If she couldn't sell the houses, at least she could sell the furnishings. Her dear friend Anna Dodge came to her aid by buying many of Eva's things: $113,855 worth, to be exact. Her selections ranged from a pair of backgammon tables in the billiard room to the eighteenth-century commode in Eva's bedroom, topped with marble, covered with ormolu and signed by Riesener. Anna, of course, had little need for additional furniture, although she did add the choicest pieces to her collection. Much of what she bought from Eva was sent to Horace in England, since St. Leonard's still had some empty space. It arrived there on the eve of World War II, and a letter to Anna's lawyer from Horace's long-time secretary, Sarah Helmick, noted, "By the way, tell Mrs. Dillman that the Stotesbury stuff is pretty mothy, and we must take extra care to keep the moths out of the carpets."

Eva also sold her jewelry, which was quietly "placed" by Cartier. She then closed the houses in Maine and Philadelphia (Whitemarsh Hall was sold within a few years) and concentrated all her resources on keeping El Mirasol going. There were rumors, strongly denied by Eva, that the house would be turned into a nightclub, but not even for that ignominious purpose could a buyer for El Mirasol be found. For much of the duration of the war, El Mirasol was closed, and Eva lived in a modest apartment in Washington—whose rent was paid by none other than Anna Dodge.

Eva returned to Palm Beach after the end of the war and gave one or two parties at El Mirasol. She died on May 23, 1946. Her things were dispersed in an auction at El Mirasol the following winter. The catalog listed the highlights:

XVI Century Ispahan Rugs
Modern Oriental and Spanish Apujarra Rugs
Chinese and European Porcelains
Fine Silver, Table China, Glass, Linens
French and English Colored Engravings
Oil Paintings of the Flemish, Dutch,
Italian, English Schools
Library of Books in Fine Bindings
Garden, Patio and Loggia Furniture
Four Thousand Potted Tropical Plants

There were crowds at the auction, but still no one wanted the house itself. Addison Mizner had died, broke, a decade earlier, and his standing as an architect was in question. Moreover, it was clear that in the postwar world it would be harder than ever to staff such a big place and keep it up. Newer houses were smaller, easier to manage with only a small staff. Eventually, El Mirasol was torn down, and an entire development of such newer, smaller homes was built on its acreage. All that remains today is the elaborate Moorish arch that was originally the entrance to the Stotesburys' fabulous home.

Anna still lived in Playa Riente during the winters, and she had added a pool on one of the patios for the benefit of grandchildren and great-grandchildren. But the part of her personality that wanted to be a leading hostess of Palm Beach died with Eva Stotesbury and was lost in her marital breakup.

Henceforth, she would play the role of matriarch.

12

The Matriarchs Reign Supreme

Anna and Matilda had been at odds from the time John Dodge divorced Anna's friend Belle to marry his former secretary. After their husbands died, relations deteriorated even further. Matilda was scandalized that Anna would give Delphine a big wedding so soon after John's death; Anna thought Matilda showed signs of wanting to interfere in the running of Dodge Brothers whenever she visited the factory. With every passing event—a wedding, funeral or society party—the rift deepened, until there was nothing left but the most perfunctory of surface civilities. The final straw was Matilda's discovery that Anna had placed the ashes of their sister-in-law, Delphine/Della Dodge Ashbaugh, in the Dodge mausoleum at Woodlawn Cemetery, against Matilda's wish to have no further association with her husband's sister.

Newspapers had always equated the two women as the Dodge widows. But aside from the coincidence of marrying brothers who were extremely close, Anna and Matilda had very little in common. As the years passed, their differences became more and more pronounced.

Thirty years after the death of John Dodge, Matilda was deeply rooted at Meadow Brook, the home that still bore traces of the strong-willed man who bought it as a country retreat. The original farmhouse, where John entertained his cronies, was still standing, and the family still played golf on his private course. The root cellar, the greenhouse and the power plant were also constant reminders of the man who earned the money for the later improvements. Even the Hall, always referred to as the Wilson residence, incorporated many elements of John Dodge's unfinished dream house in Grosse Pointe.

Yet Matilda had stamped her own personality on top of the foundation laid by John Dodge. She turned a rustic retreat into a civilized country estate, complete with prize-winning livestock and such amenities as brick pig barns where all the animals were automatically given showers as they entered. The former haunt of political and business cronies became a focus of lavish society entertainment. One of Detroit's "greeters"—the man hired to stand at the hostess's elbow and announce the names of all the guests at a party—recalled, "Mrs. Wilson could give the biggest parties I ever saw. She'd pack in 600 or 700 people without batting an eye."

But by the 1950s, grand entertainments at Meadow Brook Hall were increasingly rare. The debut of Barbara Wilson in June 1950 was one of the last big parties held there for purely private reasons. Thereafter, when the big kitchens behind the *faux*-Tudor dining room were operating at full capacity, it was most likely to be for a civic function of some sort. Most of the time, Matilda and Alfred were alone in the vastness of the mansion.

That loneliness was largely due to Matilda's own preference. Her habitual method of dealing with family problems was simply to cut off all contact with the offender. Eventually, everyone had been cut off.

Matilda's sister, Amelia, had been the first to be banished. In fact, she lived for many years with her husband in a modest house

Isabel Dodge Sloane, whose life in Palm Beach was an almost continuous house party, relaxes by the pool with a guest. (Historical Society of Palm Beach County)

in the nearby town of Rochester, and she never stopped taking an interest in the children she had frequently looked after when they were small. But from the time Amelia married "beneath her," Matilda ceased communicating with her. Thenceforth Amelia was reduced to following the doings of her relatives by reading about them in the newspaper. It was not until the two women were both widows that Matilda could once again bring herself to speak to her sister.

Matilda's breach with her eldest stepdaughter had come in the early 1920s, when Winifred had the temerity to divorce William Gray and marry Wesson Seyburn. When Isabel supported that decision and invited her sister to be married from her home in Long Island, Isabel too became *persona non grata*. The two sisters, in

Isabel Dodge Sloane (left) *and her sister Winifred Dodge Seyburn, attend a thoroughbred race in the 1950s.* (*Detroit Free Press*)

control of their own fortunes, went their own ways, maintaining only ritual contact with Matilda. Isabel never had children; Winifred had four daughters. They grew up with only minimal contact with their stepgrandmother.

One by one, Winifred's daughters married, and most of their husbands were socially prominent men. (Peggy Gray married the son of the pretender to the throne of Portugal.) The focal point of their family life was the Seyburn mansion in Grosse Pointe, where they all gathered every year for Christmas with their own children. They were closer to their cousins on the Horace Dodge side of the family than they were to the residents of Meadow Brook Hall. Their aunt Isabel was an integral part of their lives as well. Winifred and Isabel maintained their deep emotional intimacy as long as they both lived. The gregarious Isabel continued to entertain lavishly, and her Brookmeade Farm stables continued to win the most prestigious of the thoroughbred races. She lived life to the hilt until her death in 1962.

Of course, Matilda had stopped all contact with her stepson John Duval from the time of his impetuous marriage. Her own son, Danny, died in disfavor because of his choice of bride as well. Next to be ostracized was Matilda's daughter Frances, and again it was marital plans that triggered the separation. As she aged, Matilda's horror of any sort of marital irregularity increased. It would be interesting to know how she reconciled these views with her own past conduct in dating a married man and waiting for him to obtain a divorce so he could marry her. Was her extreme disapproval of divorce due to the prickings of her own conscience? Or had she kept the secret of John Dodge's second marriage so long and so well that she had virtually forgotten it ever happened? Since she never broke her silence on the subject, she took the answers to these questions to the grave.

Frances and her second husband were married at her horse farm in Kentucky, and that home became their primary residence. Frances enlarged her stables, and continued to win ribbons and races with her harness horses. Fred Van Lennep was as keen on racing as his wife was, and proved an interested and able help-meet. There were two children of this marriage, in addition to the daughter from Frances's first marriage, to Jim Johnson. Perhaps because of the children, communication was gradually re-established with Meadow Brook Hall. Eventually, Frances bought a house in Indian Village as a sort of *pied-à-terre* in Detroit, and during the last years of Matilda's life, Frances and her husband and children became regular guests at Meadow Brook over the holidays.

Matilda's adopted son, Richard, was another one who fell out of favor, thanks to his decision in 1950 to marry a Catholic and convert to that faith. Matilda not only did not attend the wedding, but also never laid eyes on his bride, and ignored his children. Richard calmly refused to be antagonized, and continued to visit his parents regularly, despite the fact that they appeared not to notice his presence. Over time, he managed to effect a limited reconciliation, although it never included his own family.

Thanks to this proclivity for thrusting people out of her life when they displeased her, Matilda found herself isolated at Meadow Brook Hall, with only Alfred for company. It appears that the big mansion became oppressively lonely, for in 1952 Matilda and Alfred began building a small modern house on the Meadow Brook property. They named it Sunset Terrace and referred to it as their "retirement home"—which says something about the burden a huge establishment such as Meadow Brook Hall can be. Sunset Terrace specifically represented the personal tastes and inclinations of Alfred Wilson. The house turned its back on grandeur and sought, instead, an atmosphere of coziness and convenience. The style of the house was imitative of Frank Lloyd Wright's work, which the Wilsons had seen in Arizona (where they had a modest winter home called Miramonte). Sunset Terrace was a sprawling two-story structure with big windows providing views of the rolling hills and a lovely terrace enhanced by a fountain and reflecting pool. The house could be maintained with a small staff, and it was altogether more domestic an environment than that provided by the high ceilings, elaborate carvings and drafty corridors of Meadow Brook Hall.

With few family concerns left to occupy her, Matilda in the 1950s turned her thoughts increasingly toward the larger community. She is even today remembered warmly as a pillar of the First Presbyterian Church in Detroit, and a portrait of her as a gray-haired woman of distinction still hangs on the wall there. The Reverend Joseph Vance—who had been intimately connected with the Dodges from the time he talked John Dodge into donating the money for a community center sponsored by the church until he conducted the simple funeral service for Daniel Dodge—had retired, but Matilda retained her close ties with the church. In addition to regular attendance at Sunday services, always accompanied by Alfred, she was also a faithful member of the Ladies' Guild. Church fund-raisers recall that she could usually be counted on to respond to requests for donations.

Matilda gradually became involved in other good works for the community. In part, her participation arose from the serious thought she gave to the question of what would become of Meadow Brook after her death. It was clear that the postwar world would be a very different one from the era in which the property had been assembled and the mansion built. Already, in the early 1950s, many estates like Meadow Brook were being sold to developers, who pulled down the great houses and subdivided the land for the maximum profit. With her usual strong will, Matilda was determined that would not happen to *her* estate.

In 1956, Matilda made a decision about how to preserve Meadow Brook. She would give the estate to Michigan State University, as the site of a new campus in Oakland County. The initial gift was 1,400 acres of property, along with $2 million to start erecting the new buildings. For the period of her lifetime, she reserved the 127 acres that were the heart of the estate, along with both Meadow Brook Hall and Sunset Terrace. After her death, this property too would pass to the newly created Oakland University.

From the moment she made her decision, Matilda found a new

and absorbing interest in life. Suddenly her calendar was full. There were dignitaries to entertain at Meadow Brook Hall, ceremonies such as groundbreakings and dedications that demanded her presence. Everywhere she went, the elderly benefactress of Oakland University was treated with a delightful deference that always put her in a good mood. She enjoyed watching the young people for whom the university was home, and particularly enjoyed their recognition of *her*. It was her pleasure to greet them with a wave and a cherry hello as she whizzed around "her" campus. So much did she identify with Oakland University that she even enrolled in a course there, one for efficient reading.

Matilda's emotional commitment to Oakland University became greater than her personal checkbook could sustain, so she began to use her connections to drum up additional financial support for the school. At her urging, Samuel Kresge and H. L. Kettering each donated the money for buildings named in their honor, and other acquaintances were tapped for sizable contributions. The rapid growth of the university owed much to the hard work of its chief patroness.

Participation in the wider world proved to be good for Matilda. The activity spurred by her involvement in the university spilled over into other areas of her life. She attended civic functions, remained committed to her agricultural breeding programs. Whatever her sorrows and losses in the family, she was too busy to brood over them.

As Matilda used the strength of her deep roots at Meadow Brook to turn outward toward the interests of the larger community, Anna Dodge grew ever more peripatetic, possibly in an attempt to escape the burden of family worries that she carried on her stooped shoulders. As the controller of the purse strings of the enormous trust left by Horace Dodge, Anna used the money to try to bribe, cajole and discipline her unruly descendants into behaving as she wished.

Like Matilda, Anna desired that her family do as she pleased. But Anna had a different strategy for bringing about that result.

No matter how annoyed she became, she did not follow her sister-in-law's example and cut off communication with the miscreant. Instead, she contacted her long-suffering (although well-paid) lawyers, bankers or men of business to arrange some economic carrot and stick. Sometimes it was enough merely to threaten. For example, young Delphine Dodge, the daughter of Horace and Lois, received the following letter in 1942, when she was planning to leave Bryn Mawr before graduation:

> I was not only shocked and bitterly disappointed at the news your father brought me that you are leaving college, but I was utterly ASTOUNDED that you should show so little foresight and so little gratitude and appreciation of the opportunity for education that has been given you.
>
> Next year will be your last one—the gayest and easiest of any college year. Your degree will mean in these uncertain times a protection and a guarantee which nothing else can give you just now. . . . Everyone has to be on his own now. Christine's husband has to support her and their baby with no help from me. The question of livelihood and the earning of one's own bread and butter is to be faced, and faced seriously.
>
> I am hoping that your innate sense of right and self appraisal will cause you to reconsider this move which can only mean a personal loss to you which can never be redeemed.

This heavy-handed letter served its purpose. Delphine graduated from Bryn Mawr the following year.

Anna's demands fell particularly heavily on her grandchildren. Friends recall that they all dreaded the so-called treat of a trip on the luxury yacht, *Delphine*; all the caviar, French furniture and organ music in the world could not dispel the uncomfortable feeling of being prisoners of their grandmother. She insisted on being called "Ma*ma*" (pronounced in the French fashion), and she de-

The Delphine *was formally furnished: the card room; a guest bedroom such as the grandchildren might occupy; the sitting room in the master-bedroom suite.* (Collection of David Agresta)

Bud and Delphine Dodge, the children of Horace Junior and Lois Knowlson, are pictured at a Detroit social event in the early 1940s. (Detroit Free Press)

manded that her grandchildren behave like proper ladies and gentlemen at all times. When they visited her at Rose Terrace, it was like going to a museum. They could not sit on the priceless chairs that had once belonged to Marie Antoinette, or touch the sculptures by Clodion, or even walk on the antique rugs that covered the parquet floors; and when they descended the grand staircase, they had to hug the edge of each step, so their feet would be on the hard marble rather than the irreplaceable blue runner.

No wonder they preferred to go next door to Horace's house to play. The gray house, although furnished in keeping with a rich man's tastes, was much more of a home, and Horace was the last man in the world to fret over the fate of a few sticks of furniture.

He liked to see his and his sister's children enjoying themselves, and he even liked to join in their fun. One of the features of his house was an underground passage from the basement out to the secret party room under the front lawn, which provided an ideally creepy spot the kids all loved. One of Horace's favorite tricks was to hide in the passageway and scare those walking through it; after the screams of delighted terror, he'd sweep the victims up in a big hug. The next move was usually a suggestion that they go out in the boat, and boat trips with Horace were full of thrills and high speed. There might even be a pretty "aunt" along to fuss over everyone.

As the children grew older, the gray house offered the opportunity to listen to popular music, to have friends over without benefit of chaperons, perhaps even to raid the bountiful supply of liquor. It was much more fun than Rose Terrace, where the daily schedule was arranged to suit the convenience of an elderly valetudinarian.

As a father or uncle, Horace was all charm and irresponsibility. His mother felt it was her duty to act as a counterbalance in the children's lives by emphasizing duty and discipline, qualities they rarely saw demonstrated by the adults around them. The combination proved a bad one for the children, who were by turns indulged, disciplined and ignored. Today, Anna Dodge's grandchildren express their appreciation of her willingness to accept the responsibility for them when no one else seemed interested or willing. But even the descendants who speak of her with the most gratitude are unable to remember many genuinely warm moments in their relationship with their grandmother.

In view of the way these "poor little rich kids" were raised, it is not to be wondered at that the members of this generation of Dodges were attracted to the idea of setting up their own households as soon as they were old enough—or even before. In the love of a spouse and the independence of their own homes, they hoped to find the warmth, the stability, and the control over their own lives so obviously missing in their childhoods.

Christine Cromwell, Anna's oldest grandchild, was also the first to marry. The eighteen-year-old "debutante of the year" made headlines by eloping with young Frederic P. White on May 12, 1941. They were married by a justice of the peace in Elkton, Maryland, and told their families informed only several days later. Fred, a few years older than Christine, was the son of a New England banking family that went to Palm Beach every winter, so he and Christine had known one another for years. They settled down on Cape Cod, and Fred joined the navy when the United States entered World War II. Their daughter Marilynn was born nine months after the wedding, and a son, Frederic P. White, Jr., a year after that.

But the marriage, so impetuously begun, foundered quickly; in fact, Christine and Fred separated even before the birth of their second child, in the spring of 1943. They were divorced in Florida two years later. Custody of their two children was given to Fred White's parents. Christine rarely saw the two children of her first marriage until they were nearly grown, at which time she exclaimed over the perfections of Marilynn, telling Anna Dodge that the girl was everything she had ever hoped for in the previous generation. At the urging of Jim Cromwell, who remained in touch with his grandchildren and his ex-mother-in-law, Anna Dodge augmented the senior Whites' support with funds that permitted the children to go to good schools and enjoy pleasant vacations. Yet they spent most of their time with their father and his family.

The press loved to describe Christine as "the Dodge heiress," but in fact she had almost no money of her own. After her separation from Fred White, she returned to Palm Beach. But the big houses of her two grandmothers, El Mirasol and Playa Riente, were closed for the duration of the war, so Christine lived in a room at the Everglades Club and worked as a clerk in a shop on Worth Avenue. A friend who knew her in those days remembers the youthful Christine as a warm, attractive and vital woman determined to find the happiness that had so far escaped her. Although she was already the mother of two children, she behaved

Christine Cromwell, in fancy dress and an ermine cape, is escorted to a Palm Beach party by her father, Jim Cromwell. (Historical Society of Palm Beach County)

like a girl herself. When Eva Stotesbury opened El Mirasol again at the end of the war, Christine moved in with her grandmother, and she was treated like the spoiled daughter of the house. She entertained there frequently, for she was so pretty and animated

Delphine Dodge Petz was a war bride, married at her mother's home. She and her husband later settled in Detroit and raised a family of nine children. (Detroit Free Press)

that she had lots of friends. Active and athletic, she enjoyed the chance to ride, play tennis, go out on a boat. She was also taking flying lessons, and she told friends it was for the sole purpose of dropping her wedding ring in the ocean when her divorce was final!

A few weeks after Christine won her divorce (on the grounds of cruelty), she married her second husband, Edward Williams, in an elaborate ceremony, complete with a white dress and a huge bridal bouquet. The dark-haired Christine made a beautiful bride. It was the third wedding in the family in a little over a year. Her cousin Delphine had been married the previous spring at her mother's home in White Plains. The groom was Robert Petz, a native of Detroit, who, like many young men at that time, was in the army. The former Lois Dodge gave her daughter the rose-point lace that had embellished her own 1921 wedding dress to wear on this special day. Since her divorce from Horace in 1927, Lois had married and divorced two more husbands; at the time of her daughter's wedding, she was on her fourth marriage. Her first husband was present to give their daughter away, resplendent in his major's uniform. Anna Dodge was among the honored guests at the small ceremony.

Delphine Petz had nine children. She and her husband settled down in Grosse Pointe to raise their large family, and their eldest daughter, Virginia, was married just one month after the death of her great-grandmother Anna Dodge. Delphine and Robert were subsequently divorced, in 1971, and she retired to live quietly on a farm outside Detroit. Her children still play an active role in Detroit society.

Even smaller than Delphine's wedding was the ceremony that united Horace and Lois's son, Bud (Horace Elgin Dodge III), to his fiancée, Margery Gehman, on October 26, 1945. The artistic daughter of a college professor, Margery seemed unimpressed by the newspaper headlines about the Dodge fame and fortune, and told reporters she and Bud simply looked forward to a quiet domestic life. But Horace Dodge somehow got it into his head that Margery was interested only in Bud's money (of which, of course, there was none at the time; not even Horace had any money to call his own, and his son had nothing but his military pay). Still, Horace—who certainly ought to have become expert at recognizing people who marry for money—opposed the match.

Due to the exigencies of wartime, Bud's wedding was to take place in Denver. Horace set out to go there for the sole purpose of preventing the nuptials. En route, he was somehow sidetracked in Louisville and never got any farther. Inquiring reporters were turned away at the door of the house where he was staying by an attractive blonde named Betty Tinsley, who was none other than the sister of his future wife, Clara Mae. Six years later, this same

Betty Tinsley would sue Horace for $250,000 for assaulting, beating and bruising her. It seems his relationship with his sister-in-law was even more tempestuous than that with his wife.

Now, Betty announced that Horace was "resting." He did rouse himself long enough to telegraph poor Bud's commanding officer and ask him to confine the young lieutenant "until he comes to his senses." Bud and Margery were married without further ado. Several months later, the newlyweds had a meeting with Bud's father, at which time Horace was thoroughly captivated by Margery and dropped his opposition to the marriage. The rapprochement was capped when Horace posed for photographs sitting in Margery's lap.

Bud and Margery had six children, one of whom died while still a toddler and is buried in the Dodge mausoleum in Woodlawn Cemetery. They eventually settled in Southern California, where Bud went to work as an executive at General Electric, and lived the life Margery said they longed for: a quiet, simple, family-oriented existence. They remained on cordial terms with Anna Dodge, writing to her periodically, entertaining her when she was in California, and even naming one of their children Anna, after her. Margery died recently, and young Anna remains at home, keeping house for her father.

David Elgin Dodge, the son of Horace and Muriel, was another Dodge heir who yearned for the quiet life. A brilliant amateur pianist who strongly resembles his grandfather Horace, David became an architect, was associated with Frank Lloyd Wright at Taliesin West, and still spends much of his time there, promoting Wright's architectural legacy. He married a German woman, a former governess named Anneliese. They have one son, and divide their residency between Switzerland and the Southwest. In 1980, David launched the renovation of Detroit's Orchestra Hall, originally a gift to the city from the Dodge Brothers, with his own donation of $25,000 and his architect's interest in the plans for rehabilitation.

David's sister, Diana, turned out to be another horse fancier in the family. In her teens, she always begged to be permitted to use her allowance to buy and care for horses, and today she alternates between a horse farm in North Carolina and an even larger one in Virginia. Something of a recluse even as a child, Diane seemed uncomfortable with the social demands of being a young heiress. She fled the party scene as soon as she was old enough to act independently. She has never married and is closer to her horses than she is to any human being except her brother.

While the children of Horace Dodge tried to find their adult happiness in lives of relative stability, Delphine's daughters were still making headlines. Christine, still looking for Mr. Right, married and divorced a series of husbands in rapid succession. She and Ed Williams were divorced in 1950, in an atmosphere of great bitterness (although her ex-husband continued to write affectionately to Anna Dodge for some years, addressing her as "Mama Dear"). Christine was given legal custody of their son, Ned, but he was sent to boarding school at age six and spent his vacations with his father, so her contact with the boy was minimal. In the late 1950s, Jim Cromwell commented with amazement on the fact that Christine's children from various marriages had never met.

Christine's next husbands, in order of succession, were Bob Hoffman (divorced on the official grounds that he was "chiefly interested in her money"), Ray Asserson (also known as Bob Ellis, a nightclub singer from the Virgin Islands), and another Virgin Islander, John Christiansen. The last suffered a mental breakdown, and Christine had to fight to try to preserve his assets. Her last marriage was to the captain of her yacht. As they sailed away on their honeymoon, Christine told the press that this was the marriage that would last forever, but by the time they sailed back again, she was ready to file for another divorce. With each husband, Christine was sure that she had finally found Mr. Right, but none of the marriages endured for more than a few years. Warm-hearted, affectionate and romantic, she suffered from the repeated disillusionments. Pictures taken in the 1960s and 1970s show her still-beautiful face embedded in an obese body, her curly dark hair long and unkempt. Yet her eyes are still those of a girl, dreaming of future happiness.

Her tendency toward marital mishap had its price in divorce settlements. It was money she didn't have, since her father had successfully tied up much of her interest in the Horace Dodge estate in an irrevocable trust, to keep it out of the hands of the series of husbands, whom he distrusted as fortune hunters. Desperate to find a way to pay her mounting bills, Christine in 1953 instituted a lawsuit against Anna Dodge and the Detroit Bank and Trust. The charge was mismanagement of her grandfather's estate, in which she had a future one-fourth interest. She claimed that the fortune left by Horace Dodge had been too conservatively managed. The bulk of the trust was invested in tax-free municipal bonds rather than common stocks that might have experienced a capital gain in the rising postwar market, and thus the principal was smaller than it ought to have been.

It is not easy to convict the trust department of a major bank of excessive conservatism, since that is exactly why people choose them to administer a trust. Nor was it likely that a court was going to penalize the elderly Anna Dodge for trying to safeguard the inheritance of her grandchildren. Her testimony was taken at her own home because she was pronounced too old and frail to go to court. Photos show the white-haired matriarch in one of her antique chairs, looking tired but still in control, despite the badgering of the opposition's lawyers.

In an interesting revelation, Anna told the court that all of her decisions as a trustee had been dictated by the late Horace Dodge's wishes:

> I have followed his instructions in this estate from the time that he died. Everything that I have done has been because he told me to do it that way. He told me that they eventually would probably have to sell Dodge Brothers if anything happened to him, and that the other estate [the heirs of John Dodge] would want to get some money out of it,

and that I'd have to sell. "If you do that, then I want you to invest in municipal bonds and tax exempts." He said, "There is money enough in the estate for everybody," but evidently there is not enough for Christine. . . . He earned the money, he had the right to tell me what to do.

The outcome of the lawsuit was slow but inevitable. In 1954, the court found that Anna and the bank had acted correctly.

The ingenious Christine subsequently came up with a new way to raise the money she needed: She began to sell "futures" in her eventual inheritance. Through a formal document of absolute assignment, she granted speculators a fixed share in the money she would inherit from the Horace Dodge trust after her grandmother died, in return for their cash payments to her. This brainstorm was to net Christine more than $9 million over the next fifteen years. Of course, no one, including Christine, knew exactly how much she stood to inherit. It all depended on how much Anna had, how she spent it, and how much longer the elderly matriarch would live.

The lawsuit severed relations between Christine and her grandmother for a time, but by 1957, Christine had resumed letter-writing, to keep Anna abreast of developments in her eventful life, including another divorce and subsequent remarriage. Anna responded by sending her granddaughter a Saint Christopher's medal for protection! At about the same time, Anna decided to try to curb Christine's sale of her inheritance by granting her a monthly allowance of $2,500 later raised to $4,000, to be counted as an advance against her share of the estate. In essence, it was the same program Christine was already following, trading future expectations for present cash, but it was with relatives instead of strangers. Anna's ledgers show that by 1967, the money Christine had been advanced already totaled $820,000.

At the time the lawsuit for mismanagement of the trust was decided, Anna also ended her legal guardianship of Christine's half-sister, Anna Ray Baker, who had previously announced to the family that henceforth she was to be called "Yvonne." By the time of her twenty-first birthday, Yvonne had already run away from home, found herself a husband and produced children. Kenneth Allinson was a news announcer on a Virgin Islands radio station whom she had met while visiting her half-sister. Yvonne and Kenneth Allinson had two children: Anna Yvonne, born in 1952, and Kenneth Junior, born in 1953. That marriage ended in divorce, and Yvonne married again. Her second husband was Thomas Bason, who became the father of her daughter Rhonda, born in 1957. Yvonne divorced Bason in 1959. Her third marriage, in 1961, was to Jim Ranger, whom she had met through their mutual interest in horses. In Jim, Yvonne found the strong man she had been looking for, and since their marriage, he has taken control of their shared existence. Gentle, friendly, and somewhat vague, Yvonne today is content to live the life of a quiet homebody in California, and to leave most of the major decisions to her husband. He has shown a special interest in collecting many of the Dodge family possessions that might otherwise have been scattered, like so much of the family's past: old Dodge cars, boats, furniture and warehouses full of other items from the various Dodge houses. Included are pieces from their own Detroit house, once the residence of Horace Junior, which was demolished in the early 1980s.

However difficult some of the grandchildren might be, they could not hold a candle to Horace when it came to creating problems for Anna Dodge to solve. Typically, the solution most in demand was more money.

Mother and son were together in Palm Beach in the winter of 1950–51, and pictures show Horace with the stout physique of his father and uncle but the pouched eyes and blurred features of a bored roué. Before the winter was over, he was in Good Samaritan Hospital because of a heart attack. It was an intimation of the toll his self-destructive behavior was beginning to take on his body and spirit. Even with the best of medical care, Horace was slow to recover, and from that time forward, he was never free of health problems. Directly or indirectly, they were related to his heavy

drinking, and some of them were severe enough to curtail his freedom for months. For example, he fell and broke his leg while he
was on a binge, and the complications that ensued were so dire
his doctors thought at one time they might have to amputate the
leg. After weeks of hospitalization and months of convalescence,
he was still permanently in need of a cane, or, when he needed to
go any distance, a wheelchair.

But even such drastic limits on his mobility could not keep him
out of trouble. A story told about Horace by a Palm Beach historian involves a night of carousing in 1962. He was then living in
the elegant Palm Beach Towers, and his wife hoped to keep him
there, so she gave instructions that if he had a few drinks and
called for a wheelchair, the doorman was to say they were all in
use. Nothing daunted, Horace rang for a bellboy to help him dress
and went downstairs to take a cab next door. While paying the
cab driver, he dropped a $10,000 bill on the street, where it was
later found by a dishwasher at the hotel's restaurant. Typically,
Horace didn't even notice that the bill was gone. The police traced
the serial number back to him, a feat the chief said they managed
simply by asking themselves what citizen of Palm Beach would be
most capable of the folly of carrying such a large bill around with
him. They discovered that in fact it had been one of six $10,000
bills the family lawyer had brought Horace from Detroit only that
morning.

Horace much preferred hotels to homes, perhaps because hotels
were the only places he could get the kind of service to which he
had become accustomed. He often played tricks on the staff. Once
during a stay at New York's Madison Hotel, he ordered hard-
boiled eggs from room service and kept sending them back because they were raw. When the room-service manager came to
apologize, he discovered that Horace had bought a dozen raw eggs
at the grocery store and was substituting them for the ones sent
up from the hotel kitchen. Even his amusements were those of a
boy.

Throughout the decade of the 1950s, the high-spirited Horace partied, he drank, he spent money he didn't have, he concocted wild get-rich-quick schemes, he fell madly in love . . . and none of it made him any happier. He was truly one of the saddest cases in a generally sad family. Young Horace Dodge started out with more advantages than most people get in one lifetime. When he was in grade school, the family was comfortably well-to-do, and by the time he entered his teens, his father was a multimillionaire. In addition to all the privileges that money could buy, Horace Junior had natural assets as well. He had a quick mind, a prankish sense of humor. His immense charm and *joie de vivre* drew others to him. He was fun to be with.

Perhaps what was most remarkable about Horace was that, throughout a life that grew progressively more disreputable, he retained a romantic vision of the world and his place in it; surely that was the source of his inner sadness. He wanted so much to be everyone's knight in shining armor. That was his attitude toward every woman he married (and many he didn't). He loved the process of courtship, and he enjoyed giving a woman everything she had ever wanted. Underlying the drunken buffoonery, there was an innate warmth and tenderness that were just as attractive to women as his willingness to spend his money on them.

The woman that he wanted most to be able to protect and care for, of course, was his mother. He did his best to play the cavalier in her eyes, and he was happiest in the moments when that dream could come true—when, for example, he played the host at her wedding to Hugh Dillman, when he was her dashing escort to a society party in Palm Beach, and when he thrilled her with one of his racing victories. When a reporter inquired about the name Horace had given his most successful boat, *My Sweetie*, he quickly and unself-consciously identified his mother as the honoree. All during his life, Anna Dodge *was* her son's sweetie and occupied the place of honor in his heart.

But the sad truth was that he was unable to live up to his idealized vision of himself. He wanted to achieve the status of his father, with the success and respect the auto pioneer had won, but

The ailing Horace Junior escorts his mother, his only true "sweetie," to a Palm Beach society ball. (Collection of David Agresta)

the reality was that every business with which he became involved lost money. He intended to cherish and protect his wives, but sooner or later the romance would wear off and the fights would begin: He was much better at being a lover than a husband. His greatest failure was with his mother. He wanted to be independent and manly, to dazzle her with his accomplishments, to impress her with his acumen. He imagined that he would look after her in her declining years; instead, he remained her bad boy until the end of his life—a constant burden and concern to the elderly woman. She, in her turn, manipulated him through her control of the family fortune, and kept him in a state of childlike dependence.

Horace's troubles escalated significantly when he divorced his fourth wife and married his fifth. He and Clara had separated in October 1950, before he suffered his heart attack. But, following his usual pattern, he made no move to obtain a divorce until he wanted his freedom to marry someone else. There was a separation agreement, later ratified in a Michigan divorce court, that gave Clara what was reported to be a million-dollar settlement; that seemed to be the accepted price for giving Horace his freedom.

In the early 1950s, there was widespread gossip that Horace's next wife would be his former sister-in-law, Florence Sisman. Florence had been a telephone operator from Alpena, Michigan, when she married Muriel Sisman's brother Buhl Andrew, at about the same time that Horace Dodge married Muriel. On the face of it, Andrew did not seem like a great catch: A diving accident had left him with a hunchback and delicate health. His earning capacity seemed questionable, and his inheritance was not likely to be large. Although Sisman *père* was a respected Detroit businessman, his financial affairs were shaky, as evidenced by the fact that as soon as his daughter had married into the Dodge family, he tried to borrow money from Horace and Muriel. Later, his company was given the contract to make tool boxes for all Dodge cars.

The talk in Detroit was that Florence had married Andrew because her job gave her the opportunity to overhear Horace's telephonic courtship of Muriel. Aware of the future connection between Sismans and Dodges, she aggressively pursued Andrew as her avenue of entrée into the moneyed world. This bright idea worked for a while, but then Horace and Muriel separated acrimoniously, and people named Sisman were no longer welcome at any Dodge home.

Slowly, Florence worked her way around this barrier. She hung around Horace until he grew to tolerate her presence. To increase the propinquity, she set up a little company that did packing and shipping, on the strength of a contract with Chrysler arranged by a friend. The premises of Kenneally and Sisman were located in the warehouse district down by the waterfront—and just across the street from Horace's boatworks. Thus she was able to see Horace often, in the relaxed atmosphere of heavy drinking and salty language where Horace most felt in control. Almost intolerably peppy, Florence was willing to run any errand, carry any message, and help with any scheme that Horace asked her to.

Where Horace always needed the most help was in his finances. He began to send Florence as an emissary to his mother, to pave the way for his next request for a "loan." At first, Florence was only allowed to use the back stairs of Mrs. Dodge's residence, but then Anna, too, came to recognize her usefulness as an intermediary. Through Florence, Anna's painful business of bargaining with her son could be conducted without the involvement of her lawyers, who always made their disapproval of Horace's conduct palpable. Over time, Florence was first tolerated and then needed, as an adjunct to the relationship between Anna and her son.

Evidently Florence had hoped that her efforts to cultivate a relationship with Horace would culminate in marriage. But her hopes were dashed in late 1951, when Horace fell madly in love with the woman who would be his fifth and last wife.

She was a beautiful blonde actress—Gregg Sherwood. Born Dora Mae Fjelsted in 1926 back in Beloit, Wisconsin, she got her career start when she and a girlfriend she was visiting in Raleigh entered

Gregg and Horace Dodge share an affectionate moment in the early days of their relationship. (Detroit Free Press)

a beauty pageant as a lark. Dora Mae won the title of Miss North Carolina. She was immediately signed by the famous modeling agency of the 1940s, John Robert Powers, and went to New York in search of fame and fortune. Powers had the idea that with her brown hair and regular features, she would photograph like another Rita Hayworth. A few shooting sessions proved that assumption erroneous, so he suggested that she dye her hair blonde. At the same time he helped her choose a new name, Gregg Sherwood. As a blonde, she was quickly successful. She posed for magazine covers and did a well-known Chesterfield ad. Modeling led to offers to appear as a showgirl in the Vanities revue, and in Mike Todd's revue called "As The Girls Go." She was the Colgate Comedy girl on television, appearing in sketches opposite such stars as Eddie Cantor and Abbott & Costello. After that came Hollywood, and a contract with Twentieth-Century Fox.

It was just about the time she signed her movie contract that Gregg agreed to model elegant and expensive clothes in a charity fashion show in Palm Beach. Anna Dodge had bought tickets for the affair and asked her son to escort her. Horace was instantly captivated by the glamorous blonde model, and caught her attention with a typically lavish gesture: He bought all the outfits Gregg had modeled, including a fabulous sable coat, and sent them to her as a gift. When Gregg went to Hollywood (where she appeared in five movies, including *Tomorrow Is Another Day,* in which she costarred with Ruth Roman) Horace continued to pursue her. In the spring of 1952, Horace gave her a trip to Europe—her first— that culminated in an engagement party in Cannes, where their betrothal was announced to the world, although Horace was still technically married to Clara Tinsley. The announcement was sealed with a 32-carat diamond ring worth more than $100,000.

But the course of this romance was anything but smooth. Even before the wedding, Horace and Gregg argued and made up with such intensity that it seemed they would surely destroy one another. They quarreled so bitterly on the night of their engagement party that Gregg threw her ring out the window. Horace had all the employees of the hotel on their knees searching the shrubbery for the valuable diamond, but Gregg refused to accept it again after it was found. Later, Horace bought her another engagement ring, of similar size, from Harry Winston in New York.

Another widely publicized blow-up came when Gregg was visiting Horace in Detroit. After a night on the town, they went back to the gray house and had a tremendous row. Gregg stormed out of the house with her luggage, and Horace promptly called the police and accused her of stealing four gold lighters and a box of candy he had put in her hat box. She retaliated by dashing to New York for a date with Joe DiMaggio. Horace had some friends call her and announce that he was seriously ill, to which she replied,

Anna held her son's fifth wedding, to Gregg Sherwood, on the patio at Playa Riente.
(Collection of David Agresta)

"Call a nurse." Eventually the tiff was resolved, and Gregg added a diamond and emerald necklace from Cartier to her growing jewelry collection, which was eventually to be worth more than $3 million.

Despite such dramatic evidence of incompatibility, the wedding plans proceeded. Horace got his divorce from Clara on February 11, 1953, in a suit charging her with mental cruelty and a violent and ungovernable temper. Three days later he and Gregg were married at a small but elaborate afternoon ceremony on the patio at Playa Riente, in the very same spot where Anna had once greeted the Duke and Duchess of Windsor. The twenty-seven-year-old bride wore a bouffant blue lace dress with a Peter Pan collar that came from society designer Mainbocher and wept copiously. The freshly

A loggia at Playa Riente lets in the light and air fom the central courtyard. (Historical Society of Palm Beach County)

divorced groom was fifty-two and looked every minute of it. The matron of honor, in overdone pink chiffon, was none other than Florence Sisman. The wedding pictures show Gregg looking demure, Horace content, and the mother of the groom—in a ridiculous flowered hat and a dress of gray and rose silk—rather bemused. (Anna had just left the hospital in order to attend her son's fifth wedding.) After the ceremony, conducted by the pastor of the fashionable Royal Poinciana Chapel, Gregg and Horace left for a honeymoon in Cuba—with her family following in a separate plane.

In retrospect, the pictures of the wedding convey a sense of impending doom. The first to succumb was Playa Riente itself. The big mansion was simply too much for Anna to manage. At the time of the wedding, she was almost eighty-two years old, and she no longer had any great interest in entertaining, or in the work that running two huge houses entailed. In Palm Beach, she preferred to live in a comfortable apartment in one of the elegant new condominiums going up along the oceanfront. She decided to put Playa Riente on the market, but her experience was the same as Eva's: There were no takers for such big white elephants. The heyday of the mansion was long gone.

This property rejected by all purchasers may have been Addison Mizner's masterpiece. It was built on a sandy ridge overlooking the ocean, and encompassed twenty-seven acres. The massive double front doors framed a tunnel that provided a carefully composed view of the breaking surf. The stone entry hall was sixty feet long and two stories high, with a rib-vaulted ceiling. The house was a rectangle, with the long side facing the water, and in the center was a huge patio. The exterior was faced with cut and polished coral stone from the Florida keys that Mizner had submerged in the ocean for months, to obtain just the right antiqued look. Loggias on all sides of the central patio provided a transition from the outdoors to the indoors, and they were ideal locations for setting up a luncheon table in the winter sunshine. Gothic arches made of filigreed cast cement framed the loggias and the entrances to the house.

The sparkle and lightness of the loggias gave way to an impressively regal interior. The high ceilings were adorned by antique beams salvaged from the old University of Seville; the main staircase was grand enough for a royal procession. The dining room featured ceiling and wall frescoes by Florentine artists that were a copy of the decoration in the Davanzati Palace there. The master-bedroom suite was located at the top of its own private tower, with a separate entry hall, and the bathroom there was entered through doors that came from tenth-century Persia. Yet most of the hallways and rooms had a feeling of openness and airiness and gave constant glimpses of the outdoor spaces. The cool tiled floors mimicked ancient cobblestones, and visitors were warned to wear comfortable walking shoes.

The furnishings were a fit match for the house. When Anna bought Playa Riente in 1926, she paid as much to keep the furniture and decorative objects as she did for the house itself. Mizner had accompanied Nell Cosden on trips to Spain to select many of the pieces. Among the most remarkable of their purchases were several thronelike chairs and a living-room rug more than sixteen feet long, with a raised floral pattern, handmade by Spanish nuns in 1595 for the cathedral in Grenada and valued at more than $50,000. Nell Cosden had also bought a set of nine huge murals— all over sixteen feet high—painted by Spanish artist José Sert, a foremost practitioner of mural decoration in the 1920s. The murals, oil and gilt on canvas in dramatic dark reds, black and silver, depicted various adventures of Sinbad the Sailor and were originally executed for King Alfonso of Spain. By the time the murals were completed, the royal exchequer was bare, and the king was unable to accept delivery. On the advice of Addison Mizner, Nell snapped them up and installed them in the ballroom.

When she found she could not sell the estate as a private residence, Anna Dodge hoped to turn Playa Riente into a club. The new Palm Beach Country Club, with an eighteen-hole golf course, had been built at the bend of the road that marked the southern end of her property; if there could be one club in the neighborhood, why not another? But the zoning board refused to allow a second club, and the newspapers ridiculed Anna's pleas regarding the financial hardship of keeping up and paying taxes on such a large and valuable property. Syndicated columnist Malcolm Bingay wrote:

> Not since I was a wee child and read the sad, sad story of "Nellie, the Little Match Girl" have I suffered such grief, as when I read the distressing tale of Mrs. Horace Dodge. The poor dear, down to her last $150,000,000, has been

forced to dispose of her $5,000,000 palace at Palm Beach because the taxes have reached $28,000 a year and the insurance is another annual bite of $10,000. Of course, she might dispose of her $5,000,000 ocean-going yacht, but then what is a woman going to do if she gets the idea she would like to go to sea and has nothing to go to sea in? And you could hardly expect her most delectable son, Horace, if he heard the call of the sea, to use a rowboat.

Those two reactions brought out Anna's mean streak, and she decided to carry out her threat of razing the house so the land could profitably be sold to developers.

On March 10, 1957, Anna Dodge threw her last party at Playa Riente. She invited 125 members of Palm Beach society to help her say farewell to the mansion. The invitation was for cocktails, dinner and dancing. For the space of an evening, it was as though time stood still, and the glorious days of the 1930s had returned: Tables in the loggias held a rich buffet supper, champagne flowed, music played, the tall beeswax candles that were custom-made in Rome at a cost of $100 apiece burned in the great wrought-iron candelabra, the beautiful people in their fancy clothes mingled and chatted. When the party was over, Anna got in her limousine to drive to her new accommodations, a suite at the Everglades Club. As the car turned from the driveway onto the road, she instructed the chauffeur to circle back past the house one more time in a final salute to all she was losing.

A few days later, everything went on the auction block, from the gold-lined sink in the master bedroom to the piano on which the party music was played. The Sert murals were purchased by Anna for $100,000. She later gave them to the Detroit Institute of Arts, but since Sert's stock has fallen in the art world, they have never been put on permanent display. In April, the house itself was razed: the masonry broken and crushed flat, then covered with sixteen inches of dirt.

What memories the house took with it for Anna! Did she think

The dining room at Playa Riente dwarfs a table big enough to seat fourteen people.
(Historical Society of Palm Beach County)

about the days when she was a rich widow and decided to buy the house to consolidate her social climb? Hugh Dillman, who helped her make the purchase and taught her how to live in the style Playa Riente demanded, had been out of her life for decades, and had in fact died just the previous year. Her idol, Eva Stotesbury, had been dead for ten years, and El Mirasol was an empty shell. Delphine, the high-spirited, popular daughter whose marriage had paved Anna's way into Palm Beach society, was also long dead. Anna had survived past the collapse of the world she had known.

Hoping that movement and change would help her forget, she went on cruises, tried a change of air for her health, stayed in her suite at the Waldorf-Astoria or her apartment in Palm Beach or Horace's castle in England. But no amount of travel could separate her from the ghosts of the past, or the sorrows of the present.

Her son Horace was all Anna Dodge had left, and he was scarcely an unalloyed pleasure in her old age. At the time that Anna was bidding farewell to her Mizner mansion, she was also dealing with the problem of Horace's debts. Thanks to his desire to impress his new wife and shower her with gifts, a pack of creditors was angrily hounding the Dodges. The bills he and Gregg had run up since their marriage were huge: $216,964 to Cartier, $83,148 to Bergdorf Goodman, more than $100,000 to a jeweler in Beloit and countless thousands to other smaller creditors. The magnitude of the debts made it necessary for Anna to send her lawyers to try to deal with the situation. They made neat lists of the most pressing bills, negotiated agreements with the major creditors to take a down payment (provided by Anna) and subsequent installment payments as Horace's allowance would permit. But even as the lawyers talked to Horace like Dutch uncles and tried to find ways to contain his financial problems, the debts continued to grow. A letter from one lawyer exclaimed: "You may imagine my surprise when I was informed by Cartier that instead of the indebtedness being $150,000, it had increased to $220,000; and all of the bills had the authorization of Horace." Those bills were for a diamond necklace and a diamond ring for Gregg, perhaps to ease the pain of the planned economic stringency in their future.

Unsurprisingly, the stringency never materialized, and the pattern of spending themselves into insolvency continued. A year later, Gregg was writing to her mother-in-law to tell her they had no money to buy food, the cleaners wouldn't accept their clothes unless they paid cash, the Palm Beach Bath and Tennis Club was about to throw them out because they couldn't pay their dues, and the household help was leaving because their salary checks were always late. Gregg warned that it would all break in the newspapers soon and ruin the Dodge name. She added that this profligacy was chiefly Horace's doing.

In his own letter written later that month, Horace asked Anna for an additional $300,000 to clear up this year's problem, and

A holiday in the sun unites Anna Dodge, Florence Sisman, Gregg Dodge, and Horace Junior. (Collection of David Agresta)

stated self-righteously that most of the indebtedness had been incurred by Gregg. He closed the letter:

> I don't want to worry you by appealing to you again, but I promise that if you help me out at this time I will never approach you again for any future financial assistance. . . . Without your help, Mother, I don't know what I will do.

A touching postscript in Horace's own hand added, "I do love you, Mommy."

It was a hopeless case, made even worse by Anna's own erratic attitudes. For example, in June 1953, when Gregg and Horace were still newlyweds, Anna cabled her lawyers from England: HOLD UP PAYMENT OF BILLS FOR H. AS I TOLD SARAH UNTIL I RETURN NO BOATS TO BE BUILT. A few weeks later, after she had talked to the errant Horace, she told her lawyers to release the money. When they tried to clarify the situation to make certain they had understood her wishes correctly, she denied that she had ever instructed them to withhold any money from Horace. Her irrationality extended to her own expenses as well. The lavish parties were a thing of the past, Rose Terrace was always partially closed, her household bills struck her as distressingly high. The yacht *Delphine* never left her anchor off Rose Terrace (Gregg Dodge later joked, "I thought it was a mural for years") because Anna thought it cost too much to run. On the rare occasions when Anna was coaxed into giving a party, her hospitality was downright cramped: She didn't want to serve food or hire musicians or buy flowers. Of course, she didn't want Horace to do these things either.

Anna had it in her power to stop the childish game she and her son were playing any time she wanted to. Although the terms of the $40 million trust set up by Horace Dodge in 1919 had created the problem by denying Horace Junior either interest or principal during his mother's lifetime, Anna had by this time—nearly forty years later—accumulated an estate of her own that was nearly as large as her late husband's. She could have recognized that the intention of the trust—set up when her son was still a minor—was surely not to keep him dependent on his mother throughout his entire life, and she might have given him enough money to be truly independent. Instead, she chose to treat a man in his fifties like a delinquent child. He retaliated by behaving like one.

Given this background, it's hardly surprising that as soon as the lawyers settled one financial crisis for Horace, they were at it again, making more neat lists that divided the bills into groups labeled "Most Urgent Accounts" and "Current Accounts." Most of the new bills were from the very same tradespeople and shops that Anna had paid off before. Although one of the lawyers wondered aloud at the willingness of these merchants to extend so much credit to Horace and Gregg, the record shows that by and large it was a wise decision. Horace couldn't pay the bills, but Anna would.

The financial problems that faced Horace and Gregg had a de-

Horace Dodge escorts his wife, Gregg, to a Palm Beach party. (Photo courtesy of Gregg Dodge)

bilitating effect on their relationship. If you believed what you read in the papers, Mr. and Mrs. Horace Dodge were one of the happiest couples in the world. Gregg, who had a real talent for publicity, gave interviews that made the Dodges sound almost as wholesome as June and Ward Cleaver. She was photographed in the newly redecorated gray house in Detroit, which she had made lighter and brighter and easier to live in: "I just knocked out walls and opened up everything to the lake." She talked about how much she and Horace were still in love, and demonstrated it by throwing a huge party for their second anniversary. It was a memorable Palm Beach extravaganza with an Oriental theme that was photographed for *Life* magazine and reported to have cost over $16,000. Gregg looked gorgeous decked out in a fortune of jewelry, an antique silk kimono she had ordered custom-made in New York at a cost of $5,000, and face powder laced with real gold sprinkles. Horace looked old and ill and tired in his $7,500 Mandarin's robes.

But the papers carried other stories that revealed a darker side of the marriage. Only months after the wedding, there were reports that the pregnant Gregg had gone home to Beloit, declaring that her health and that of her unborn child were threatened by the constant friction over the couple's finances. Another reconciliation followed, which Gregg described to reporters: "He'd been phoning constantly, but I wouldn't accept the calls. Then he flew up and we saw each other for the first time in a month. I won't tell exactly what he said, but he told me I was right." With that victory, Gregg returned to the Florida sunshine with her husband to await their child's birth, musing, "I must get one of those books on the care of babies."

But that reconciliation, and the subsequent birth of the baby, couldn't keep the relationship on an even keel. Horace seemed to be drifting farther into his own fantasy world. An old friend of the family went to see him and reported back to Anna:

> For the first time since I have known Horace I was really apprehensive about his health. He spoke of disappearance, of flight, and of secreting himself somewhere on this earth where nobody could find him. I have found him very impatient of any questioning of the correctness of his plans of action. He believes he is far from well and thinks his heart isn't too sound.

Horace's old friend and former brother-in-law Jim Cromwell wrote to Anna about his concern over Horace's physical and psychological welfare. As a way to take Horace's mind off his financial and marital problems, Jim proposed that the two of them go into business together (some scheme about uranium deposits) and work in "double harness, just like the Dodge Brothers." Jim painted an attractive picture of the fortune they would earn, along with renewed respect for the Dodge name.

Horace didn't ever get into the uranium game, but he did go to England by himself and live quietly and soberly for a time, causing those who saw him to marvel over how well he was looking. Said one of Anna's lawyers, "Horace looked very well and while he is confined to his wheelchair his face showed strength and resolution and the results of living a normal life in England." Then he returned to the States, and the trouble started all over again. After another fight, Gregg went home to Beloit once more, and promptly got into trouble with the police. According to a story in the *Detroit Free Press:*

> Home for the holidays, blonde ex-model Gregg Sherwood Dodge went on a police-baiting spree early Tuesday with these rapid-fire actions. She sped away at 60 mph from two policemen who stopped her when she ran through a red light. When the two policemen caught up with her, she swore at them until they sent for the sergeant. The sergeant, called all sorts of dirty words, got slapped twice and kicked in the shins. Gregg finally accepted a traffic summons and was led away by a young fellow who had been nightclubbing with her. In a final fit of anger, she turned, pulled what she thought was the traffic summons from her coat pocket, and tore it into shreds. She had torn up her Michigan driver's license instead.

If Gregg could go off to Beloit, then Horace, too, could disappear. Cables to Anna from Gregg indicate that Horace disappeared for four days, and that when the Detroit police located him, he still refused to divulge his whereabouts to his wife.

Horace seemed miserable, unable to live with his wife or without her. Gregg, too, was unhappy. Nothing could have prepared her to face the reality of marriage to Horace Dodge. Often drunk and disorderly, he was a public embarrassment. She still vividly remembers the night he stood on the open roof of a Palm Beach restaurant and urinated on the Duchess of Windsor, sitting at a table below in a white silk dress. In private, he was a weak man who seemed unable to counter or resist his mother's manipulations. Gregg had tried hard to conciliate her mother-in-law, spending hours attempting to entertain her with the latest gossip or a game of cards that Anna was allowed to win. It makes the blood run cold to imagine some of those long evenings *chez* Dodge, with Horace behaving like a drunken buffoon, Anna sitting as silent as a stone with a disapproving look on her face, and Florence running in and out asking if she could take home a ham, an ashtray, or some of Gregg's unwanted dresses. Yet in the end, Anna treated her daughter-in-law with enormous hostility—and Florence did her best to exacerbate Anna's hard feelings. Anna had told Gregg before she married Horace, "Once you become a Dodge, you will be a lonely woman." The prediction was coming true.

Perhaps the chief victim of the whole situation was the son of Gregg and Horace, young John Francis Dodge, who was born on March 18, 1954.

Johnny Dodge was an adorable golden-haired child, just as photogenic as his mother, who frequently sent Anna Dodge studio portraits of the sweet-faced tyke. Horace doted on the child, treating him with the same mixture of winsome charm and neglect that characterized his paternal behavior toward all his children. But Johnny's young life was shadowed by the financial problems of his parents. In a newspaper interview, Gregg once referred to her son as "the richest little boy in the world." It was true that he would eventually inherit a grandchild's share of the large trust fund left by Horace Dodge, and that he could also expect to inherit from his own father once his father inherited his grandmother's estate. Meanwhile, however, Johnny lived in a house that couldn't be maintained because there were old bills to be settled before any new ones could be incurred. He did without medical care because the doctor hadn't been paid. Even his pet could not be looked after properly because the Dodges still owed money to the local vet. The contrast between the public image and the private reality was all too painful.

In 1961, Horace Dodge filed for a divorce from his fifth wife. He charged that Gregg preferred the company of other people and

Horace Dodge helps his son Johnny celebrate his first birthday at their home in Palm Beach in March 1955. (Photo courtesy of Gregg Dodge)

spent most of her time away from him. The subject of her extravagance also came up, as did her temper, which he claimed made him fear for his physical safety. Gregg contested the divorce, and there were hearings in the case. News photos show Horace slumped in his chair, looking unwell and terribly depressed. His lawyers brought in a heart specialist to sit by his side and make sure his health would permit him to testify.

According to Gregg Dodge, the divorce action was a scheme pressed on Horace by Florence Sisman as a way of mollifying his mother and getting her to agree to pay more of Horace's debts. Whatever the inner truth of the couple's relationship, the divorce action was dropped in November 1963. In Gregg's possession is a letter dated November 26:

> Dearest Gregg:
> I do not want a divorce or any other legal proceeding and when the present case comes up I will not appear and you

may proceed to obtain a dismissal of my present action against you.

All my love,
Horace E. Dodge

The latter accompanied a witnessed statement that guaranteed Gregg a monthly allowance and also gave her the right to void any prenuptial agreements should she care to do so.

Horace died on December 22, 1963. At his Detroit bedside were his daughter Delphine Petz, his long-time secretary Sarah Helmick, and Florence Sisman. As his condition worsened, due to the combination of heart problems and liver failure, Anna was summoned from Palm Beach. Gregg says that Horace asked Florence Sisman to summon Gregg as well, but it was a call that Florence never made. Anna Dodge's plane had not yet arrived in Detroit when her son died. His last words were "Where's Mother?"

Poor Horace had become the victim of his "expectations." For thirty years, he had lived with the assumption that his inheritance was right around the corner. He loved his mother, and he certainly didn't wish for her death. But it was a natural assumption that she would die before he did, and that the event, painful though it would surely be, would take place while he was still young enough to enjoy the money to the fullest. His mother was old, she was often ill . . . and the years crept by, and still she lived on, and still Horace had no money of his own. For his entire life, he had nothing to live on except the allowance his mother gave him.

At ninety-two, Anna had lost the last person she ever cared about. Horace's funeral was held at the Jefferson Avenue Presbyterian Church, attended by scarcely more than 100 people. Gregg flew up from Palm Beach for the occasion, and made her appearance dressed in deepest black and protected by a mourning veil. According to newspaper accounts, "she sat apart from other members of the Dodge family." There were flowers from Anna; from Horace's ex-wife Clara (who would herself be dead in a few months);

In a candid press photo taken during their divorce proceedings, Gregg Dodge appears radiantly confident, while Horace seems alarmingly old and ill; he died soon after. (*Detroit Free Press*)

and the biggest floral arrangement of them all, from his son Johnny Dodge.

No more than five cars of mourners made the trip to Woodlawn Cemetery to see Horace laid to rest in the family mausoleum.

13

The End of
an Era

The last years of the two Dodge widows were pathetically lonely.
Yet they seemed to prefer the isolation from their families.

Matilda lost the companionship of her second husband, Alfred
Wilson, when he was stricken with a fatal heart attack in the spring
of 1962, at their winter home in Arizona. The funeral was held in
Detroit, and Alfred was buried in the new Wilson mausoleum at
Woodlawn Cemetery. Constructed of rather feminine pink granite
in a vaguely Art Deco style, it was located on the plot next to the
Dodge mausoleum. Matilda had given a great deal of thought to
the question of which husband she should be buried with, and
opted for Alfred. She had been married to him for a longer period,
and the truth was that she was more comfortable with him than
she had ever been with John Dodge: John ruled her, whereas she
ruled Alfred. At the time of Alfred's death, she moved the bodies
of her two Dodge children, Anna Margaret and Daniel, into the
Wilson mausoleum. That would fill up three niches, leaving the

Judy Johnson prepares to receive guests at her Meadow Brook Hall debut; she is accompanied by her mother, the former Frances Dodge, and her stepfather, Frederick Van Lennep. (Detroit Free Press)

fourth for her, so the rest of the family would have to find other resting places.

After a suitable period of mourning, Matilda moved out of Sunset Terrace, which had been her concession to Alfred's preferences, and back into Meadow Brook Hall. She was all alone in its splendor except for her dogs and her servants. Her daughter Frances observed the proprieties and gave a big party for her on her eightieth birthday, but the relationship between mother and daughter was no longer warm or intimate. Her adopted son, Richard, saw her regularly, but could not be happy about her determination to ignore his wife and children. Matilda had severed contact with her adopted daughter, Barbara, after Barbara got a divorce and talked about going into the nightclub business. Amelia Rausch Cline had moved to Arizona for her health, and even when Matilda was out there in the winter, they saw each other only once or twice a season.

In real need of companionship, Matilda arranged for her twenty-one-year-old granddaughter Judy Johnson, the daughter of Frances's first marriage, to join her. She had always been a favorite with Matilda, from the time she lived at Meadow Brook Hall for several years as a little girl. Matilda had arranged for Judy to make her debut there in the summer of 1960. It seemed that she would make an ideal companion for her grandmother.

Judy, like her mother, loved horses, and Matilda was quick to indulge the young woman by buying her a string of thoroughbreds and planning to build a race track on the estate where Judy could train her race horses. Together, the two women went out for drives with Matilda's hackney horses and planned new additions to the stables of the Belgian draft horses. There were a few happy months, and then the old pattern reasserted itself. Judy fell in love with the local veterinarian, of whom Matilda disapproved because he was older than Judy and especially because his first marriage had ended in divorce. When Judy realized that her grandmother was never going to agree to the match, she eloped. That, of course, was the end of any communication between Matilda and her.

All Matilda had left was Meadow Brook, and "her" university. She was surprised and delighted when the students of the first class at OU gave her a birthday luncheon, complete with a big birthday cake, and touched when the party turned into an annual tradition. She reciprocated by giving the class of 1963, the first to graduate from OU, a dinner dance at Meadow Brook Hall and buying every one of the 175 students a class ring. Her health remained sound, and she continued to work to raise funds for Oakland University, where there was now an enrollment approaching 4,000 students, and to take pride in the growing campus. If she thought about the future at all, she at least had the satisfaction of knowing that Meadow Brook would be safe, and appreciated.

In the fall of 1967, Matilda made a carefully planned trip to Europe. One of the most important stops on her itinerary was Belgium, where she intended to look at some draft horses to buy for the Meadow Brook stables. On September 18, while in Brussels, she suffered a serious heart attack and died. Significantly, it was not a member of her family who flew to Brussels to bring Matilda back home, but three students chosen for the honor by Oakland University. On the campus, all flags flew at half-mast, and a well-attended memorial service was held for the woman who had been the institution's chief benefactress. The public recognition of Matilda's passing left nothing to be desired.

Privately, mourners were few. Frances flew in to Meadow Brook Hall from Virginia, Richard and Barbara were there, and Amelia came from Arizona as a last gesture of reconciliation. The funeral was held at the First Presbyterian Church, with interment in the Wilson mausoleum. Matilda was placed beside Alfred. Her first husband was her next-door neighbor, in the larger Dodge mausoleum, in the company of his first wife, Ivy, their children Isabel and John Duval, and his beloved brother, Horace, as well as Horace Junior, Delphine and Andrew, a young son of Bud and Margery.

The definite preference for identifying herself as a Wilson, rather than a Dodge, that Matilda showed in her burial arrangements was echoed in her will. The bulk of her fortune—all, of course, earned by John Dodge—was left to the Matilda R. Wilson Fund, to be used by its trustees for educational and religious purposes. Through sizable gifts to Oakland University, the Detroit Institute of Arts, the Detroit Zoo and the First Presbyterian Church, the $21-million fund kept the name Matilda Wilson in the public consciousness. It was as if she hoped that posterity would finally erase the memory of her connection to those hard-drinking, heavy-spending, rough-cussing, marrying-and-divorcing Dodges.

Only tiny amounts of Matilda's own money were left to relatives and servants. Frances was given the right to take from Meadow Brook Hall the furnishings and art objects that had been hers or were purchased by her father. Richard and Barbara Wilson each received $10,000, and an educational fund was set up to send their children to college. Sister Amelia, old and nearly blind, got just $7,500. (She lived on until 1984 in a small rented apartment in Rochester.) Of course, Frances had already been given a share of the much larger trust fund left by John Dodge, and her heirs would share in its distribution after the death of the last surviving child of John Dodge, so it was certainly reasonable for Matilda to conclude that she was already well provided for. The others had no further expectations, so her testamentary dispositions were the punishments she meant them to be.

Frances, Richard and Barbara tried to challenge the will, although it stated clearly, "I have been especially mindful of financial provisions that have been made by me and others for my children and I have concluded that each is already well provided for." They tried to prove that the will was vague and did not reflect Matilda's true wishes, but the court ruled in 1969 that Matilda's intentions were unusually clear, and the legatees had to be content with the small amounts they had been left.

Since Matilda had left her two homes, Meadow Brook Hall and Sunset Terrace, to Oakland University, there was little of her estate to be dispersed. The only major dispersal came when about half of her collection of fine paintings, bought in a ten-year period after her marriage to Alfred Wilson, were sold by her executors to raise more money for the Matilda Wilson Fund. Friends had suggested to Matilda that she should leave them as a group to the Detroit Institute of Arts, but she vetoed the idea emphatically, due to a rebuff she felt she had received from the museum in the 1940s. Her will left the paintings as part of her estate, without any direct stipulation as to their disposition, but she apparently envisioned them forever hanging in their accustomed places at Meadow Brook Hall. Trustees felt the risk of that course of action was too great, since the paintings could not adequately be protected against theft or the ravages of humidity and dirt.

Accordingly, they selected the best of the art and arranged to have it auctioned off. A group of thirteen paintings by European masters was sold by the Parke-Bernet galleries in New York in October 1970. The group included Rembrandt's "Portrait of a Soldier," a Van Dyck portrait, Sir Joshua Reynolds's portrait of Winston Churchill's ancestress, the Duchess of Marlborough, and portraits by Lawrence, Gainsborough and Romney. The auction resulted in generally disappointing prices; in fact, the bids for the Rembrandt were so low that Parke-Bernet decided to pull the picture from the sale. The total raised for the fund was only $178,000, a fraction of what Matilda had paid for the pictures, and far below Parke-Bernet's estimate of their value, placed at $500,000. Puzzled gallery officials said there was "no ready explanation" for the unusually low prices. Several months later, two of Matilda's paintings by American artists—a George Washington portrait by Gilbert Stuart and a famous Remington on the subject of moose hunting—were sold by the same auction house, for $310,000.

Only the paintings were removed from Meadow Brook Hall; everything else remained. The university, fretting over the $7,000 to $8,000 a month it took to keep Meadow Brook Hall open, applied to the Matilda Wilson Fund for money to help defray the cost of the building's upkeep. At the same time, in an effort to make the mansion pay its own way, it was decided to use Meadow Brook Hall as a conference center, and also to open the house for tours. Thus most of the furnishings have been left exactly as they were, and visitors can look at Matilda's French-style bedroom, the desk where Danny Dodge did his homework, the organ that played for the parties and weddings and funerals held in the house. Curators are still at work sorting the thousands of letters, preserving the fabric of Matilda's gowns, determining the meaning of the symbols used in the carvings and stained-glass windows. Thanks

During a recent antique-car show, John Dodge's 1919 Dodge sedan was drawn up to the front door of Matilda Wilson's Meadow Brook Hall. (Collection of David Agresta)

to Matilda Wilson's foresight, the great house has been beautifully preserved and is a place to learn about the past as well as enjoy the present.

Although Matilda did her best to submerge the Dodge name under her Wilson identity, the building of Meadow Brook Hall and the purchase of all its splendors were of course financed by the widow's share of the John Dodge trust that Matilda won in court in 1920, and her share of the remaining trust income. Visitors to Meadow Brook proved to be as interested in the Dodges as in the Wilsons. The original farmhouse, the golf course and its clubhouse and the sturdy little greenhouse that John Dodge built are all still in use, and the staff at Meadow Brook Hall has accumulated a wealth of anecdotes about the man who made the fortune that Matilda Wilson had at her disposal.

The bulk of the trust left behind by John Dodge was not to be distributed until the death of the last of his children. That turned out to be Winifred: The first of the Dodge children to be born was also the last to die. In Florida to celebrate her twenty-second wedding anniversary, Frances Dodge Van Lennep died of a sudden acute hemorrhage in 1971, at the relatively young age of fifty-six, and was buried in the Dodge mausoleum at Woodlawn. Winifred's husband, Wesson Seyburn, died in the same year as Alfred Wilson, but she lived until January 1980, dying at the age of eighty-six. Her death opened the door to the final distribution of John's fortune. The trust at that date was worth $44 million, or about the same as its value forty years earlier; it generated an income of $1.3 million annually.

The trust principal might have been smaller than expected, but it was still large enough to stimulate lawsuits by people who hoped thereby to obtain a share. Most of the claims were based on an ambiguous phrase in John Dodge's will regarding the trust. It read, "I direct my said trustees to convey my said estate to the heirs of my said children." Broadly interpreted, this sentence might mean that anyone who had inherited any sum of money from any of John's six children might thereby have a claim to a share of the trust. Among the claimants were the two Wilson children, the Matilda Wilson Fund, the daughter of John Duval Dodge, and the widow of Daniel Dodge. The court reached a decision in October 1980 that divided the money in the following way:

Estate of Winifred	16%
Estate of Frances	16
Heirs of Isabel	8
Matilda Wilson Fund	.78
John Duval's daughter	8
Fred Van Lennep	8
Judith Johnson	5
Fredericka Van Lennep	5
John F. Van Lennep	5

The judge ruled that Daniel Dodge's widow had already sold her full interest in the estate and was therefore entitled to nothing. The Wilson children also saw their claim rejected, since they were not considered heirs of John Dodge.

The only question remaining today about the estate of John Dodge is whether or not Pat Mealbach, the woman who believes she was born a Siamese twin of Frances Dodge, will ever succeed in making a claim. It seems unlikely now that her case will go any farther.

After the death of Matilda, there was only one Dodge matriarch left. From the day that her son, Horace, died, Anna Dodge had little left that she truly cared about. Aged and ailing, she gave up traveling and became a veritable recluse within her limestone mansion, in Grosse Pointe. For the most part, she stayed upstairs in her private suite of rooms—bedroom, bath and sitting room—from which she could look out on her gardens and watch the boats go by on the river. It was her custom to start the day with a huge breakfast, including hot cereal, juice, bacon and eggs. One of her three doctors visited her daily, and then Gertrude Draves, her personal secretary, came from the office in downtown Detroit where her affairs were managed, to bring any correspondence and documents that needed her attention or signature.

A real burden of work had fallen on her when her son died. His will named Anna Dodge as an executor of his estate. She once commented on the "unbelievable horrors" of estate transfer: "the money, the power, the corruption, the conniving, the scheming, and the intrigue." And Horace's estate was certainly a case in point, not finally settled until 1968, five years after his death. The problems involved in sorting it out were myriad.

They were also extremely expensive. Anna had to spend nearly

The beautiful yacht Delphine *rides at anchor alongside the dock in front of Rose Terrace.* (Collection of David Agresta)

$1 million to buy back much of the property in Horace's estate, including his house, the *Delphine*, his boatworks—all things she had originally given him herself. Then, once they were back in her possession, she had to decide what to do with them.

She soon learned that the yacht had become another white elephant, too expensive to run and impossible to sell to anyone else. Unwilling to bear the expense of hiring a crew to stand by in case someone might want to use the boat, Anna put it in dry dock in Detroit while a broker tried to locate a possible buyer. There was some interest in operating it commercially, but nothing ever worked out. In 1967, Anna decided to donate the *Delphine* to Project Hope, for the $56,000 tax deduction it would provide, along with the end of the need to spend more than $20,000 a year to keep the ship in dry dock.

St. Leonard's Castle was sold, along with all its furnishings. Sotheby's was chosen to conduct the sale, and the net proceeds were $339,000. Anna decided to keep the villa in Cannes, perhaps with the vague thought that she might someday want to make one last trip to the sunny Riviera. The boatworks was closed and the buildings sold to Florence Sisman, to provide more space for her packing-and-shipping business.

The drain Horace had exerted on Anna's income was indicated by the losses she declared on her taxes after his death. Her loss on his hobby, the boatworks, was listed as about $2 million, and she also claimed a deduction of more than $9 million in worthless notes her son had signed every time she gave him more money. Nevertheless, she had loved him, and she wanted to honor his memory. She decided in 1965 to give the city of Detroit money to establish a riverfront powerboat facility, containing launching ramps, a service area and a small spectators' tower, to be known as the Horace E. Dodge Memorial Pits. The gift commemorated the only real achievement of Horace's sad life. In the field of powerboat racing, his collection of trophies and his record of wins was impressive.

One other problem connected with Horace's death was the lawsuit filed against Anna by Gregg Sherwood Dodge. Horace's widow filed a suit against Anna Dodge for $11 million. According to Gregg's complaint, $1 million was due her through a prenuptial agreement in which Anna had promised to pay her daughter-in-law that amount in the event Horace predeceased his mother. The other $10 million was for the alienation of Horace's affections. Gregg alleged that Anna had done everything in her power to break up the marriage, and added that Anna's demands on Horace to account for every cent he spent made him so worried and anxious that it had shortened his life.

Questioned about the suit, Gregg told reporters:

> I feel that I am doing this as much for Horace as for myself. He lived constantly in fear of his mother, but because someone had to pay the bills, he didn't want to make trouble. Neither did I. In 1959, Anna Dodge evicted us from our $300,000 lakefront house in Palm Beach on which she

held the mortgage. You learn about mortgages when you deal with a woman like Mrs. Dodge.

Anna Dodge settled out of court. Gregg's life since the death of Horace Dodge has been a panorama of highs and lows. She has been a leader of Palm Beach society, and she has suffered financial reverses. For a time she owned the luxurious estate in Connecticut that is presently the residence of Leona and Harry Helmsley. She married again, and then had the sorrow of losing her handsome husband when he took his own life during a period of depression. Through it all, Gregg has remained a Palm Beach institution.

As Horace's executor, Anna also sent a check to Lois, his first wife, in return for her signature on a release that would deny her any further claim against the estate. Anna asked her lawyers to make the same arrangement with Horace's second wife, Muriel, but Muriel refused to sign the release, and the check was destroyed. Muriel's refusal seems to have been a case of cutting off her nose to spite her face. Her need for funds was made clear by the fact that she continually asked her children, David and Diana, to help her (and her husband, who apparently was unable to support her). Eventually, they offered to set up a trust fund to give their mother a modest permanent income, on the condition that she would refrain from ever asking for more. Muriel died in the late fall of 1987.

Handling these affairs was a real burden on an old woman who spent most of her time in bed. Anna Dodge had three TV sets in her bedroom and generally kept them all going at once. Her favorite program was "Bonanza," which she watched devotedly. She became a great fan of Lorne Green, keeping his picture on her bedside table, and he once came to visit her. She liked to watch the Detroit Tigers; she still bought box seats at their stadium every year but contented herself with viewing the games on TV. She also followed football, and she was glued to her set during Detroit's boat-racing season. When none of these was on, she watched the daytime soaps and news programs. She was so devoted to her

TV viewing that visitors were allowed in only during commercials, summoned by the nurse from a bench in the hallway where they were forced to wait.

But other than people who worked for her, Anna's visitors were few and far between. Her granddaughter Yvonne had bought the house next door (with a loan from Anna) after Horace died, and she and her children were generally there in the summers, holding big parties for 300 or 400 people during the boat-racing season. It was Anna's wish that Yvonne's husband, Jim Ranger, carry on the family boat-racing tradition. As she explained in a letter:

> In November of 1965, I told Jim that I would like to have him purchase a boat and to enter unlimited racing competition with either Jim or someone else driving the hydroplane. I did this for my own pleasure, because I have always loved boat racing and because I wanted the Dodge name to continue in championship caliber hydroplane racing. As I instructed, Jimmy formed a corporation to own the boat, and I was to lend the corporation all money in excess of $25,000 that it needed to buy and operate the boat, so that if the prizes and advertising income were not sufficient to pay costs, I would bear the loss.

Jim Ranger did as she instructed, and Anna followed the fortunes of his boat with interest, but she rarely saw the family and no longer attended the parties.

For the most part, Anna's attitude toward her descendants ranged from the critical to the negligent. She complained about one grandchild, "It would seem the only thing she cares about the Dodges is the money she gets," but in fact, at that point in Anna's life, money was virtually all she was willing to give. Her grandchildren David and Diana were regular visitors, and the only ones who brought her little personal presents. But she was not particularly appreciative of the effort they made, and they were forced to wait their turn until commercial time, just like all the business visitors. Christine continued to write to her grandmother—always amusing, chatty letters, often with drawings enclosed, that expressed her affection (and, indirectly, her own loneliness). They were remarkably similar to the letters she used to write from boarding school, and they met with the same old silence as a response. Christine, now in her late sixties, has finally found some measure of peace. She lives quietly in Florida and has apparently sworn off marriage. Christine never found the love she was looking for, but she seems finally to have been wise enough to give up the search.

Most of the great mansion was shut up, the museum-quality furniture covered by dust sheets, all cared for by her maid who had been with Anna Dodge for decades. The kitchen, staffed by a single elderly woman, produced meals only for Anna, the nurses, and a few other staff members. No chauffeur was needed, since Anna never went anywhere. There was one man in charge of maintaining the entire estate, as well as looking after the Ranger house next door. He was aided by only two gardeners. The formal gardens were no longer kept up, but the roses that gave the house its name were carefully pruned and sprayed and watered, and every year several dozen had to be replaced. Whenever they bloomed, there was always a big silver bowl of roses in Anna's bedroom. On good days in the summer, Anna liked to be wheeled out to the steps facing the water, to enjoy her views and her flowers.

The loneliness of Anna Dodge's last years created a vacuum, and into that vacuum stepped the dynamic Florence Sisman. A woman of tremendous energy, Florence was able to work all day at her own packing-and-shipping business, Kennelly & Sisman, and still have the zest to go out on the town for a long evening. After Horace was gone, Florence began to influence more and more areas of his mother's life. She hired (and fired) the people who worked for Anna, and she was the one who gave them their instructions. Florence regulated access to Anna, so that even her grandchildren found themselves having to go through Florence to enter her bedroom. In her daily visits to Rose Terrace, she went

Magnificent wrought-iron gates guarded the private world of Anna Dodge at Rose Terrace. (Collection of David Agresta)

over all of Anna's business affairs with her. The orders to buy this or sell that, to send a check for charity or take a box at the opera, were all written in Florence's hand. Even the decisions about what size check to send great-grandchildren on their birthdays were made by Florence.

Florence was unfailingly generous with Anna's support of charitable causes in Detroit, and in return she enjoyed the rewards of Anna's contributions. Florence was the one who used the tickets to the opera, the passes for the pits during boat-racing season, the invitations to the charity balls. As Mrs. Dodge's "representative," she would dress to the nines (often wearing Anna's jewelry) and mingle with Detroit society.

Anna (right) *attends a charity event accompanied by Florence Sisman.* (Collection of David Agresta)

Florence Sisman stands in for patroness Anna Dodge at a charity event.

In an interview given a year after Anna's death, Florence talked about her relationship with the Dodge dowager:

> Years ago Mother Dodge wanted to adopt me. But I refused. After all, I had a mother. She asked me to at least call her mother. Horace called her "the queen." Mother Dodge was a lonely woman, you know. Her children were

always traveling around the world. She'd think nothing of calling me at 5 o'clock and insisting, "Florence, come right over." I was never too busy to give her some time. Mother Dodge wanted me to come live with her. I didn't want to be that close to her, though. So Yvonne suggested I live next door in her house. . . . Mother Dodge was just a very good friend. I miss her terribly. She taught me a lot— all the social graces. She was very well read. She made me read about European history—she was an authority. She wouldn't let me read novels.

Incidentally, when Florence visited the gray house next door to Anna's, she always stayed in the master bedroom that had been Horace's and Gregg's. She told the family that the ghost of Horace often came to her when she was in bed.

Most evenings, Florence would stop by Rose Terrace at dinnertime to be with Anna. Using Horace's term of endearment for his mother, she would rush down the hallway shouting, "Where's my queen?" The two women would have a bourbon highball, drinking liquor that came from big barrels in the basement vault that were the legacy of the first Horace Dodge's preparations for Prohibition. Then Anna would eat, with a hearty appetite, a meat-and-potatoes dinner with homemade coffee ice cream for dessert. If Florence was going out that evening, she wouldn't eat herself, but she often asked for something to nibble on later. When Anna's dinner was over, Florence would kiss her "queen" good-bye and rush out again, to be overheard muttering under her breath, "When's the son of a bitch gonna die?"

Despite precarious health, Anna hung on. She was in and out of Detroit's Jennings Hospital, she was taking a long list of medications and the bills for the attention of doctors and nurses ran into thousands of dollars every month. But she lived on and on, in terrible fear of death, saying over and over that she didn't want to die. The attachment to life exhibited by this sick and lonely old woman was truly impressive.

Mourners at the funeral of Anna Dodge included her granddaughters Christine (second from left) *and Diana* (center left), *and her niece Winifred* (center right). *(Detroit Free Press)*

The struggle finally ended on June 2, 1970, when Anna died in her own turquoise bedroom at Rose Terrace, with only a nurse in attendance. Obituary notices said she was 103, but in truth she was well over a year short of her century. She had always felt free to alter her age to conform to other people's expectations. Like her sister-in-law, she died without family or friends nearby, and she was mourned more as a symbol of an era than as a human being. Her funeral was a large one, for she had seven grandchildren and more than twenty great-grandchildren. The funeral was held at the Jefferson Avenue Presbyterian Church, conducted by her own pastor, the Reverend Allen Zaun. He called Anna "a queen mother, regal in dignity" and recollected that he had visited her just a few days before her death and joined her in singing "What a Friend I Have in Jesus." Then her one-and-a-quarter-ton bronze casket was slipped into the waiting niche beside Horace Dodge, the husband whose death preceded hers by fifty years.

But few of the people who followed the big black hearse down the curving driveway of Rose Terrace really knew Anna, and even fewer had had any contact with her in the last years of her life. Their letters to her were answered by her secretary, Gertrude Draves; their wedding presents were chosen by Florence; the timing of their visits was dictated by the TV schedule. Her passing left no gap in anyone's heart.

But it did, of course, leave some money to be distributed. Anna left a large estate in her own name, built up through fifty years of receiving the income, millions of dollars every year, from the trust left by Horace. Rarely, even during the years when she was building and furnishing the second Rose Terrace, did she spend the entire income. The excess was invested in tax-free municipal bonds that gave her a personal income of more than $1.5 million a year by the time of her death—without any tax bite. So her death called for the distribution of her own estate, and it also paved the way for the distribution of the trust itself.

It seemed to be a virtual tradition that the settling of estates in the Dodge family was always accompanied by at least one or two lawsuits, and this one was to be no exception to the rule. The terms of the trust established so long ago by Horace Dodge were unequivocal enough. The five children of Horace Junior would split half of the $48-million trust, giving them each almost $5 million. The other half would be divided between Delphine's two daughters, Christine and Yvonne.

Neither Christine nor Yvonne stood to profit greatly from this distribution. As soon as Anna Dodge died, Christine's creditors took legal action to secure their interests in her inheritance. Petitions showed that there were more than 600 people who had some claim on the $12 million that was to come to her, estimated by her creditors at anything from $9 million to $14 million. Those suits went on for months, with more than 150 lawyers arguing the rights of their clients to a share of Christine's money. The total claims actually exceeded the amount of her inheritance. Her lawyers tried to put the inheritance into the trust Jim Cromwell had set up for his daughter in 1949, but the court ruled such an action would be unfair to the creditors. Eventually, about $9 million was paid out to those whose claims were judged to be valid. Trustees of Anna's estate at Detroit Bank and Trust revealed that Yvonne had also borrowed heavily against her future inheritance. She owed the estate some $6.6 million, and owed the bank another $1.3 million.

It was the disposition of Anna's personal estate, valued at about $15 to $20 million, that caused the most trouble. Anna's will set up a trust for her grandchildren, allowing them to collect their share of the income when they reached the age of thirty-five, and provided that the principal would remain in trust for *their* children. But her will specifically stated that her granddaughters Christine and Yvonne were not to be included in that trust; they were to inherit nothing from her estate.

Did Anna take this step because she thought Christine and Yvonne were improvident? Or did she feel that she had already given them help enough? In addition to the large loans she had made to these two daughters of Delphine Dodge, she had also given them a number of outright gifts. For example, Yvonne was allowed to "buy" the Catherine the Great pearls that had once belonged to Anna and then to Delphine and were valued at nearly $1 million by simply signing a note for $400,000 and then picking up the pearls from the bank's office and stuffing them into a brown paper bag. Three years later, Anna wrote her to say:

> As I am sure you remember, you signed a note for Four Hundred Thousand Dollars for the "Catherine the Great" pearls which you have in your possession. I have previously set up trusts for Horace's children but I have not done anything like this for you, so I am now forgiving this debt and as of now this note to me is cancelled. I hope you

use and enjoy the pearls in good health for many years to come.

John Francis Dodge was also left out of the trust set up by Anna (although he, like Christine and Yvonne, would get his share of the Horace Dodge trust). Her will provided only for a gift to him of $25,000. The three excluded grandchildren quickly filed suit to break the will. They claimed their grandmother was mentally incompetent at the time she made the will, and that she was "under the mistaken impression" that the will she signed provided for all her grandchildren to share equally. Christine and Yvonne also filed suit against the Detroit Bank and Trust, charging it with mismanaging the Horace Dodge trust. Choosing to invest solely in tax-free municipal bonds, the bank had, they charged, "ignored possibilities of investing in conservative, gilt-edged common and preferred stocks of major corporations, whose value has kept pace with the national economy."

It was the same complaint Christine had made ten years earlier, and it proved to be equally unsuccessful. Johnny Dodge got nothing from his grandmother's trust, but he would still inherit one-fifth of one-half of the original Horace Dodge trust. After a year of litigation, the judge also ruled against Christine and Yvonne and upheld the will. He concluded that Anna had been in complete control of her faculties at the time she made the will.

Anna's will was a curious document, much amended by codicils written during the last years of her life, in the isolation of her bedroom at Rose Terrace. Some of the changes were to strike out bequests: for example, Horace's loyal secretary Sarah Helmick (about whom Anna once commented, "I never will understand her being such a fool") was left nothing, and she too sued Anna's estate. Cynics will not be surprised to learn that many of those codicils—drawn up by Florence Sisman, witnessed by her and signed in a shaky hand unrecognizable as Anna Dodge's—benefited Florence and her family. Florence was left $50,000, an an-

Florence Sisman poses with the Gerald Kelly portrait of her benefactress, Anna Dodge.
(*Detroit Free Press*)

nual income of $12,000 a year and the villa that had been Horace's in the south of France. Florence's sister, Maxine, too got an income of $12,000 a year, still being paid as of this writing. Another provision canceled the balance of Florence's debt for her purchase of Horace's old boatworks, although she had paid no more than

10 percent of the agreed-upon price. There are reports—perhaps malicious in their motivation—that she also helped herself to a few little pieces of jewelry and nickknacks from Rose Terrace.

Considering the size of Anna's estate, very little of her money went to charitable causes. She left the contents of the music room to the Detroit Institute of Arts, plus an outright gift of $1 million to help them install the room properly. The Children's Hospital in Detroit received $1 million for the construction of the Anna and Horace E. Dodge Floor of the hospital. She also gave the city of Detroit $2 million for the erection of a Dodge Fountain in downtown Detroit as a memorial to her husband and son. Other bequests included:

Good Samaritan Hospital	$150,000
Jefferson Ave. Presbyterian Church	50,000
Manlius Military Academy	25,000
Lois Knowlson	10,000
Mickey Devine	10,000
Mickey's 3 children, each	5,000
Robert Petz	10,000
Jim Ranger	10,000
Gary Clements, son of Maxine	6,400
Rev. Allen Zaun	5,000

Anna's will showed her to be as unsentimental in death as she had been in life. All her possessions were to be sold and the money added to her estate for distribution to her heirs. Any member of the family who wanted so much as a silver-framed photo or a little memento of Rose Terrace had to buy it from the estate at the appraised value. Grandchildren David and Diana Dodge made major acquisitions. Christine bought a jade crane, a huge Irish silver rose bowl, a Meissen cupid and some other pretty trifles. Yvonne bought some valuable memorabilia.

The dispersal of the estate took years and the efforts of large numbers of people; an amusing story about it in the *Wall Street*

Journal was entitled "Mrs. Dodge's Bundle: Liquidation of an Estate Turns into an Industry." The trustees selected the British firm of Christie's to handle the sale of Anna's jewelry, furniture and art objects. Christie's dispatched thirteen experts from England, who spent nearly a month appraising every single thing inside Rose Terrace. The jewelry was sent to Geneva, to be sold in a big Christie's auction there; it included the pearl necklace and the emerald-and-diamond necklace Anna had bought from the estate of Edith McCormick, as well as sixteen other important pieces. That sale realized $857,472. The best of the furniture (134 pieces) and *objets* were solicitously packed into two jumbo jets and flown to England, to go on the auction block in London. The furniture brought a total of $1,685,000, and one of the tables Anna had bought from Duveen sold for $415,000, setting the world-record price at that time for a single piece of furniture. The Chinese jade Anna and Hugh had bought on their trip to Peking, when they had Jade Street in their sitting room for days, went for $206,491, and Anna's silver collection brought $226,580. Some paintings were sold separately: a pair of large Bouchers for $1,016,000 and a Van Dyke portrait for $215,000.

The remainder of Anna's possessions were auctioned off at Rose Terrace in 1971, after thousands of people had filed through the house to gawk at its contents. It was the first time Christie's ever conducted a house sale in the United States, and they needed two auctioneers and a staff of forty-five to accomplish it. The three-day sale brought buyers from all over the Western Hemisphere; a fleet of big private planes was lined up at the Detroit airport every day. Antique dealers and gallery owners came from New York; Lamar Hunt flew up from Dallas and bought a table for $3,200. Detroit society came too; the records of the auction show sales to the Chrysler and Keller families. Delphine Petz bought a number of her grandmother's possessions, and John Duval's daughter, Mary Ann, picked up a souvenir of the family she hardly knew. Anna's custom-made Chrysler limousine, with a body by the Italian firm of Ghia, fetched $8,000. Horace Dodge's last car, the 1920 sedan with his initials on the door, went for just $1,200. The highest price at the Rose Terrace auction was paid for a thirty-eight-by-twenty-one-foot Aubusson rug, which a London dealer bought for $13,000.

Rose Terrace itself was also on the market, for an asking price of $1.25 million—with predictable results. Despite glossy brochures enumerating the glories of the house, from its antique paneling to its ice-cream-making machinery, no one wanted to live in a house that cost a bare minimum of $12,500 each month just to keep open. Anna had apparently given some thought to providing for the mansion's preservation by giving it to the Detroit Institute of Arts. They were responsive, but lacked the funds to keep up such an expensive building and decided they could accept it only if it was accompanied by a $10-million fund for that purpose. That was the end of Anna's interest. After her death, there was an effort on the part of the local community to find a way to save Rose Terrace, but zoning regulations and lack of funds doomed all attempts.

Rose Terrace was sold to developers in 1976, and they arranged the last big sale that summer, putting the very structure of the house on the auction block. Auctioneer Frank Boos remembers the event with amusement. "I met the buyers at the front gate and started selling then and there." After selling the gates ($6,000) and the fence, he went on to sell the Belgian stone blocks of the driveway, the three miles of eight-inch underground copper pipes that watered the lawn, the 150-year-old boxwood hedge that had been imported from England, and even the rose bushes. Moving inside the house, he auctioned off the paneled walls ($20,000 for the library), the marble floors ($500 for the card room), the basement vaults, the marble tubs and the curving marble staircase ($22,500). A news photo shows him hanging out of one of the third-floor dormer windows, bullhorn in hand, selling the two-inch-thick lead off the rooftop ($200).

The wrecker's ball hit Rose Terrace just one month later. Once the mansion was gone, the site was subdivided into twenty-five lots for executive homes. Several years later, Yvonne Ranger sold the Kahn house next door to the same fate. Nearly fifty families now live on the spot where Anna Dodge once reigned supreme.

A visitor to Detroit today is struck by the fact that so little remains of the Dodge name or influence. Traveling along the Walter P. Chrysler Freeway, stopping in at Henry Ford's museum, passing the large factories and test tracks of Ford, General Motors and Chrysler, there is no reminder of John and Horace Dodge and their legacy. Thanks to Henry Ford's genius for public relations, and the untimely deaths of the two brothers, the fact that the Dodges built the first Fords and laid the foundation for all of Ford's prosperity has faded from the public consciousness, and most people are incredulous to know that Henry Ford had to sell those first cars on the strength of the Dodge reputation for quality work. The Dodge brothers were among the most influential of the automotive pioneers. They set the early standards of quality and durability in the industry and taught the public how high their demands of automakers should be. Circumstances robbed them of the credit they deserved. The family's decision to sell the company finished what Henry Ford started, the erasing of the memory of the achievements of John and Horace Dodge.

The heirs of the brothers did nothing subsequently to rescue the family name. The few accomplishments they could boast were limited to the elite world of sports of the rich, boat racing and horse breeding. Their names were in the papers because they held fabulous parties, married and divorced with a maximum of scandal, and sued one another with disgusting regularity. They indulged in conspicuous consumption of the sort that tends to rouse the ire of the public, as when they built big houses, cruised on their yacht, and enjoyed multimillion-dollar shopping sprees in the depths of the Depression. They didn't work, and they didn't even know how to make their money work for them.

Their lack of a generous spirit is particularly noticeable, and of course it is another reason that the Dodge name has sunk from view. A surprisingly small portion of their fortune has been used for the public good (with the exception of Matilda's fund, and she took pains to keep the Dodge name out of that philanthropy). Thus there are no Dodge hospitals, or museums, or other public buildings. The men who earned the money gave it freely, but those who inherited it were much less charitable.

No wonder, then, that the Dodge contribution is mostly forgotten. Here and there, a few bronze plaques memorialize a long-ago gift, and old-timers in Detroit still relish relating a malicious anecdote or two about some Dodge drinking and carousing. But even in the places where the family was once best known, little remains beyond ill-natured gossip. For example, a recent inquiry in Palm Beach about Anna Dodge brought the response, "Anna Dodge? Anna Dodge . . . Let's see . . . didn't she marry one of the Dillmans?" How Hugh McCaughey, son of an Ohio tailor, would have laughed!

Little splinters of past grandeur are embedded in the lives of the grandchildren and great-grandchildren, into whose hands the fragmented Dodge fortune has now passed: a grove of jade trees on a bookcase shelf, gold-rimmed dishes from the yacht in a cupboard, a key chain from which dangles the bejeweled portrait of Catherine the Great that was once a pendant to her pearls. At worst, they drink and take drugs and try to forget the way things used to be; at best, they have learned to live quietly, with modest aspirations and low profiles. They are like the survivors of some terrible tragedy—and yet the worst thing that happened to the Dodge family was that they achieved the American dream.

A Note on the Sources

The starting point of this book was a wealth of documentation preserved in the estate of Anna Thomson Dodge. These filing cabinets full of papers included both sides of her correspondence with a wide variety of family members, friends and business advisers. Among the most illuminating of her correspondents, and the ones most frequently referred to in the book, were Leo M. Butzel, Christine Cromwell, James H. R. Cromwell, Hugh Dillman and his sister Mary, Bud and Margery Dodge, David Dodge, Horace Dodge, Jr., Eva Stotesbury, Frank Upton and Philip T. Van Zile.

Other useful documents in this trove included Anna Dodge's account books and ledgers; her travel diaries; her social lists and the notebooks her social secretary kept, which detail every occasion of hospitality at both her houses; blueprints for Playa Riente and Rose Terrace, as well as all the bills for the art and furnishings she bought for those two great houses; family photographs and films; and letters from strangers asking for money.

This huge collection of original material was supplemented first by informal interviews with some family members, who gave the project their encouragement, and then by a number of interviews with those who had been close to the family and its various activities. Public documents, such as wills, certificates of birth, marriage and death, and real estate transfers and taxes helped to fill in some of the gaps. So did archival research, utilizing the Burton Collection at the Detroit Public Library, the records at the Edison Institute of the Ford Museum, the archives at Chrysler Corporation and files at the Historical Society of Palm Beach County, the Grosse Pointe Historical Society, and the major Detroit newspapers: the *Detroit Free Press*, the *Detroit News* and the *Detroit Times*.

Books have been helpful sources of corroboration and explication. Especially valuable were:

Brannock, Earl. *Queen of the Chesapeake and Hudson.* Cambridge, MD: Brannock Maritime Museum, 1986.

Collier, Peter, and David Horowitz. *The Fords: An American Epic.* New York: Summit Books, 1987.

Curl, Donald W. *Mizner's Florida.* New York: Architectural History Foundation, 1984.

———. *Palm Beach County.* New York: Windsor Publications, 1986.

Ferry, W. Hawkins. *The Buildings of Detroit.* Detroit: Wayne State University Press, 1980.

Hyde, Charles K. *Detroit: An Industrial History Guide.* Detroit: Detroit Historical Society, n.d.

———. " 'Dodge Main' and the Detroit Automobile Industry 1910–1980," *Detroit in Perspective*, Spring 1982.

Johnston, Alva. *The Legendary Mizners.* New York: Farrar, Straus & Young, 1953.

Lacey, Robert. *Ford: The Men and the Machine.* Boston: Little, Brown & Co., 1986.

Maher, James T. *The Twilight of Splendor.* Boston: Little, Brown & Co., 1975.

Marzolf, Marion, and Marianne Ritchie. *Matilda R. Wilson.* Rochester, MI: Meadow Brook Hall Publication, n.d.

Pitrone, Jean Maddern, and Joan Potter Elwart. *The Dodges.* South Bend, IN: Icarus Press, 1981.

————. *The John Dodge Story.* Rochester, MI: Meadow Brook Hall Publication, n.d.

Acknowledgments

The best thing that can happen to authors is to find people who are willing to give generously of time, knowledge and enthusiasm in support of their projects. In that regard, this book was truly blessed.

Our thanks to these people who shared with us their firsthand information about the subject matter: Agnes Adams, Frank Boos, Joan LeGro Bushnell, Virginia Wills Chauvan, Fred Cleaver, Clara Cogley, Howard M. Davidson, Gregg Dodge, Gertrude Draves, Donald R. Egan, John Griffen, Charles Hyde, Bill Kennedy, Frank Kerbratt, Judge James Knott, Pat Parish McKenzie, Pat Mealbach, Leo and Virgie Mucutza, Dick and Carl Perry, Robert Petz, Jr., Jim Ponce, Pris Posselious, Neal Shine, Dr. Werner Spitz and Mark Stevens. Special thanks are due to the late George McCall, the dedicated chronicler of the Ford and Dodge families, who managed in a few sadly short years to collect a treasure trove of archival materials, to visit and photograph every site linked with the Dodge family and to record hours of fact-filled interviews with Amelia Rausch Cline.

Archival research can be a time-consuming and frustrating process without the help of the skilled professionals who keep the archives in order and lead confused authors to the very document or photograph for which they are searching. We would like to thank Nan Dennison, who maintains the files of the Historical Society of Palm Beach County in impeccable order and seems to know what is in each one of them; Barbara Thorpe at Meadow Brook Hall, who guided us through countless boxes of material without ever losing her zest; Marilyn Brooks at Meadow Brook Hall, who is herself a veritable repository of information about the family that lived there; curator George Bird at Meadow Brook Hall, who generously shared his knowledge of the great house and its furnishings; David Crippen, archivist of the Edison Institute, who led us to documents we did not know existed; Carla Rosenbusch, the very helpful archivist at Chrysler Corporation; all the people at the Burton Collection in the Detroit Public Library; Jean Dodenhoff at the Grosse Pointe Historical Society; Linda Bohr at Woodlawn Cemetery; Alan Darr and Peter Barnett at the Detroit Institute of Arts; Pat Zacharias at the *Detroit News*; Sharon Hite at Good Samaritan Hospital; and Joseph Bedway at Albert Kahn Associates. Our search for photographs was assisted by Marcia Eymann and Cynthia Read-Miller at the Henry Ford Museum, and the incredibly helpful Vivian Jiunette at the *Detroit Free Press*.

There were others who smoothed the way for us, or led us to resources we were not aware we should be looking for. We are appreciative of the help of Mike Skinner, Ron Fox, Peter C. Smith, James Hammond, Jo Anne Smiley, and, especially, Mike and Vivian Boutell, who could not have been more gracious.

We would also like to thank our agent, Alice Martell, for her support and encouragement, and our editor, Marie Arana-Ward, for her total professional commitment from the very beginning.

David Agresta

This story has become a ten-year effort for me. The first eight years, I searched for a coauthor as able as Caroline Latham. There are many people to whom I owe more thanks than I can express here. Alicia Johnson who introduced me to this life and much much more. Gertrude for her trust, honesty and sincerity. Silvio and Pat because they were always there for me, and always have been. James V. Bellanca, Jr., has been my anchor, coach, adviser and best friend throughout. Don Colombo and Ramon Lascano, for their encouragement and an infinite list of selfless support to me, I thank from the deepest part of my heart. Steve and Maxine, from the first day I came to New York. Monsignor Wilbur F. Suedkamp, Donald R. Egan, Christina Young, Leo and Virgie Mucutza, A. Y., Chelsea, my good buddy Mia, and finally my Lainie, for all of the above, and for maintaining my rational half this past year. I don't blame you.

New York City
April 1988

Caroline Latham

My primary thanks must go to David, for bringing me such a fascinating subject and a wealth of material to document it. All that's left to add is my love and thanks to Tony, for all the times he cheerfully found something else to do while I worked on the weekend, and all the Chinese take-out he brought home for dinner as deadlines drew near.

Hudson, New York
April 1988

Index

Italicized page numbers refer to photographs.

er eror